Ghana: Transition to Democracy

D1826294

Ghana: Transition to Democracy

Edited by
Kwame A. Ninsin

CODESRIA BOOK SERIES

Ghana: Transition to Democracy

First published in 1998 by CODESRIA

Copyright © CODESRIA

CODESRIA is the Council for the Development of Social Science Research in Africa, headquartered in Senegal. It is an independent organisation whose principal objectives are facilitating research, promoting research-based publishing and creating multiple fora geared towards the exchange of views and information among African scholars. Its correspondence address is:
B.P. 3304, Dakar, Senegal.

ISBN: 2-86978-091-5 (Soft back)

Cover designed by Alla Kleekpo
Typeset by Marie Therese Coron-Diouf, CODESRIA
Distributors: ABC, 27 Park End Street, Oxford OX1, IHU, UK

CODESRIA would like to express its gratitude to the Swedish International Development Co-operation Agency (SIDA), the Rockefeller Foundation, the International Development Research Centre (IDRC), the Ford Foundation, the Canergie Corporation, the European Union, the Norwegian Ministry of Foreign Affairs and the Danish Agency for International Development (DANIDA), the Dutch Government and the Government of Senegal for support of its research and publication activities.

Printed in Great Britain by
Antony Rowe Ltd, Chippenham, Wiltshire

Contents

Acknowledgements

The essays in this collection are the result of a research project that was initiated and supported by the Africa Leadership Forum (ALF) and the Global Coalition for Africa (GCA). Actual financial support came from the Overseas Development Administration (ODA) of the United Kingdom. The Department of Political Science, University of Ghana hosted the research. The Ghana study was part of a cross-national African study involving nine countries. The director of the continent-wide study was Boubacar Barry. The project was concluded with a final workshop at Gorée in Dakar, Senegal at which several useful comments were made on the draft report from which this collection emerged. I thank the Overseas Development Administration (ODA), the Africa Leadership Forum (ALF), and the Global Coalition for Africa (GCA) on behalf of the Ghana Team for making the study possible; and to the participants at the Gorée workshop for their valuable comments on the draft report of the Ghana Team.

This book comprises a selection of five of the reports (revised) whose main theses were considered central to the democratisation process in Ghana, and two chapters which were written on invitation. My role in all of this was that of a facilitator first as co-ordinator of the Ghana project and later as editor. I wish to thank the contributors for enduring my relentless demands to meet several deadlines. I am most grateful particularly to Robin Luckham who acted as a peer reviewer and adviser to the research team, and also for agreeing to contribute the chapter on the military when it was urgently needed. I am equally grateful to Kwame Karikari for responding to a belated invitation to write the chapter on the press specifically for this book. Godfrey Mantey of the Department of Political Science, University of Ghana assisted with the typing of the revised papers. He was assisted by Daniel Noi of the same department who ran several errands especially in preparing for the numerous internal workshops held by the Ghana Team to review progress of work and discuss findings. I thank them for their invaluable services. Finally, I acknowledge with gratitude the financial support of the GCA for this publication.

But all said and done, neither the Department of Political Science of the University of Ghana, the Overseas Development Administration, Africa Leadership Forum, nor the Global Coalition for Africa is responsible for views expressed in these chapters. The authors are individually responsible for any views expressed in their respective chapters.

Kwame A. Ninsin
African Association of Political Science,
Harare, Zimbabwe
September 17, 1997

Contributors

Gilbert Keith Bluwey is Senior Research Fellow and Acting Director of the Legon Centre for International Affairs, University of Ghana, Legon.

Kwame Boafo-Arthur is Senior Lecturer in the Department of Political Science, University of Ghana, Legon.

Charles Jebuni is Research Officer at the Centre for Policy Analysis (CEPA) in Accra, Ghana.

Kwesi Jonah is Senior Lecturer in the Department of Political Science, University of Ghana, Legon.

Kwame Karikari is Senior Lecturer and Acting Director, School of Communication Studies, University of Ghana, Legon.

Robin Luckham is Professor of Political Science at the Institute of Development Studies, University of Sussex, Brighton, UK.

Kwame A. Ninsin was Professor and Head of the Department of Political Science, University of Ghana. He is currently the Administrative Secretary of the African Association of Political Science (AAPS) based in Harare, Zimbabwe.

Abena Oduro is Lecturer in the Department of Economics, University of Ghana, Legon.

Abbreviations

ARPS   -   Aborigines Rights Protection Society (1897)
NCBWA   -   National Congress of British West Africa (1920)

1947 - 1960

UGCC   -   United Gold Coast Convention
CPP   -   Convention Peoples Party
NLM   -   National Liberation Movement
NPP   -   Northern Peoples Party
UP   -   United Party

1966 - 1969

PP   -   Progress Party
NAL   -   National Alliance of Liberals
PPP   -   Peoples Popular Party

1979 - 1981

PNP   -   Peoples National Party
PFP   -   Popular Front Party
UNC   -   United National Convention
KNRG   -   Kwame Nkrumah Revolutionary Guards
AYC   -   African Youth Command
NDM   -   New Democratic Movement
KNWS   -   Kwame Nkrumah Welfare Society
KNF   -   Kwame Nkrumah Foundation

1982 - 1991

INCC	-	Interim National Coordinating Committee
NDC	-	National Defence Committee
PDC	-	Peoples Defence Committee
WDC	-	Workers Defence Committee
NCD	-	National Commission for Democracy
DOA	-	District Organising Assistant
CDR	-	Committees for the Defence of the Revolution
CDO	-	Civil Democratic Organisation

1992 - 1994

NPP		New Patriotic Party
NDC	-	National Democratic Congress
PNC	-	Peoples National Convention
NIP	-	National Independence Party
PHP	-	Peoples Heritage Party
NJP	-	New Justice Party
NCP	-	National Convention Party
EGLE	-	Every Ghanaian Living Everywhere
PPDD	-	Peoples Party for Democracy and Development
DPP	-	Democratic Peoples Party
GDRP	-	Ghana Democratic Republican Party
NGA	-	New Generation Alliance
NSP	-	National Salvation Party
PCP	-	Peoples Convention Party
NCCN	-	National Coordinating Committee of Nkrumahists
MFJ	-	Movement for Freedom and Justice
CCDF	-	Coordinating Committee of Democratic Forces
ADF	-	Alliance of Democratic Forces
UNICRAWL	-	United Clubs for Rawlings
INEC	-	Interim National Electoral Commission

1

Introduction

Kwame A. Ninsin

A Profile

Ghana is bounded on the west by Côte d'Ivoire, on the north by Burkina Faso, on the east by Togo and on the south by the Atlantic Ocean. It changed its colonial name, The Gold Coast, to Ghana on the attainment of independence in 1957.

Its population, which is currently estimated at about 14 million, is a vast mosaic of big and small ethnic groups. The major ones are the Akan who constitute about 44.1 per cent of the population, the Mole-Dagbani 15.9 per cent, Ewe 13.0 per cent, Ga-Adangme 8.3 per cent, Guan 3.7 per cent and Gonja 3.5 per cent. Despite its rich ethnic diversity, easy geographic and social mobility have scattered peoples from various ethnic groups throughout the country without destroying or weakening their ethnic bonds. The Akan occupy almost one-third of the country stretching from the lower fringes of the northern savannah through the entire forest belt to the central areas of the southern savannah. But there is an Akan speaking person in almost every corner of the country. Similarly, the Mole-Dagbani and Gonja who are concentrated in the northern savannah zone could be found in most parts of the country. And so are the rest of the ethnic groups.

The ethnic map of Ghana is almost coterminous with its religious map. Christians who constitute about 45 per cent of the population are found largely in the southern sections while the 12 per cent Moslems live mainly in the northern sections. Animists are evenly distributed among the various ethnic groups throughout the country. The spatial distribution of the two major foreign religions, Islam and Christianity, almost coincides with the division of the country into the northern half that is poor and disadvantaged, and the southern half which is wealthy and more developed.

Brief Political History

On 6 March 1957, Ghana became the first Black African country south of the Sahara to achieve independence from colonial rule. Its first democratically elected government was formed by the Convention People's Party under the leadership of Kwame Nkrumah who became the country's first president in 1960. Its independence constitution was democratic: it was based on the rule of law; enshrined a number of fundamental rights including the habeas corpus, freedom of the press, association, speech and assembly; and guaranteed the independence of the judiciary, among others.

Multi-party politics and spirited public debate were key features of the country's politics before and immediately after independence. The vigour of democratic life was reflected in the diversity of political parties that existed prior to 1964 when the country adopted a constitutional one-party socialist system. For example, there were 11 political parties at one time or the other during the 1954-1964 period. The change to a one-party socialist regime in the early 1960s aborted this vibrant pluralist democratic life, and prepared the ground for the *coup d'état* of 24 February 1966, which ushered the country into a long winter of successive military interventions in its politics. The Provisional National Defence Council (PNDC), which seized power on 31 December 1981 and ruled the country until January 1993 — a total of 11 years — was the latest of the military governments.

Between March 1957, when Ghana attained independence, and 3 January 1993, when the new civilian administration of the National Democratic Congress was sworn into office 4 military governments — with a total tenure of 22 years and 3 months, and 3 civilian governments — which shared a total of 13 years 9 months in office, had ruled the country. Apart from the successful direct military interventions the country experienced several abortive military coups.

Evidently, this tradition of government by military regimes and failed coup attempts has not been conducive to the growth of democratic culture and practice. For, invariably, the fledgling democratic institutions, laws and procedural rules were either set aside en masse; or they were brutally subverted. Nor have civic associations and political parties been allowed sufficient time to gain roots, form democratic habits and practise such norms. It is in the context of this history of constant abortion of democratic institutions and rules of behaviour, followed by a relapse into authoritarianism that the current transition to democracy is taking place.

The Problem

As could be inferred from the above outline, the current transition is not the first in Ghana's 35 years of independence from colonialism. The similarities between the present and past transition processes are striking. In almost every instance, the incumbent military government acceded to demands to return the country to constitutional democracy only after considerable pressure had been piled on it. In each case a constitutional body was set up to write a new democratic constitution; and the transition to constitutional rule was invariably controlled by the incumbent military government.

This history of incomplete transitions naturally poses a serious question about the current transition to democracy. If previous transitions had several things in common with the present but failed, what elements in the current process are so unique as to strengthen the chances for successes? Does the current transition promise to give rise to a stable democratic order?

Definition

The transition politics dates back to the first few months after the military government of the PNDC came to power on 31 December 1981. It continued thereafter with varying degrees of intensity and mass involvement. However, it was only after 1988 that the pressure for political reform became strong enough to compel the military government of the PNDC to agree to liberalise politics and introduce a democratic constitution. The thrust of the demands of the democratic forces was the replacement of the authoritarian military-based government institutions, rules and procedure with democratic ones, based on consent obtained through electoral processes in which the universal franchise applied, as well as government based on the rule of law. This was the substance of the transition politics.

A political transition does not necessarily consummate a democratic order. Rather, it marks an important beginning of a long and difficult process. On 3 January 1993, this process of reconstitution was initiated. But the outcome is unpredictable because the norms, ideas and sentiments associated with the old regime could not be replaced immediately with the new: these die rather slowly. Even though the outcome cannot be inferred from what took place on 3 January 1993, the act of physically replacing the old with a new political order is a conscious attempt to redefine modes of behaviour in politics and restructure existing political relations. Therefore, some indications of future possibilities could be deduced from a review and analyses of the process of reconstitution and of prevailing trends and tendencies. The papers in this collection identify and discuss the institutional and non-institutional factors, both domestic and external, which impinge on the current transition process; they also isolate those that have the greatest potential to sustain it. From their individual perspectives the authors assess the problems, obstacles and prospects for a successful transition, as well as the opportunities for consolidating the strengths of this process.

Issues in the Political Transition

The term 'political transition' is used here with reference to a period in a country's development when conscious efforts are made to overcome a political order characterised by institutional disarray and normative incongruence, recurring political instability, institutional breakdown as well as extreme civil disorders by substituting it with one that is institutionally coherent and stable, and above all, capable of responding adequately to the demands emanating from an interplay of social interests and claims.

As indicated in the preceding section, the political transition in Ghana took a quantum jump forward on 3 January 1993 when the authoritarian military-based regime was replaced with a new one based on the 1992 Constitution. The success of this protracted process would depend on the extent to which the principal political actors would agree on the institutions and rules that are necessary for efficient mediation of competing claims, and be able to reshape attitudes and norms in line with the new political order that is envisaged. Among the responsibilities of such groups is the need to undertake the painful process of gradually but systematically redefining the boundaries of state and society, and instituting appropriate regulatory rules, norms and procedure that will ensure responsible government and safeguard the rights and interests of society. The literature on democratic transformation and consolidation attributes this function to civil society. According to Diamond (1994:7):

> The first and most basic democratic function of civil society is to provide: 'the basis for the limitation of state power; hence for the control of the state by society, and hence for democratic political institutions as the most effective means of exercising that control'. This function has two main dimensions: to monitor and restrain the exercise of power by democratic states; and to democratise authoritarian states.

Postulates like this do not take cognisance of the complexity of a transition process and the diverse factors which mediate and determine its direction, especially in underdeveloped countries like Ghana. It should be recalled that the idea of civil society has a specific socio-historic origin which gave it a particular connotation. In its seventeenth and eighteenth century origin, the term implied the emergence of a definable social class, with settled socio-economic and political rights and capabilities and, above all, class identity. This class was the bourgeoisie whose emergence also marked the rise of capitalism.[1] The central point of this argument is that the idea of civil society was associated with the rise of the bourgeoisie. Their struggle against the state was not merely to separate and protect the private sphere of life from state interference. It was above all a struggle to dominate the public sphere. Laissez faire in politics and the economy were the ideological justifications for the hegemony of the bourgeoisie. Hence, some African writers (e. g., Nzimande & Sikhosana 1995:20-45) have questioned claims in the literature on democratisation which argue that civil society has the capacity to secure freedom and democracy for all members of the political community rather than freedom and democracy for this dominant class, and repression for the rest.

From another perspective, Bangura and Gibbon (1992) have argued that the concept ignores the fact that civil society is a product of the existing social structure; and that the authoritarian tendencies inherent in particular social structures are ultimately reproduced in the civic associations that constitute civil society. That is, civil societies could also become the realm of unfreedom. It is therefore erroneous to attribute to them intrinsic democratic tendencies. This point becomes poignant particularly in underdeveloped countries where:

(i) the emerging social forces lack sufficient autonomy from the state, and easily become instruments for enforcing the political domination of the ruling elite; or where

(ii) the prevailing attitudes and norms are regulated to a significant degree by traditional authority structures and corresponding ideologies.

In either case, the emerging social forces are an easy target of state manipulation and control.

Therefore, civil societies in such social formations may not be able to function as free agents capable of transforming the authoritarian political structures of society into free and democratic ones. Bayart's caricaturisation of state-society relationship as 'the politics of the belly' (Bayart 1993) captures the essence of such socio-political ambiguities which epitomise everything that compromise rather than safeguard the liberties of members of the political community against the state.

In a similar vein, Mamdani (1995:3-5) cautions against the danger of taking 'a one-eyed vision of social and political processes' that are so complex and dynamic. He identifies the traditional sector of African societies as an obstacle to democratisation — that is, assuming that there are social forces in the modern sector that are committed to the democratisation of state power. The thrust of Mamdani's point is self-evident. The incompleteness of capitalist modernisation has left in its trail a modern sector in which the leading social classes — the capitalist and working classes, best described as incomplete classes — are a composite of traditional and modern elements dominated by an equally delicate mixture of traditional and modern attitudes and norms. Peil's (1972) description of the Ghanaian working class as a proletarianised peasantry is therefore apposite.

In fact, whole social structures exhibit such amalgam of cultures in which class differentiation and behavioural characteristics are not clearly defined; and at best confused. At the economic level, that morbid sector which is euphemistically called the informal sector is a remarkable product of this pervasive confusion in the social structure of developing societies; and its dramatic expansion during the last decade[2] illustrates the weakness of the social classes. As I will argue below, this weakness in the social structure is reproduced at the level of political action. The point is that in an underdeveloped society like Ghana, the conceptual distinction between the modern and traditional sectors is untenable. The two have a symbiotic existence; what is modern contains within itself the strengths, weaknesses and dangers of the traditional; and vice versa. The caution raised by Bangura and Gibbon (1992) and Mamdani (1995) is about the dynamics of this relationship; particularly, the tendency of the traditional elements to obstruct the modern sector's potential for growth and expansion.

This is why civil societies that are constituted in backward societies could not be regarded with certainty as agents of democratisation. The ease with which regimes have created civil societies or co-opted existing ones into state-centred patronage networks, as in the Ghanaian case under discussion, illustrates the point graphically. Furthermore, the ease with which civil societies melt away with the first shot from a soldier's gun, are co-opted by the state or absorbed by political parties whose main pre-occupation is not just to secure control of the state but also become part of it, reinforces this point.

In the Ghanaian situation these problems of the social structure were compounded by an entrenched military-based authoritarian government, the Provisional National Defence Council (PNDC) headed by Flt. Lt. J. J. Rawlings, which had been in office for about 10 years before the democratisation process actually took off. This government had constructed and nurtured an authoritarian regime at the centre of which was the personality of Rawlings (Hansen 1991; Yeebo 1991). And by 1991 when the democratisation process got under way, the government had successfully intimidated and disorganised the middle classes of professional and business people and suppressed their civic associations, including political parties. The PNDC government had employed legal, extra-legal and political means such as the National Investigations Committee, Public Tribunals, Citizens Vetting Committee, and Defence Committees combined with organised confrontation, physical attacks, and intimidation to achieve its objective.[3] The government had also succeeded, by and large, to intimidate, weaken and divide or suppress political and quasi-political groupings which had given it militant support in the initial phase of its rule — for example, organised labour and student organisation, as well as left-wing and radical organisations such as the New Democratic Movement, June Fourth Movement, and People's Revolutionary Youth League of Ghana.(Graham 1989; Ninsin 1989;

Yeebo 1991; Gyimah Boadi *et al.* 1993) The upshot of it all is that the organisations that could be mobilised by the most powerful social forces to influence the content and direction of the reform process had either been neutralised or considerably weakened.

To strengthen its monopoly of the political space, the government had successfully mobilised an alternative civil society comprising grassroots civic associations and quasi-political organisations whose members had been recruited from urban workers and the unemployed, informal sector operators and small business people. Prominent among them were the defence committees, 31st December Women's Movement, the Mobisquad, and several organisations of informal sector operators.

Added to these was the government's success in mobilising thousands of grassroots politicians — numbering over 6,500 — through the local government reforms and the elections which followed in 1988/89. By giving these small politicians access to political office, regular income and political patronage, the government could count on their support in the impending political contest between it and the opposition prodemocracy forces during the transition. For example, during the nationwide debate which was organised by the National Commission for Democracy (NCD) on the search for 'true democracy', most of these grassroots politicians were mobilised by the PNDC government to advance its own version of the democratic project. As the reform process gathered momentum, the possibility that such social forces would be mobilised to abort freedom and democracy became quite strong. When the government packed the assembly which drafted the 1992 Constitution with representatives of these social forces that possibility became very real.[4]

It should be recalled that the Rawlings government had come to power with the promise of replacing 'paper guarantees of abstract liberty' with 'popular democracy' in order to ensure the 'involvement and active participation of the people in the decision-making process'.[5] In the light of the government's position on the issue of democracy, it could be argued that its sponsorship of an alternative civil society was a critique of existing civil society on the grounds that it had denied a vast majority of Ghanaians of their rights as citizens of the country and excluded them from the political process. Rawlings' declaration, when he seized power, that he would install a regime that would be based on the consent of the people, and restore their fundamental rights was an unqualified indictment of the system he had overthrown.[6] As Seligman (1992:106) explains, the denial of equality and other rights, is a denial of citizenship; and that it usually leads to the growth of syndicalist ideas and movements whose activities threaten the existing social order. Viewed as syndicalists, it was inevitable that the civic associations that constituted this alternative civil society would become instruments of struggle against the social forces which supported the status quo or attempted to obstruct the realisation of the PNDC government's own democratic project which conflicted with liberal democracy.

On the issue of Rawlings' commitment to fostering a 'new' or 'true' democracy in Ghana, writers like Yeebo (1991), Shillington (1992), and Folson (1993) have argued from entirely different, often opposing, theoretical and empirical positions that Rawlings was not interested in effecting structural changes that would transform Ghanaian society and politics, including the fostering of a new democratic order. The fact that his government mobilised an alternative civil society was therefore simply an opportunistic strategy designed to enable him to consolidate his power. In other words, the Rawlings government employed alternative civil society as a Machiavellian strategy to substitute the existing political class with himself and his collaborators. It may be argued that this was the motive behind the Rawlings second coup d'état which aborted the country's 1979 Constitution. Borrowing from Max Weber, Hutchful (1991:184-85) has described such a strategic intervention in politics by soldiers, like Rawlings, as a 'charismatic moment'. He defines a charismatic moment as comprising:

> [first], the de-legitimisation and loosening of pre-existing structures and relations of power and authority; and second the opportunity to more or less extensively reorganise these relations. The defining characteristic of the charismatic moment is its appearance as a 'new beginning in national political life, signified by the rhetoric of revolution. ... A new constitution .... (enables the military) to redefine the formal context and space within which politics may be practised and to infuse the state with reserves of legitimation.

That Rawlings was least interested in, or committed to constitutionalism, was a fact which he did confess umpteen times during the life of his regime. In this sense, his regime could be seen clearly as an obstacle to democratisation and a grave threat to the most ardent civil society actors. The issues in the Ghanaian transition politics were therefore extremely complex and daunting.

Furthermore, different social classes espousing different political agendas were engaged in the process. In terms of objectives in the transition politics, these different social forces pursued a democratic project that had different meanings. On the one hand, for different opposition groups the movement for political reform was a fight against military dictatorship; it was for either constitutional rule, civilian rule, human rights; or a combination of a number of these. For the Rawlings regime and its supporters on the other hand, the issue at stake in the transition politics from the early 1980s, was simply a struggle for power: that is, whether or not the Rawlings regime should relinquish power. The rhetorical question which Rawlings posed early in the 1980s: 'Return power to whom?' underscored his conception of the key issue(s) in the political transition not for the moment but through to the 1990-1992 period. The alternative civil society that the regime mobilised was intended to ensure the retention of power by any means rather than facilitate the establishment of a new type of democracy. Authoritarianism was part of the strategy to retain power at any price. It may be argued that this original conception of the transition politics as a struggle between the pro-Rawlings and anti-Rawlings social forces had by the early 1990s changed but only in form and not in content. Hence, as the transition politics progressed the question which was posed silently by many concerned Ghanaians was whether or not the process would consummate in the transfer of power at all.

These are some of the key issues in the political transition which are addressed in the chapters that constitute this volume. The chapters by Bluwey, Jonah and Ninsin dilate on these ambiguities and dangers in the country's transition politics. According to Ninsin, at the critical juncture when the pressure for political reforms was gaining momentum, it became apparent that the 'existing civil society' was reconstituting and positioning itself for a struggle against the military regime of the PNDC. But in contrast with previous transition politics when middle class professional associations dominated civil society, this time it was the student organisation, National Union of Ghana Students and the trades union congress that spearheaded the struggle.

The relentless challenge which the Bar Association gave the government was the only exception to that general situation of abstention by middle class civic organisations from the movement for democracy. Another feature of the moment was the vigorous role played by leaders of the Christian Churches; namely, the Christian Council and the Catholic Bishops Conference who intervened openly on the side of the movement for reform, and actively mobilised their congregations to press for political reforms. Complementing the efforts of these leading actors were the quasi-political organisations which had been sponsored by existing political interests. The engagement of the latter groups, including the formation of the Movement for Freedom and Justice, in the transition politics marked a turning point in the process. As Jonah argues, these new, but covert, organisations were based on the political traditions of the proscribed political parties. If the primary aim of Africa's political parties is not just to win political power but also become part of the state apparatus once in power then, as noted by Ninsin and Jonah, this phenomenon of sponsored civic organisations was likely to deplete the ranks of the pro-democracy civil society and make the struggle for democracy more difficult. As happened soon after April 1992, the political parties that had sponsored the civic organisations simply absorbed the latter in their pursuit of political power; and so the struggle for democracy was deflated even if for a while.

The critical role played by the leadership of the two orthodox Christian Church organisations in precipitating political reforms also raises new questions about the character of Ghana's existing civil society. The role of the Church has traditionally been to offer spiritual and moral guidance. By advocating drastic changes in the structure of state power, including safeguards for the fundamental rights of the citizen, the Christian Council of Ghana and the Catholic Bishops Conference had departed from their traditional role to engage in direct and partisan political activity. Could such intervention in the transition politics by the Christian Churches signify a change in the composition and strategy of the Ghanaian pro-democracy civil society?

It is arguable that during the 1982-1992 period the repressive policies of the PNDC regime had forced, especially the vocal sections of the middle class to abandon the traditional middle class organisations, like the Association of Recognised Professional Bodies, to seek protection against political persecution and repression in the Christian Churches, where they hold key offices, as a strategic move to use the Churches as alternative instruments of political action. If this is tenable, and an indication of the future political role of the Christian Churches then we should expect a more activist political stance from them, especially in defence of good government. But if the Christian Churches should become instruments of good government, which is essentially a middle class project, it is unlikely that they would become advocates of the rights of the poor — which would place them in stark contrast with the tradition of liberation theology of Latin American Churches.

Jonah's argument regarding the positive role of political tradition in the democratisation process is equally noteworthy. In fact, this proposition should balance our earlier view about political parties as ultimately part of the state machinery and therefore instruments of rule. Jonah seems to argue that the party system as tradition afforded the Ghanaian middle class another haven in their struggle for democracy. Rather than expose themselves to the ravages of the authoritarian regime they opted for the security of the party political traditions even as the system hibernated pending the restoration of the right to form political associations and engage in open political activities. In this connection, the growth of 'political funerals' and the formation of quasi-political associations — the various welfare clubs formed in 1990-1991, may be regarded as one more of the strategies employed by the pro-democracy social forces to reform the state.

These roles of the orthodox Christian Churches and political parties in Ghana's transition politics calls for a revision of the conventional view which attributes to civil society — excluding these two social organisations — the exclusive capacity to initiate democratic reforms and act as watch-dog of the rights of the citizen. The definition of pro-democracy civil society should take into account the valuable contributions to the struggles for liberty which organisations like these could make. Alternatively, the concept of civil society should encompass a plurality of social structures that could interact with the state at different levels and in different instances. First, it is clear that the political role that the middle classes put the Churches, as well as political parties as tradition, in their struggle for democracy when party political activity was proscribed, enabled them to realise the gains which ultimately led to the elections, and finally to constitutional government in January 1993. As Jonah forcefully argues, Ghanaian political parties, both as tradition and specific organisations are committed to securing the institutional bases for a multi-party democratic regime. The same may be said for the orthodox Christian Churches.

The chapters by Bluwey and Ninsin provide additional insight into the complexity of Ghana's transition politics. The two draw attention to the extent to which an authoritarian regime could go (i) to mobilise alternative civil society to undermine the pursuit of democracy, and (ii) use key state and quasi-state organs also to obstruct the demands for liberal democratic reforms. Bluwey's paper raises an important element in the political equation of the transition: an authoritarian government which is keen to succeed itself. Surely, a government that has such a big stake in the transition process would employ every tactic to undermine the pro-democracy movement. According to Bluwey, the PNDC succeeded in its grand design of self-succession by employing a number of state institutions to gain political advantage. Apparently, the institutions which were employed by the government included even quasi-state organs whose autonomy is guaranteed by the 1992 Constitution — like the 'democracy commissions'. In such situations where the key institutions which should mediate the politics of the moment are appropriated and controlled by the incumbent government the entire transition process loses its integrity; and its legitimacy becomes doubtful. The crisis of the transition immediately before and after the 1992 elections may be attributed in part to this loss of integrity and legitimacy.

Discussions on democratisation suggest the existence of a homogenous and autonomous civil society,[7] whose role is facilitative. The chapter by Ninsin, however, seems to suggest the contrary: namely, that an authoritarian regime could mobilise or create an alternate civil society. The factors underpinning this development are not far-fetched. As argued earlier, in liberal democracies, civil societies are autonomous political realms because the social forces which constitute such arenas are themselves autonomous and powerful. In contrast, Ghanaian society provides an example of social forces that cannot assert themselves as autonomous political agents. Rather than the free-market reforms of the post-1982 period reversing this situation they exacerbated it, inducing a massive expansion in social forces that are impoverished, and too weak economically and politically to be independent of the state. The stupendous growth of the informal sector points at the dramatic changes in the country's social structure during the 1980s and early 1990s, changes that spanned both the lower and middle classes. It was the rise of these less autonomous social forces that provided the Rawlings regime with the material for constituting an alternative civil society.[8]

As argued above, civil societies which are constituted by less autonomous social forces are incapable of functioning as agents of democratisation. They tend rather to become state-controlled instruments for frustrating and ultimately aborting the process of democratisation. To sum up, the politics of Ghana's transition reveals contradictory tendencies: pro-democracy and anti- democracy tendencies which were always in conflict — were each spearheaded by their own civil society, and consisted largely of weak or less autonomous social forces.

As an integral part of civil society, the mass media or press must also not be viewed as a single, homogenous and autonomous institution. The chapter by Karikari is emphatic on this point: the Ghanaian press was divided between the pro-democracy and pro-government forces; and the latter was controlled firmly by the government which regarded it as an instrument for perpetuating its political domination. The contribution of the press to the democratisation process was therefore as contradictory as the civil societies it represented.

One can indeed argue that the practice of the pro-democracy and pro-government sections of the media followed a long tradition of division and fragmentation on issues of public policy. It may be argued that, like the political parties that Jonah studied, this tradition of division and fragmentation within the media is structured by deep-seated normative, ideological and political divisions in Ghanaian society. Such tendencies should reinforce similar developments in civil society to facilitate the growth of divergent views, and freedom of choice. Without doubt these are positive attributes for the pursuit of a democratic order; for it is out of diversity and contention of ideas, claims and interests that freedom prevails.

The military factor has not featured much, if at all, in the debate on the future of the democratisation process in Africa. Borrowing largely from the experience of Western countries, students of African politics have shown a striking pre-occupation with civil society's role in democratising the political order. The reason for this indifference towards the military factor has been summarised by Diamond (1994:4-5): 'the stimulus for democratisation, and particularly the pressure to complete the process, have typically come from the "resurrection of civil society"...'. The 'extensive mobilisation of civil society was a crucial source of pressure for democratic change.' To understand the democratisation process therefore we must understand the workings of civil society.[9] This neglect is puzzling in many ways, especially because of the military's predilection to intervene in the politics of the continent.

In the few instances where the subject has been broached the discussion has been oblique. For example, in a discussion of the state and democracy in Nigeria, Jibrin Ibrahim (1992:105-128) could merely pose the ancient question about whether the military would remain in, or retreat from, politics. It is Hutchful, with almost a life-time interest in the militarisation of African politics, who provides a sombre perspective on this nagging problem. He argues that:

> even in instances where a military regime's project of constitutionalism implies complete civilianisation of politics (the military is constrained) both in terms of technique (manipulation of constitutional instruments), the type and scope of problems that it has to address, and the extent to which it opens up the political structure to deprived groups. The overriding political objective has been state preservation and the reconstruction or reinforcement of modes of political dominance (Hutchful 1991:185).

The Luckham chapter seems to concur with Hutchful. Luckham cautions against hasty conclusions about the eventual civilianisation of Ghanaian politics: the country's democratisation process is still inconclusive, he argues. Its future hangs thinly on 'how the military can be prevented from intervening ...'. On the one hand, members of the military have become intoxicated with power and acquired an insatiable appetite for wealth through politics; so that the military has become almost a military political party in disguise. On the other hand, the grounds for democratic civilian control of the military are thin indeed. Not only was there little or no debate during the constitution-making phase of the transition about this crucial imperative and how to address it; but what ultimately emerged as the Fourth Republican Constitution simply reproduced the old constitutional framework governing civilian-military relations without untying this Gordian knot of the military's growing dominance in Ghanaian politics. Therefore, attempts at re-professionalising the military may not promise the expected antidote against the prospect of a return of the 'military party' to abort another infant democratic experiment by converting its 'gun power' into political power.

The preceding analysis of the issues in Ghana's transition has so far proceeded on the assumption that the process of political reforms was pushed forward by autonomous internal social forces; that, indeed, the process itself was autonomous. Two chapters: one by Jebuni and Oduro and the other by Boafo-Arthur, provide a different perspective on the autonomy, or lack of it, of the internal forces and the transition process itself: they expatiate on the role of external forces in propelling the transition process forward. Both contributions agree on the important role played by the donor community in precipitating the crucial phase of the transition process and keeping it on course against internal odds, particularly the military regime's antipathy towards democracy. They further argue that the significant inflow of foreign financial resources and the fact that the government became extremely dependent on crucial external economic resources exposed the government to the political conditionality of the donor community so much that it could not ignore the possibility that economic sanctions might be applied against it should it renege on the demands for political liberalisation. What is missing from the two contributions is analysis of the prospects for political reforms if there were no internal pressure for them. Nonetheless, the two chapters raise questions about the autonomy of the transition process from external forces.

Jebuni and Oduro raise two equally significant factors that affected the transition process — a political and economic factor. Even though these two factors are internal, it is not their contribution to the success of the transition process(es) that is discussed but their negative impact on it. The discussion raises important policy issues. In particular, the interplay of the two factors in the transition process raises the rather controversial question of the relationship between political liberalisation and economic liberalisation. Briefly put, Jebuni and Oduro argue that, on the one hand, the lack of a forum for openly debating the economic austerity policies of the government was a strong reason for the agitations for political liberalisation. And on the other hand, the pressure for political liberalisation fuelled a dramatic expansion in government expenditure which consequently jeopardised the economic reform policies.

These observations raise serious questions about the theoretical underpinning of current liberalisation policies. The pertinent literature has for a long time postulated an immutable relationship between democracy and markets. According to Lindblom (1977), for example, capitalism promotes and reinforces democracy. This, I believe, is why the economic reform policies that are currently being implemented in several African countries have been strongly defended as a solution to Africa's political crisis: economic liberalisation would create the impetus for political liberalisation, and vice versa, runs the chorus. It would seem that the support given by the donor community to Ghana's transition process was driven by this dictum. But, in fact, what Jebuni and Oduro saw as a potential danger to the economic reform policies raised the embarrassing question as to whether or not the economic liberalisation policies should be sacrificed for political liberalisation, and vice versa. It was not a pleasant dilemma; for it exposed a serious flaw in the liberal argument. In particular, it questioned the veracity of the thesis that economic reforms towards capitalist markets would promote democratisation. If the Ghanaian experience has proved anything at all, it is that liberal economic reforms could provoke people to fight for their democratic rights rather than the reforms following an iron logic of liberalising an authoritarian regime.

But more fundamentally, the dilemma identified by Jebuni and Oduro does not pose an either or question: economic or political reforms? First the Ghanaian experience testifies to the extremely complex nature of any transition process; and the need therefore to avoid simplistic theories and postulates. What has become clear from the Ghanaian experience is that there were two transitions — the economic and political — going on simultaneously; and that the economic transition does not provide the magical formula for a successful and stable political transition. Second, it is politically unwise to pursue the economic reforms without any regard for the political interests and aspirations of the people. Similarly, it is foolish to embark on political reforms regardless of the economic interests of the people. Too often, as in the Ghana case, the two reforms are unavoidable just as providing for the economic and political rights and interests of the citizens have become imperative and inseparable. This is the heart of the matter.

Either the economic or political transition has great potential to mobilise social forces that could easily undermine the other. The danger of this happening is strongest where the contending forces have few reasons for compromises. Clearly, the lack of political will among Ghana's contending social forces — the pro-democracy and government forces — to compromise and reach a consensus on the direction of public policy was a real threat to the two transitions. Equally important is the need for all the contending parties in the transition to agree on adequate guarantees of security and benefits for both losers and winners. In the Ghanaian situation the absence of sufficient guarantees of security for the leading personnel of the liberalising authoritarian government almost precipitated a crisis both before and after the 1992 elections.[10] The dogged efforts by the military government to win the elections at any cost and constitutionalise itself was the result of the profound sense of insecurity that gripped the members of that regime. In the end, the fear of perpetuating the rule of the outgoing authoritarian regime by default obliged the pro-democracy groups to abandon their resolution to boycott the fledgling democratic authority structures which had been established under the 1992 Constitution. It was evident that the price of returning the country to authoritarian rule would be far greater than the price of living under an imperfect democratic order and learning patiently to purge it of its imperfections and abuses. The resolve of the opposition forces now to contest the 1996 elections is a clear testimony of their commitment to the course of democracy in the country.

Moreover, there should also be core institutions outside the ambit of civil society-state and quasi-state institutions, which are capable of mediating even the most intractable conflicts. In the Ghanaian transition the judiciary and mass media have prevailed as key conflict mediating institutions. The period following the 1992 elections shot the judiciary and the mass media on to the centre-stage of politics. In spite of their obvious limitations, these two institution have been transformed into an extension of the political arena where political conflicts would henceforth be fought.

Yet another development that could provide a mechanism for peaceful management of political conflict is the growth of small citizens rights associations, and a seeming upsurge in mass consciousness. The proliferation of citizens associations and the most recent explosion of mass public demonstrations against unpopular laws and policies — both economic and political — underscore the fact that it is only when citizens become aware of their democratic rights and obligations, and are prepared to take concerted action in defence of such rights and obligations that dictatorship would be kept at bay. It is this level of popular vigilance and organisation which, if sustained, could compel elements within the state system — like the military, to gradually accept the golden rule in democratic politics: that sovereignty emanates from the people through the ballot box; and not from the barrel of the gun.

Notes

1. For a critique of the uses and abuses of 'the idea of civil society' see Seligman (1992).
2. See Ninsin (1991) for an analysis of the origins and growth of the informal sector in Ghana. He argues that the informal sector, its growth and dramatic expansion in recent times, is the direct result of the crisis of Ghana's perverse capitalist economy.
3. For a discussion of the impact of these and other measures see Oquaye (1993).
4. This fear explains why there was so much criticism and agitation against the composition of the Consultative Assembly resulting the in the boycott of that body by influential civic associations and key actors in the transition politics such as the Ghana Bar Association and the National Union of Ghana Students. For the declarations of their views on the Consultative Assembly and other issues in the transition politics refer to Ninsin (1996).
5. The first 2 radio and television broadcasts to Ghanaians which he made in January 1982 - that is, immediately after seizing power.
6. Ibid.
7. The possible exception is Bayart (1988; 1993).
8. It should be recalled that Kwame Nkrumah achieved a similar political feat by mobilising social forces which were equally less autonomous to propel his party to power in the elections of 1951, 1954 and 1956; and later mobilised the same social forces to consolidate his power.

9. African political scientists also seem to have shown the same indifference. The following works by African political scientists, who are based on the continent and write from there, illustrate the extent of their neglect of the military factor in the current democratisation processes on the continent, See Anyang' Nyong'o (1987); Mamdani and Wamba-dia-Wamba (1995); and Chole and Ibrahim (1995). It is remarkable that none of the contributors in Osaghae (1994) could discover the presence of the military in the political space between the state and civil society.

10. For example, the motive behind the Rawlings government's decision to entrench blanket indemnity clauses in the 1992 Constitution, and the angry denunciations of that action by the most articulate sections of the Ghanaian public, especially by leading members of the pro-democracy movement clearly illustrate the grave sense of insecurity that gripped the Rawlings military government on the eve of the elections of 1992.

2

Structural Adjustment Programme and the Transition to Democracy

Charles D. Jebuni and Abena D. Oduro

Introduction

As in the 1960s when the wave of decolonisation swept across the African continent, in the 1990s there is a wave of political liberalisation involving a movement to pluralistic democratic systems. Following closely the wave of structural adjustment programmes sweeping across the African continent, there is a natural tendency to link the two; namely, the movement for political liberalisation and the structural adjustment policies. For example, the Provisional National Defence Council (PNDC) Law 252 establishing the Committee of Experts (Constitution) to draft proposals for the constitution of the fourth republic provided *inter alia*, that the proposals shall 'provide for directive principles of state policy that shall ensure participatory democracy, and the sound management of the national economy'. Whether this provision in the law was the result of conviction in the soundness of the principles of economic management under structural adjustment or as part of the increasing trend among a number of less developed countries to link the two, the PNDC established a link between economic management and the transition to democracy.

But it must also be said that this provision of PNDC Law 252 was based in part on an emerging consensus in the Ghanaian society that 'the most secure democracy cannot be one that depends on a massive protective military or police presence but one that assures the basic necessities of life for its people as a fundamental duty' (NCD 1991:43). These developments raise a number of issues about the possible relationship between structural adjustment and the transition to democracy sweeping across Africa.

The objective of this paper is to examine the relationship between the implementation of a structural adjustment programme and the transition to democracy in Ghana. In the first section we examine the literature in order to derive the basic hypothesis to be tested in this paper. Section 2 provides a discussion of the structural adjustment programme in Ghana, examines the initial conditions leading up to the implementation of SAP, the reasons for its implementation, and then presents an outline of the programme. Section 3 examines the outcomes and its relation to internal demands for political liberalisation and the role of external donors. Section 4 examines the link between SAP, governance and the transition to democracy. Section 5 analyses the effect of the transition to democracy on SAP and Section 6 concludes the paper.

Transition to Democracy: Theories and Issues

The internal demand for political reform, it is argued, usually arises during periods of crisis or discontent. Urban groups and the middle class tend to be in the forefront of demands for improvements in their standard of living which, in their view, had been eroded by the economic measures being pursued. This discontent is then exploited by opposition groups which broaden the call for change away from the particular interest of individual groups. Economic discontent within the context of open corruption will fuel further the demands for political reform on the grounds that the failure or poor performance of the economic programme is due to corruption which has been facilitated by the type of political regime. In some cases the demand for the introduction of political liberalisation and eventual democracy may be based on the simple fact that the populace want a change from the previous regime which they consider to have failed them.

However, it is not only during conditions of economic crisis or discontent that the calls for democratisation of the political system is made. Economic growth and the improvement in economic well-being in an autocratic political regime can also provide grounds for the demand for an increase in political liberalisation and eventually, democracy. Economic liberalisation, a result of the implementation of SAPs, changes the role of the state in the economy. The removal of controls transfers the decision-making process concerning the allocation of resources from the state to the market place (Hofmeier 1991). Individuals will perceive that they are becoming increasingly responsible for their economic outcomes. The increase in the ability of the private sector to generate wealth could fuel demands for democratisation if the decision on how revenues are allocated and taxes levied is determined by a small clique which is not necessarily the group that produces the national wealth. Thus the demand for increased political liberalisation may be based on the need for a widening of the decision-making process.

It is therefore not clear *a priori* whether it is economic prosperity or economic decline which is necessary to trigger domestic demands for political reform. Nor is it clear whether incumbent autocracies are more likely to respond to these demands when they are made during periods of crisis compared to periods of prosperity.

Developments in the international political environment have also been identified as important in explaining the current move towards democracy (Bratton and van de Walle 1992; and Hofmeier 1991). These developments have not only impacted directly on the domestic populace but have also been important in explaining the emergence of the international donor community as a strong and in some cases effective lobby of political reform. The collapse of the Eastern European Socialist bloc and the institution of democratically elected governments seriously flawed the logic of the one-party and military autocracies in Africa and the rationale for the ban on multi-partyism. Elsewhere in Africa, the multi-party elections in the newly independent Namibia and the moves towards universal suffrage in South Africa must have strengthened the resolve as well as the arguments for democracy amongst local opponents of the autocracies.

The fall of the socialist regimes of the world has allowed human rights issues to become important considerations in the aid disbursement process amongst Western governments. For example, at the Franco-African summit in 1989, President Mitterrand of France stated in clear terms that development aid would henceforth be linked to progress on political reform. Similar sentiments have been expressed by ministers of other Western governments. The World Bank in its long-term perspective study on Africa had this to say, 'Underlying the litany of Africa's development problems is a crisis of governance. By governance is meant the exercise of political power to manage a nation's affairs. Because countervailing power has been lacking, state officials in many countries have served their own interests without fear of being called to account. ...This environment cannot readily support a dynamic economy' (World Bank 1989:601). In contrast with writers like Przeworski and Limongi (1993) who link regime type with international development aid, the World Bank does not place emphasis on the type of regime it assists with development aid. It nonetheless emphasises the importance of politics, and the need for some political liberalisation which involves transparency and accountability.

The expression of dissatisfaction with the autocratic regimes in the developing countries must have further strengthened the position of the external donors. Concurrently, the struggles of local population must also have been encouraged by the sentiments expressed by the donors thus contributing to a virtuous circle in the demand for political liberalisation.

The recent calls for democratisation are not the first in the post-independence history of African countries. We should therefore explain why incumbent governments had become responsive to them during the 1989-93 period. Bratton and van de Walle (1992) have argued that governments respond positively to these demands when it will ensure their political survival or more generally if it is in their best interests to do so. They identified three determining variables of importance. The first is whether dissatisfaction is expressed by support groups critical to the government's survival. The second is whether government has access to resources which will allow it to continue to dominate the political process even after reforms. The third is the degree of dependence on foreign inflows. A fourth variable which may be included is the ability to repress the manifestations of dissent.

What then is the role of SAP in the transition to democracy? To begin with, the demand for political reform at home will be linked to the impact of the SAP on the populace because of the impetus it may have given to demands for democratisation. The SAP is also relevant in determining whether and how governments respond to such demands. SAPs may affect government's control over resources; and secondly the implementation of the programme may affect the government's dependence on foreign inflows and thereby increase the leverage of external donors.

Once the process of transition has been embarked upon it can influence the structural adjustment programme. The transition process itself may require an increase in expenditures as institutions are created to facilitate voter registration, education of the populace and elections. Second, as argued by Hofmeier (1991:106) '... within the framework of an incipient process of democratisation, taking notice of the most articulate political groups can mean a considerable hindrance to making the necessary economic structural changes'. Haggard and Kaufmann (1989:64-65) also find that 'democratic transitions are associated with difficulties in managing the macro-economy': and that 'eight out of the ten transitional democracies had higher budget deficits during the transition year than in the period prior to the transition'.

Prelude to the Structural Adjustment Programme

The ten-year period prior to the implementation of the Economic Recovery Programme (ERP) was characterised by increasing controls and regulation of economic activity, particularly in the tradable goods sector. The Acheampong government of 1972-79 reversed the economic liberalisation programme which had been initiated in 1967. The government partially revalued the currency and unilaterally repudiated some of Ghana's debts. Comprehensive import and payment controls were reintroduced, the scope and coverage of price controls were widened. The overall principle of government was self-reliance and a reduction in dependence on external resources. Economic policy had moved full circle to the command economy of the Nkrumah era. Except for brief periods between 1979 and 1980 when some attempt was made at liberalising the trade regime with a devaluation of the cedi in 1978, these controls remained in place up to 1983.

As these policies began to take effect, the rate of inflation almost tripled within four years from 11 per cent in 1972 to 30 per cent in 1975. The real depreciation in the currency achieved with the devaluation of 1971 was eroded. The value of the cedi appreciated sharply in subsequent years. The highly overvalued exchange rate discouraged exports and intensified price and trade controls thereby worsening an already precarious economic situation. Furthermore, despite the highly favourable terms of trade between 1972 and 1979 both import and export volumes declined (Table 1).

With an expanded role for the state, government expenditures increased. To finance these expenditures the government instituted high excise duties, export taxes, import duties and an array of complex income and profit taxes. These developments encouraged both rent-seeking activities and the expansion of parallel markets in commodities and currency transactions. The official economy shrunk and with it government revenues. The tax base on both imports and exports declined sharply and tax compliance also decreased. Government revenues as a proportion of GDP declined throughout the period 1975-1983 from 15.5 per cent in 1975 to 5.6 per cent in 1982 (Frimpong-Ansah 1991:160). While occasional attempts were made to cut expenditures they remained relatively high largely on account of recurrent expenditures.

Table 1: Some Key Economic Indicators 1970-1983

(a)

Year	GDP Growth	Fiscal balance GDP Ratio	Investment GDP Ratio	Inflation Rate	Credit to (A)	(B)
1970	6.78	0.1	13	3.68	0.291	0.115
1971	5.56	0.4	13	9.28	0.289	0.12
1972	2.49	5.4	9	11	0.358	0.168
1973	5.55	4.4	8	17	0.376	0.231
1974	6.85	7.4	12	19	0.584	0.338
1975	12.43	11.8	12	30	0.924	0.295
1976	3.52	13.3	9.8	55	1.57	0.393
1977	2.26	13.2	9.4	116	2.78	0.423
1978	8.47	9.1	6.4	73	4.52	1.11
1979	3.77	5.8	6.7	55	4.90	1.63
1980	0.23	6.1	6.1	50	6.51	1.96
1981	3.17	6.1	4.7	116	10.64	3.39
1982	5.85	5.9	3.5	22	11.05	6.08
1983	4.33	2.5	3.7	123	28.05	1.34

(b)

Year	Export	Import	Official	Real**
	Volume Index (1975=100		Exchange Rate Cedis per US$*	Effective Exchange Rate
1970	154.7	165.3	1.02	28.1
1971	108.7	138.8	1.82	28.4
1972	130.7	71.7	1.28	22.1
1973	118.5	85.4	1.15	25.7
1974	97.7	115.2	1.15	27.4
1975	100.0	100.0	1.15	30.8
1976	104.5	96.3	1.15	46.8
1977	86.3	100.0	1.15	90.8
1978	71.1	82.9	2.75	102.0
1979	67.8	63.0	2.75	75.77
1980	70.0	64.3	2.75	100.0
1981	70.1	72.5	2.75	220.5
1982	81.6	48.4	2.75	276.8
1983	58.8	37.4	30.00	242.0

(External Indicators)

Sources: Statistical Services, *Quarterly Digest of Statistics*, various issues, Accra. IMF, 1993, *International Financial Statistics Yearbook 1992*, Washington DC.

* End of period.
** An increase means an appreciation.
(A) is net credit to the central government by the banking system in billions of cedis.
(B) is credit to the nonfinancial public institutions by the banking system in billions of cedis.

One lesson most Ghanaian governments had learnt was that political success depended on the ability to minimise the discontent of the politically active urban classes. As the rate of inflation accelerated and the control system failed to supply commodities either in sufficient quantities or at controlled prices, urban unrest developed. To placate these groups government expenditures financed by borrowing from the banking system increased, especially from 1975 onwards. Government spending had no relationship to budgetary plans with most years realising large budgetary deficits rather than the planned surpluses.

The policies pursued since 1972 resulted in heavy taxation of the exportable sector. There was a transfer of resources from exporters as a group, in particular cocoa farmers, to the group responsible for the allocation of licenses and foreign exchange and the group which had access to the subsidised import licenses and foreign exchange. The subsidies on petroleum, other imported items and utilities probably benefited urban dwellers who tended to consume a significant proportion of these commodities.

The coup d'état of December 1981 which brought the PNDC to power did not initially stop the economic decline. This is because the radical populist approach to economic recovery adopted by the new government in its first fifteen months did not address the underlying causes of the economic crisis. Output plummeted further in 1982 and the investment rate declined whilst the black market premium increased (Table 1).

Thus, by the start of the structural adjustment programme, Ghana had experienced a continuous decline in growth of GDP as a result of these policies starting from 1975. After this period, for every single year, except for 1977 and 1978, real GDP actually declined. The external position of the economy was precarious. Gross external reserves as a ratio of GDP stood at 0.7 per cent by 1982.

Explaining the Economic Policy Change in 1983

Theories abound to explain why economic policy change occurs. Economic policy change may occur when there is a change from a weak state to a strong state. This may coincide with a change in leadership. Lal (1987) argues that it is the failure of previous economic strategies which provides the impetus for policy change. Bates (1983) on the other hand, argues that policy change occurs when a political pact amongst various interest groups unwinds as the losers from the pact exit from the economic system transferring the costs of the pact to the intended beneficiaries. Change is more likely when it is the government which bears the cost of the breakdown of the pact.

The policies pursued prior to 1981 may be considered as a pact between the government, traders and import-substituting groups to generate resources from the export sector through the trade and exchange rate policies and the cocoa pricing policy. This pact began to unwind however as cocoa producers exited the system through smuggling, for example, and as export volumes in general declined. The decline in government revenues resulting from the trade and exchange rate policies acted as a constraint on government's ability to maintain support through the use of discretionary expenditures.

The failure of the populist strategy implemented in 1982 whilst maintaining the controlled regime (that is, without dismantling the previous pact) made it abundantly clear to the Rawlings government that there was the need for policy changes. The ability to convince the leadership that the new alternatives would improve the revenue generating capacity of the state as well as address the leadership's concern about societal injustice was also important in ensuring its acceptance of the economic reform package. The policy change however was not the result of a compromise, but came about as a result of an internal struggle in which the elements against reform were marginalised.

In summary, Rawlings and his PNDC came to power as a result of economic discontent which created fertile grounds for political change. On the other hand the failure of his populist economic strategy, the disappearance of rents and the threat to the survival of his regime forced him to adopt a liberal economic system.

The Reform Programme

There were three immediate requirements for reforming the Ghanaian economy in 1983. First it was essential to reduce the rate of inflation from the three digit level to reasonable levels. Second there was the need to increase production, particularly of traditional exports both as an input into reducing the balance of payments deficit and reducing inflation.

Finally it was critical to increase government revenues sharply. As discussed earlier, the previous policies had depleted government revenues. Increased revenues were therefore essential to restore the state's governance capacity.

In addressing these immediate concerns and for almost all the adjustment period, the strategy was to address simultaneously issues of policy design and implementation. Not only would the policy initiative require institutional changes but also arrangements aimed at addressing the issue of adequate compensation or incentives to induce the relevant response at each stage.

Trade and Exchange Rate Reform

Fear of the political consequences of an outright nominal devaluation delayed the use of this instrument by government to correct the currency overvaluation. Instead a multiple exchange rate system was introduced. The nominal exchange rate remained fixed at its 1978 level but a system of surcharges and bonuses was introduced which increased the actual exchange rate. As a result of the system of surcharges and bonuses, traditional exports and imports of crude oil, essential raw materials, basic foodstuff and capital goods were subject to an actual rate of C23.75 to the US dollar. Non-traditional exports and other imports faced a rate of C25.975 to the US dollar. The exchange rate was unified in October 1983 at C30 to the US dollar. These policy measures were then followed within the same year with fiscal retrenchment and dis-inflationary monetary policies.

Whilst these macro-economic policy initiatives were taking place, and providing the relevant incentives for production, government also took measures to remove the immediate supply constraints to the traditional export sector. Roads and railways leading to cocoa, timber and mineral producing areas were rehabilitated. Foreign loans were procured for timber and mineral producers.

Having achieved a certain level of stabilisation in the initial years the programme moved into trying to remove micro-economic distortions. Significant changes in trade and exchange rate policy have been undertaken since 1983. Following the initial unification of the exchange rate, incentives were maintained through periodic devaluations of the exchange rate. These announcements became increasingly difficult for government to make. In September 1986 a multiple exchange rate system based on an auction system (Window II) and a fixed exchange rate (Window I) was introduced. The objective of the new system was to allow the exchange rate to be determined by domestic demand and supply factors, promote trade liberalisation and divert foreign exchange held outside the banks into the banking system. Three months later the exchange rate was unified and all transactions took place at the auction rate. Liberalisation of the exchange rate system went a step further with the introduction in 1988 of the forex bureaux. Since then an inter-bank market in foreign exchange has been introduced and exchange rate regulations relaxed. These measures resulted in a substantial depreciation of the real exchange rate especially in the first three to four years of the programme (Table 2). The incentive structure is now more favourable towards exporting compared to the strongly anti-export bias which prevailed prior to the introduction of the reforms.

Previous experience in Ghana had shown that serious balance of payments consequences could follow from trade liberalisation. At the same time, it was thought that imports should go into relieving the critical import needs of the production sector. Therefore at the initial stages of the programme, import liberalisation in terms of reducing tariffs occurred within the context of import programming. This was pursued until 1986 when import programming ended. Import tariffs were reduced further after 1986. At the same time the negative import list was reduced and in 1989 import licensing abolished. Further trade reform involved the streamlining and lowering of nominal tariff rates to provide uniform incentives for industries. An export promotion package was put in place and the Ghana Export Promotion Council was revitalised in order to encourage non-traditional exports.

Fiscal Reform

Critical to governance capacity of the state was the generation of financial resources. But as noted earlier the tax base had shrunk as a result of previous policies. At the time of introduction of the ERP it was recognised that there was a large potential for revenue generation. One of the principal elements of the Ghanaian success story was the ability of the government in raising tax revenues substantially. Rather than focus on cuts in expenditure as a means of dealing with the budgetary crisis emphasis was put on revenue generation. Real government expenditures had declined to such low levels that further cuts in expenditures were not perceived to be viable. The poor state of the economic infrastructure was suggestive of a need to increase government expenditures. On the other hand the potential to increase government revenues was significant given the low levels to which real revenues and the ratio of revenue to GDP had fallen. The objective of the tax reform system was to improve the efficiency of tax administration, broaden the tax base, reform the punitive system of taxation and shift the burden of taxation from the wage earners and cocoa farmers to consumers of luxury goods — the affluent members of society.

The devaluation of the currency and the trade reform measures could be expected to increase explicit tax revenues. Compliance and an increase in efficiency were essential if these were to be realised. To increase the revenues arising from these measures a number of institutional reforms were made in the tax collection agencies. Extreme measures were taken initially to ensure that individuals and organisations which were required to pay their taxes did so. The restructuring of the tax collecting organisations and the activities of investigating committees to check for tax evasion as well as the requirement to produce evidence of tax payment before important documents (for example passports) would be released were important in improving the generation of taxes.

Novel means were devised to generate taxes from groups in the informal sector which normally escaped the tax net. The informal sector consists largely of illiterate and semi-literate entrepreneurs who do not usually keep accounts. They could not therefore be expected to complete tax forms for their incomes to be assessed and taxed. To overcome this difficulty, standardised tax rates for various trades were established. The assistance of artisan groups, for example, the Ghana Private Road Transport Union of the TUC (GPRTU), was solicited to collect taxes on behalf of the Internal Revenue Service.

Government expenditure policy was not geared towards cutting expenditures. Instead it was directed at achieving levels of outlays or expenditures consistent with macroeconomic stability (Chand 1993). The budgetary process in Ghana usually consists of four interrelated stages, i.e. formulation, authorisation and approval, implementation and evaluation. This process had fallen into disuse during the pre-ERP period. It was reactivated and strengthened as a basis for control and rationalisation of expenditures.

Several other policy initiatives were taken to achieve expenditure objectives. The wage determining process was rationalised and government made it clear that large wage increases would not be granted. From 1986, wage increases in subvented institutions were to be based on inflation, productivity and profitability. In subsequent years wage payments were computerised to remove the names of a substantial number of non-existent workers from the payrolls. Several allowances which were granted in response to political pressures in the previous period were consolidated into a basic wage or salary.

While these measures could substantially reduce the growth of government expenditures several subsidies existed in the system, the public service was overmanned and non-functioning state enterprises constituted a drain on the budget. To reduce their budgetary burden a phased removal of subsidies and liberalisation of agricultural input prices was introduced and public service labour retrenchment began in 1987.

Policy towards the state enterprises had several dimensions. The first was divestiture and outright liquidation. There was also the re-organisation component which involved initially the signing of performance contracts with the government. The laws establishing state enterprises were repealed and eventually replaced with the Statutory Corporations Conversions Bill which allows them to register as limited liability companies with Board of Directors. Their budgetary proposals have to be part of a three-year rolling plan. If deficits were incurred for three years in a row the companies would be liquidated.

Other Reforms

Reform of entry regulations and investment incentives has been slow. It was not until 1992 that there were changes in the regulatory and administrative arrangements in the industrial sector. The Manufacturing Industries Act of 1971 was abolished, the price control laws were repealed, and amendments to the Investment Code turned the Ghana Investment Centre into an investment promotion unit. However, new investments still remain subject to prior approval. The process of gaining access to investment benefits under the Investment Code is still lengthy and cumbersome.

Programme Implementation and the Transition to Democracy

In a radio and television broadcast made in 1983, Rawlings defended the programme as the transition to democracy, social justice and dignity. 'The recent budget is the only viable option to us. It is the river which we have to cross to reach the future which we have chosen, a future in which with time democracy, social justice and dignity will make freedom a reality' (Rawlings 1983:16). It is possible that the link with a transition to democracy was made as a means of winning support for the programme. The Rawlings government had overthrown a democratically elected government on grounds of economic ineptitude and corruption. It was unlikely that it could conceive of a return to the same system without any economic gains. Whatever the motive, it was clear that the democracy Rawlings talked about was not the liberal type. It was conceived as grassroots democracy in which decision-making was to be decentralised to the grassroots level. But as Jeffries (1991:164-65) has argued: 'His commitment to the latter (democracy) seems over time to have faded or at least to have taken a much lower position in the order of priorities'. Subsequently, the PNDC became 'an authoritarian administrative regime, resorting to harassment and arrest to cow its opponents and silence its critics'. Any connection between the SAP and the transition to democracy must be seen much more in the outcome of the programme rather than as a pre-conceived or visionary connection with economic welfare.

One of the reasons one could expect a reform programme in Ghana not to generate the type of IMF riots experienced in Zambia is that the rents which the predatory state and its clientele extracted through their policies had virtually disappeared. The extraction of rents had gone beyond the optimum. According to Leith and Lofchie (1993) one can identify three stages in the overvaluation of the currency. The first is the ordinary overvaluation in which no rents are generated. In the second stage of overvaluation, considerable rents are generated. In the third stage the overvaluation is so severe that the rents disappear. Ghana was in the third stage at the time of the reforms. Second, the PNDC showed inordinate propensity to suppress its critics and indeed any kind of protest. Accordingly, the incidence of industrial strikes declined sharply; and the working days lost due to strikes dropped sharply in 1982 and remained very low in the next ten years.

The Response of the Economy and the Transition

Some indicators of the performance of the economy and response to the structural adjustment programme are shown in Table 2. National income increased by 10.34 per cent in 1984 and the rate of inflation fell to 39.5 per cent from 123 per cent in 1983. Export volumes increased by 2.02 per cent in 1984 compared to the decline of 27.8 per cent in the previous year. The ratio of the current account deficit to GDP declined and there was a sharp drop in the ratio of the parallel to the official exchange rate.

The significant relative price changes caused by the devaluation, the existing excess capacity, the large parallel economy and the good rains of 1984 enabled the immediate substantial response to the programme. The existence of the parallel market allowed for a rapid supply response as the sale of output was shifted from parallel to official market channels.

Since 1984 the growth rate of national income, export and import volumes have remained positive. The trade account has been in deficit for most years. The decline in the export unit values by 33.1 per cent between 1987 and 1992 has eroded the effects of the improvement in the export volumes. The terms of trade deteriorated by 49 per cent during this period. The ratio of the current account to GDP declined between 1985 and 1989 but has since been rising. Official transfers have reduced significantly this ratio. There was an initial large positive investment response to the programme. The investment rate (both private and public sector) increased by 50 per cent between 1984 and 1985 and by 30 per cent between 1986 and 1987 (Table 2). Since 1987 however, the investment rate hardly increased: it experienced a sharp drop in 1992. Private investment almost doubled from its 1983 level by 1985. Even though it slumped by half in 1986, it has increased steadily since then. It appears that the economy has lost some of its momentum since 1990 with a slow down in the growth of GDP.

Table 2: Some Key Economic Indicators 1984-1992

	1984	1985	1986	1987	1988	1989	1990	1991	1992
GDP Growth	8.6	5.1	5.2	4.8	5.6	5.1	3.3	5.0	3.9
Agricultural Growth	9.7	0.6	3.3	0.0	3.6	3.6	2.0	4.7	0.6
Industry Growth	9.1	17.6	7.6	11.5	7.2	2.6	6.9	3.7	5.8
Services Growth	6.6	7.5	6.5	9.4	7.8	6.7	7.9	6.3	7.7
Per Capita Income									
Growth	5.9	2.4	2.5	1.2	3.4	3.3	0.5	2.0	0.9
Investment	6.9	9.6	9.7	13.4	14.2	15.5	16.0	15.9	12.6
Public Sector									
Financial Balance	2.3	3.0	3.3	2.4	2.8	2.2	2.4		
Private Sector									
Financial Balance	1.3	0.6	1.8	0.3	1.1	0.4	2.4		
Export Volume (%)	85.7	103.7	114.9	124	139	166.6	170.9	182.5	188.5
Import Volume (%)	74	82	94	106	111	119	122.1	131.8	134.8
External Current									
Account Balance	1.0	2.5	1.5	2.1	1.7	1.8	4.4		
Inflation	40	10	24	40	31	25	37	18	10
Credit to Central									
Govt. (Net)	37.46	48.05	77	157	148	110	119	87	
Credit to Nonfinancial									
Public Institut.	4.29	16.32	20	20	8	41	30	47	
Real Effective									
Exchange Rate	72.2	52.5	30.2	23.2	22.1	20.8	20.8	21.6	19.3

Source: Statistical Services *Quarterly Digest of Statistics* various issues, Accra. IMF, 1993, *International Financial Statistics Yearbook*, Washington DC.

Progress in the state enterprise divestiture programme has been slow. Government's ambiguity towards privatisation in general and foreign direct investment in particular may explain why the programme has not met with much success. There is a credibility gap because of previous government action, for example the support in the early years of the take-over of factories by workers as well as statements by the leadership. Inadequate staff capacity to prepare the corporate plans and performance agreements also initially slowed the process of monitoring firms which remained state-owned. There have been difficulties in identifying the assets and liabilities of the corporations.

The inflation rate has remained lower than the pre-1983 levels. There has been difficulty in achieving the inflation rate targets due to the rapid depreciation of the cedi, excess money supply, and inadequate food supply because of poor rainfall.

Winners and Losers in the Economic Reform Programme

Any economic reform programme must involve losers and winners. The reaction of the two groups could lead to profound political changes and can result in reversal of the reform programme. The losers from the reform programme were expected to be those who previously benefited from the controlled economic regime; namely, the bureaucrats and politicians who were actually responsible for issuing permits and licenses and operating the control system generally. The other groups expected to lose from the reform programme were the urban dwellers, basically urban workers, traders, the security forces and the import-substitution business clientele.

These groups are also the most politically vocal and powerful. One could expect that in view of the diminished rents their reaction initially would be muted. Over the medium to long-run, however, if the programme did not generate sufficient increases in welfare, one should expect demand for political or economic change from these groups. The expected beneficiaries of the reform package are producers in the export sector and producers in sectors which were subject to price controls. These expected beneficiaries however tend to be diffuse, located primarily in the rural areas. The devaluation component of the package acted as a double-edged sword. A devaluation enhances profitability in the exporting and import-substituting sector. However the extent to which profitability is increased is dependent on the extent to which producers in these sectors make use of imported inputs. This was a particular problem in the import-substituting sector where the protective element of the extensive devaluation was eroded by the high cost of imported raw materials and machinery and equipment which were required by firms in the sector. Thus producers in the import-substituting sector emerged as vociferous critics of the economic reform programme.

More critical to the interest of the urban workers is what happened to the real consumption wage, and to the prevailing poverty levels. The average growth of 5 per cent of the economy implied an increase in per capita incomes of 2 per cent per annum. At this rate the growth in incomes was slow and the level of poverty remained high. According to the Ghana Living Standards Survey, in 1987/88, about 36 per cent of the Ghanaian population lived below the poverty line. Even though rural poverty was higher than urban poverty, 26 per cent of the urban population lived below the poverty line of C36000 expenditure per annum. The results of the second report of the Ghana Living Standards Survey suggest a worsening of poverty between 1987/88 and 1990.

Real consumption wages increased immediately following the introduction of the SAP. But their levels remained on average lower than in the 1970s. The increases in real wages after 1986 can partly be attributed to the retrenchment of public sector workers and the rationalisation of employment in the private sector from 1987. The retrenchment programme concentrated on lower paid workers resulting in a decline in formal sector employment. Thus, without any increase in nominal wages, increased average earnings would have been recorded for those remaining in employment. With the introduction of the policy of cost recovery in the health, education and public utility services, real wages must be much lower. In the 1984 population census unemployment was estimated at 3 per cent. Various estimates of unemployment in 1993 put the figure around 13 per cent. With these adverse social developments opposition to the programme was bound to increase.

The decision to fund a programme to mitigate the social costs of adjustment (PAMSCAD) was agreed upon by the external donors in 1988. It however was not an integral part of the structural adjustment programme. It suffered many shortcomings, for example, insufficient funds to finance projects, which reduced its effectiveness. Inevitably therefore, the impact of PAMSCAD was very limited and unable to address the problems of the losers from the economic reform programme in any fundamental way. The slow down in the rate of economic growth, the problems faced by the import-substituting sector (resulting from the trade liberalisation and depreciating exchange rate) and the withdrawal of subsidies on public utilities used mainly by the urban population formed the basis of dissatisfaction with the programme.

The lack of a forum in which economic policy decisions could be discussed and grievances aired provided further condition for the demand for an alternative political system. Combined with the poor human rights record which accompanied the programme, these protests coalesced into demands for political liberalisation and debate on the economic direction of the country. These internal demands were weak, and could have been suppressed for a considerable period of time; but they were encouraged and made to grow stronger as external pressure for political liberalisation mounted for various reasons.

The Role of External Donors

The extent to which external donors can influence domestic policy depends in part on the degree of dependence of the country on external support. External capital flows can be crucial to the success or failure of the trade liberalisation component of the structural adjustment programme. As we show below, the structural adjustment programme increased substantially the dependence of the Ghanaian economy on external funding. When donor conditionality changed to include political liberalisation, the government was naturally under pressure to so liberalise.

Ghana's structural adjustment programme has had substantial external assistance both as programme aid and budgetary support. External programme support was co-ordinated through the Paris Club Donors Conference. According to the World Bank (1990) commitments from members and observers of the consultative group, including the International Development Agency (IDA), averaged US$420 million a year in 1984-1986 and US$740 million a year between 1987-1989. Drawings on loans increased from approximately US$272.6 million in 1983 to US$426.8 million in 1988. At the initial phases however, the programme had to rely on short-term borrowing from the IMF and other commercial sources. At this stage Ghana's credit-worthiness was low and it was difficult to attract long-term concessional financing. The share of short term credit (including IMF credits) in total external debt increased from 20.1 per cent in 1982 to 26.3 per cent in 1983 and to 40.7 per cent by 1985. As the programme progressed and credit-worthiness improved, the share of long-term concessional loans in financing the programme increased. The IMF and the World Bank have been the major sources of external financial flows since 1984. In 1985 these two agencies accounted for 58.8 per cent of total disbursements. This rose to 68.3 per cent in 1988 falling to 42.7 per cent in 1992. Disbursements are primarily from official sources.

In the initial phases of the programme external resources including suppliers credit and bilateral arrangements financed 49.1 per cent and 43.7 per cent of total imports in 1983 and 1984 respectively. In 1985 this had declined to 37.1 per cent (Ministry of Trade 1986). As the import liberalisation started in 1986, the level of foreign funding increased to 54.3 per cent in order to accommodate the increase in imports.

Ghana's total external debt stock at 1980 stood at US$1.4 billion which was approximately 32 per cent of GNP. External debt increased continuously to US$2.7 billion in 1986 to US$4.3 billion in 1992. The ratio of external debt to GNP rose to 49 per cent in 1986 and 63.1 per cent in 1992 (World Bank 1993).

The significant inflow of foreign financial resources enabled the financing of the current account deficit as well as build up international reserves. Gross inflows of loans and grants over the period was crucial in supporting the structural adjustment programme in terms of the budget, balance of payments and financing of the auction. External grants as a percentage of total budgetary revenues rose from 4.2 per cent in 1984 to 11.45 per cent in 1990, falling to 8.9 per cent in 1992 and 5.4 per cent in 1993. The finances of the foreign exchange auction from foreign sources increased from about 40.6 per cent in 1986 to 69.3 per cent in 1988 (Ministry of Trade 1988).

Dependency on external financial flows increased as depicted by the increase in the ratio of aid flows and total disbursements to GNP. The ratio of total disbursement to GNP rose from 4.3 per cent in 1985 to 7.9

per cent in 1988. Ghana's dependence on aid flows is higher than the average for African countries, for which the ratio was 4.8 per cent in 1986 and 3 per cent in 1992. With this level of dependence on external donors, political conditionality was difficult to resist.

Table 3: Inflow of External Financial Resources 1984-1992

	1984	1985	1986	1987	1988	1989	1990	1991	1992
Total Debt Stocks	1898	2226	2726	3262	3048	3296	3761	4209	4275
Use of IMF Credit	515	701	786	867	762	737	745	834	740
Debt Service Ratios (%)									
a) excluding IMF	46.7	38.5	28.9	31.1	28.2				
b) including IMF	53.3	48.7	53.9	63.3	53.4				
Reserves/Imports Goods and Serv.									
(Months)	7.0	7.1	3.0	2.7	3.7	2.3	4.3	2.5	
Concessional Flows to									
GNP ratio (%)	2.7	4.36	5.41	6.02	5.7	5.2	5.4	4.1	
Total Disbursement to									
GNP ratio	4.3	6.8	7.4	7.9	7.5	6.3	6.5	5.9	
Share of IDA and IMF in									
Total Disbu.	58.8	49.7	66	68.3	61.5	55.1	58.8	42.7	

Source: World Bank, *World Debt Tables 1993/94*. Washington, DC
World Bank, 1991, *Ghana Progress on Adjustment*, Washington, DC.

SAP, Governance and the Transition

With the end of the Cold War it was now possible for donors to link development aid to political reform, especially respect for human rights. The ultimate objective of the donors was Western-style democracy. Donors linked the shortcomings of economic management to the type of political regime in place in most African countries. Therefore, in order to ensure economic progress, it was necessary to have a liberalised political structure. Experience with structural adjustment also suggested that technically sound economic policies may generate sub-optimal responses on account of poor governance. The World Bank, it must be noted, has been careful to distance itself from the hypothesis that there is a link between political regimes and economic performance (World Bank 1992). It has however been in the forefront of the call for sound economic management which, it argues, requires good governance. According to the World Bank 'the absence of good governance has proved to be particularly damaging to the "corrective intervention" role of government' (World Bank 1992:10). Thus, good governance is necessary for governments to perform their functions efficiently. The lack of good governance could explain the slow response to policy reform. Political liberalisation, it was thought, could generate transparency, credibility of policies and accountability conducive to the implementation of adjustment programmes. This could not however, imply particular political regimes. As Przeworski and Limongi (1993) have argued, there is no clear theoretical or empirical basis to support the hypothesis that links political regime type to economic growth.

In spite of this, some donors saw a connection between good governance and particular political regimes, to wit, multi-party democracy. Competing political parties were supposed to articulate alternative options. Multi-party parliament could provide a venue for scrutiny of government expenditures and programmes and criticism of policy leading to more efficient use of resources. A freer press and open debate would force governments to be more transparent and also accountable for their actions. In general then, democratic transition was seen as necessary to improve the credibility of such programmes and create the enabling environment for better responses.

On the other hand, empirical evidence indicates that good governance is not always a feature of democratic or politically liberalised regimes. As Meier argues, political parties may be the means whereby elites control mass followings, and are not organs through which interests are articulated. These parties on the other hand, may be vehicles for the personal ambitions of individual politicians whose only goal is to acquire control of government jobs and distribute them to their followers (Meier 1991:302). The example of some South East Asian countries suggest that enlightened dictatorships can be synonymous with good governance as conceived by the donor community.

In spite of the technical soundness of Ghana's structural adjustment programme and its success in terms of macro-aggregates, implementation left a lot to be desired. Because of the security situation at the time the programme was launched, government partly used repression to dampen outward expression of dissent to the programme. In the initial phases, programme design and implementation were carried out by Task Forces and several Committees. The result was that top administrators of the policies were not involved in policy design. Both economy and nation were therefore run as a security network. According to some chief directors we interviewed, information on the economy and policies was provided on a 'need to know' basis. Communication and information is a vital part of the operation of the bureaucracy and it must be formal and written. According to the directors interviewed, communication suffered most under the ERP. It degenerated to the extent that they were expected to act on newspaper publications.

The Effect of the Transition to Democracy on SAP

Evidence from Haggard and Kaufman (1989) indicates that governments in countries undergoing democratic transition tended towards expansionist policies both in comparison to past policy and in comparison with the sample of countries they studied. A similar situation seems to have occurred in Ghana, in both the current reform programme and the previous programme of 1967-71. Table 4 presents the budgetary performance of Ghana for the period 1984-1993. Even on a narrow definition of the budget deficit, the fiscal balance worsened in 1992 and 1993 compared with the previous periods when surpluses were recorded. It is possible that this was due to the substantial fall in government revenues. But as the table shows, revenues increased during the period. The increased deficit must therefore have been due to increased expenditures connected with the democratic transition. In 1992 and 1993, current expenditures overran budgetary targets by 32 per cent and 22 per cent respectively. Part of the increase in expenditures must have been due to the huge wage increases granted to workers. These ranged from 60-100 per cent awarded to the civil service apparently to induce workers to vote for the government in the November-December 1992 elections.

To finance these deficits government resorted to borrowing from the banking system. The dramatic increase in money supply in 1992 was largely the result of such borrowing. As the data in Table 2 shows, lending to government increased substantially in 1992 compared to lending in the private sector. These resulted in substantial increases in domestic inflation, increasing depreciation of the currency and generally difficulties in budgetary control.

As discussed earlier, the transition process has implications for the expenditure side of the government budget. Donors eased the burden of the transition process by providing funding thus reducing the need to increase taxes to finance the process. These resources also reduced the pressure to print more money to finance the deficit. In addition to the above, the formation of new political parties and political debates leading up to the 1992 elections did not also result in the development of any effective alternative to structural adjustment. Instead, the debate concentrated largely on human rights issues. Partly as a result of the nature of the elections, parliament which is supposed to offer effective criticism of government policy, and act as a check on expenditure control is still under the control of the executive. Thus, 'the traditional dominance of the executive over the legislature has remained unchanged and this especially limits the scope for improvement in public expenditure management — an important economic reform' (ODI 1994). Thus, for instance, the Auditor-General's report published in 1993 was never rigorously debated in the new parliament. No committees were set up to investigate the numerous allegations of corruption and malpractice listed in the report.

Table 4: Budgetary Performance 1984-1993
(Millions of Cedis)

	1983	1984	1985	1986	1987	1988	1989	1990	1991	1992	1993
Revenue											
Total Tax	8434.2	17830.3	31841	61587.4	95399.7	125779.1	160541.9	189862.4	290528.6	301834	503395
Non Tax	1725.7	3798	6788	12037.6	15646.3	24569	35374.2	53093.2	100161.4	64422	169565
Grants	56.6	914	1394	3868	6037	11553	21343	27821	36261	32696	35931
Total	10159.9	21628.3	38629	73625	111046	150348.1	195916.1	242955.6	390690	366256	672960
Expenditures											
Current	13551.2	23313.6	39768.7	62231.8	82000.7	116008.6	153359.4	201237.7	269648	373258	605080
Compensation of Employees	3743.2	5282.2	14964.2	27895.8	38329.9	49236.1	67935.4	88116	107105.1		227600
Capital	1191.5	3367.8	5977.4	8407.4	20124.9	27888.8	43106.6	53235.3	706136	110449	186055
Total	14742.7	26681.4	45764	70639.2	102125.6	146896.6	196466	254473	3402616	510813	791135
Budget Balance	4582.6	5053.1	7135	2985.8	8920.4	6451.5	549.9	11517.4	50428.4	144557	118175

Source: Republic of Ghana, *The PNDC Budget Statement and Economic Policy,* various issues, Accra.

Economic analysis also suggests that uncertainty increases the value of waiting. This applies particularly to investment decisions (Rodrik 1990). The uncertainty connected with the democratic transition will normally tend to induce businesses to delay investment. Investment is a sunk cost and cannot be easily moved from one sector to the other. Part of the uncertainty arises from the uncertainty in terms of who wins the elections, and the possible change in policy direction. Thus, during the transition, both foreign direct and domestic investment can be expected to decline. In spite of the limited information on the breakdown of investment between private and public sectors since 1990, interviews conducted in 1994 showed that the private sector preferred short-term quick maturing assets to investment in directly productive activities: 48 per cent of the respondents preferred to invest in financial paper rather than in the productive sector if they had the resources to do so (Asante 1994).

Conclusion

The structural adjustment programme brought about improvements in most macroeconomic aggregates, i.e. growth of output, lowering of inflation compared to previous levels and a reversal in the decline in the rate of investment. However the retrenchment policy, trade liberalisation and the removal of subsidies on health, education etc., impacted adversely on the population creating discontent with the programme. Dissatisfaction with the outcome of the structural adjustment programme, the desire to broaden the economic debate on policy alternatives and to reduce state repression were important ingredients in domestic demand for political liberalisation. The capacity of the government to repress any expression of dissent whether on economic or political issues meant that these sentiments were not overtly expressed. It was only when the external donors put pressure on the government to reduce the restrictions on freedom of expression and association that the transition to democracy was given a boost. Donor pressure for political reform whether based on the value of political liberalisation in governance and the success of structural adjustment or their own predilection for particular political regimes was important both in terms of giving support to internal demands and forcing the government to liberalise.

The transition to democracy has not been without costs. It has impacted adversely on the economy and had an effect on the implementation and outcome of the structural adjustment programme. The transition has been characterised by a slow down in the growth of output. Large expenditure overruns were experienced during the transition phase which have put upward pressure on inflation, and worsened the external account. The sustainability of the adjustment programme will depend on the government's ability to regain control over its expenditures and in the ability of succeeding democratic governments to transcend short term political considerations.

3

Civic Associations and the Transition to Democracy

Kwame A. Ninsin

Introduction

The focus of this chapter is civic associations —the actors in civil society and how their actions advanced or inhibited the course of democratisation in Ghana. The term civic society, as argued by White (1994:26), has been defined and used differently in the existing literature. It has been defined either as the 'realm of freedom'; the 'intermediate sphere of social organisation or association between the basic units of society ... and the state'; or as the '"political society" in the sense of a particular relationship between state and society based on principles of citizenship, rights, representation and the rule of law'. This study was conducted on the premise that civil society is that realm of social life where organised groups intercede between the rest of society and the state with the objective of defining or redefining the bases and scope of the rights and obligations of the members of the political community; that is, citizenship.

The actions of the actors in civil society may be either in opposition to or a demand on the state; or they may be in support of the state. Civil society is therefore not homogeneous; nor is it guided by the same ideology, and vision of the political order. That is, civil society is an inclusive social structure of 'actually existing civil societies' (Bayart 1986:18). As this Ghanaian case study will show, during the 1982-92 period, a section of civil society acted to expand the realm of political society to ensure the enjoyment of political freedoms, what Dahrendorf (1988) has summarised as 'qualitative equality', by all citizens. Simultaneously, other civil society actors aimed at maintaining the status quo which was based on an exclusive political society where the enjoyment of qualitative equality was restricted. The relationship between the first segment of civil society and the state was necessarily conflictual; and that between the second and the state was corporatist.

This chapter does two things. First, it identifies and explains the actions of the civic associations that constituted the existing civil societies and assumed the responsibility to compel the state through sustained political action to expand the boundaries of political society so that Ghanaians would enjoy the rights of citizenship, and be governed by a regime of laws rather than men. And second, it identifies and explains the role of those civic associations whose actions obstructed the attainment of democracy. We have categorised the existing civil societies into three: (a) those that are active in the political sphere, and whose actions enhance the frontiers of freedom and the rule of law; (b) those who are active in the political sphere but whose actions obstruct the course of freedom and democracy; and (c) those that are least active in the political realm. The study focuses on the first and second civil societies. We call the first *pro-democracy civil society*; and the second, *alternative civil society*.

Civil societies are constituted by active social forces through their organisations which are usually called civic associations: they are the political actors which were once called pressure groups. The term *civic associations* is used here to refer to any organisations which are formed by certain social groups for the pursuit of a set of goals and objectives that are determined by the general interests of its members. A civic association may or may not be independent, organisationally and financially, of the state or the government of the day. It may or may not have clearly defined political agenda; or it may develop a political agenda only in response to particular circumstances. A civic association could have multiple goals, including political ones, as its agenda. Civic associations that develop a political agenda at one time or another are the ones which engage in civil society. This study shows that between 1982 and 1992 a handful of civic associations, those which have established a tradition of pro-democracy struggles, led and sustained the movement for democracy until the ban on political party activity was lifted to enable Ghanaians to freely organise themselves into political parties and engage in open political activity. As the handful of civil society organisations successfully dented the legitimacy of the military government and secured some political space for the exercise of political rights other civic associations entered the fray. The latter were quite militant but transitory.

A corresponding trend was the growth of new civic associations within the alternative civil society.

Civil Society Actors

The pro-democracy civil society actors were the Ghana Bar Association (GBA), Christian Council of Ghana (CCG), Catholic Bishops Conference (CBC), Ghana Trades Union Congress (GTUC), and National Union of Ghana Students (NUGS). The success of the transition to multi-party parliamentary democracy depended largely on their perseverance and exemplary struggle which, in the course of time, encouraged other civic associations that are more militant and radical, and have a greater capacity for mass mobilisation, to join.

The CBC is the synod of the Catholic Church. It has congregations throughout the country, and draws its membership from a cross-section of Ghanaian society. On the other hand, the CCG is an umbrella body of 14 protestant churches all of which have congregations in every corner of the country. Like the CBC, membership of the various churches of the CCG comprises Ghanaians from every station of life. The full list of member churches of the CCG is as follows:

Member Churches

1. Methodist Church of Ghana

2. Presbyterian Church of Ghana

3. Joint-Anglican Diocesan Council

4. Society of Friends (Quakers)

5. Evangelical Presbyterian Church of Ghana

6. African Methodist Episcopalian Zion Church

7. African Methodist Episcopalian Church

8. The Salvation Army

9. Ghana Baptist Convention

10. F'Eden Church

11. Christian Methodist Episcopalian Church

12. Evangelical Lutheran Church of Ghana

13. Orthodox Church of Ghana

14. Mennonite Church

Affiliated Organisations and Local Council of Churches

1. Young Men's Christian Association

2. Young Women's Christian Association

3. Local Councils of Churches

The GBA is the leading association of lawyers in private practice. For example, the total membership (only those who had paid their annual dues for the 1993/94 legal year) stood at about 500.[1] Its members are not just influential. Some of them occupy very key and sensitive positions in the country's economic and political institutions. Also, there is at least one member of the GBA working in every district capital of the country. Another pro-democracy civil society actor is the Ghana Trades Union Congress (GTUC), the central body for the 17 labour unions which are either affiliates or members. Before the full rigour of the military government's economic reform policies on labour were felt, the membership of the GTUC was just below 1 million. From 1985 onwards, the widespread labour retrenchment in both the public and private sectors considerably reduced its membership despite sustained resistance from organised labour (Yeebo 1991:202-217). Finally, the National Union of Ghana Students represents students of the country's universities and polytechnic. It has a floating membership of about 40,000. These organisations constitute a formidable force in Ghanaian politics if and when mobilised.

The alternative civil society actors, on the other hand, comprised civic associations like the Committee for the Defence of the Revolution (CDR), Civil Defence Organisation, Mobisquads, and 31st December Women's Movement, which were created by the military regime as an alternative to the pro-democracy civil society, in addition to other political functions.

The CDR came into existence in early 1982 as defence committees in response to the military government's calls for a popular revolution by which political power would be exercised by the ordinary Ghanaians.[2] The defence committees were the leading force in alternative civil society leading the struggle against the 'enemies of the revolution'. Members of this organisation were mainly the lower classes of unionised and non-unionised workers, self-employed workers in the informal sector, and unemployed persons. It had branches in most towns and villages of the country and, as the primary instrument of political struggle, wielded considerable political power (Hansen 1991:55-90). By 1990 it had lost much of its political influence, especially as the Rawlings revolution wore thin and turned its back ideologically and politically on its most militant supporters.[3]

The 31st December Women's Movement, whose president is Nana Kunadu Agyeman Rawlings, wife of Flt. Lt. J. J. Rawlings, head of the military government, mobilised women also of the lower classes, who were concentrated mainly in the rural communities, to support the government. Launched on May 15 1982 by Rawlings, it was reported to have about 1.5 million members by the early 1990s (Manu 1993). This made it the largest women's organisation of its kind in the country. By the 1990s, it had become the second most important actor in the alternative civil society. It had branches all over the country, and benefited from the services of state employees who were assigned to assist with its organisation. Its mobilisation drive revolved around the provision of welfare services like day care centres and income generating micro-rural industries intended mainly to benefit rural women.

By the time the politics of the transition intensified, the movement was widely perceived as the women's wing of the PNDC, and later the National Democratic Congress (NDC) when the latter was formed. 'In the absence of legalised political parties under the rule of the PNDC, the 31 December Women's Movement ... paralleled the CDRs as the nearest thing to a legal political party in Ghana since 1982' (Shillington 1992:156). The image acquired by the 31 December Women's Movement as an extension of the PNDC/NDC government was sufficient to attract a massive following of lower class individuals and groups as these struggled to gain access to the rewarding patronage networks which the movement controlled by virtue of its association with the government.

About 26 women's associations were reported to have been affiliated with this movement before the transition process gathered momentum. They included Accra Market Association, Regional Administration Staff, Zion Women's Union, Bator Women's Union, Police Wives Association, Prison Officers Wives Association, Armed Forces Wives Association, Achimota Brewery Ladies Club, GNAT Ladies Association, Power Queens, Media Ladies Club, Ghana Hairdressers and Beauticians Association, etc. (Manu 1993:195). It later took over the National Council of Women and Development (NCWD) so that the key positions on the governing body of the NCWD were usually occupied by loyal supporters of the 31st Women's Movement.

This and the other alternative civil society actors were state-sponsored organisations. Their members did not hide their loyalty to the military government, loyalties which were more openly demonstrated in the months before and during the 1992 election.

On the eve of the 1992 elections the PNDC government inaugurated another major civic association — the Council of Indigenous Business Associations (CIBA), to augment the existing alternative civil society. The CIBA, was formed as an umbrella organisation for over twenty associations of small scale business operators in the informal sector. Among CIBA's membership were associations of garage owners, dressmakers, chop bar operators, drinking bar operators, bakers, federation of Ghanaian jewellers, refrigeration mechanics, traditional healers, market women, and traditional caterers.[4] At its inauguration on 31 March 1992, the CIBA was alleged to have over one million people. A Deputy Minister for Mobilisation, Labour and Social Welfare, Peter Vaughn Williams, was its chairman.

The strategy of co-opting these associations of informal sector operators dates back to the late 1980s when about 30 of them were created by the government, allegedly to collect taxes from their members on behalf of the Internal Revenue Service. Among them were the Ghana Chemical Sellers Association, Musicians Union of Ghana, Ghana Tape Recorders Association, Chop Bar Keepers and Cooked Food Sellers Association, Sandcrete Block Manufacturers Association, Second Hand Cloth Dealers Association, Butchers Association, Second Hand Car Dealers Association, Ghana Co-operative Distillers Association Ltd.,

Traditional Healers, Fetish Priests, Mallams and Drug Peddlers Association, etc.[5] When the time came for the country to have a new constitution written, the government gave several of them an impressive representation on the constitutional assembly that wrote the 1992 constitution[6], an act which was denounced by the main pro-democracy actors. Furthermore, the PNDC government intensified its dealings with the Pentecostal churches largely through their leading organisation, the Ghana Pentecostal Council (GPC). The GPC has 78 member churches, spread throughout the country.

The third and final category of civil society actors comprised mainly apolitical and development oriented civic associations — village, community, self-help and ethnic associations, occupational, vocational and business associations; youth and old-boys clubs; the numerous non-governmental organisations, and others. For example, civic associations like the Association of Ghana Industries, Ghana Chamber of Commerce, and the Ghana Union Traders Association acted as pressure groups primarily regarding matters of economic policy; especially where such policy was perceived as having the potential to adversely affect their business interests directly or indirectly. Compared to civic associations in the first two categories, this third category of civil society actors did not engage in the transition politics as a vocation. Where they did, neither the liberalisation of political power nor consolidation of the existing power structure was its primary concern. Especially, the numerous village, self-help and ethnic associations in the country were not moved by the prevailing political struggles to abandon their habit of remaining aloof from partisan politics in general, and the transition politics in particular. Generally their occasional entry into politics and interaction with politicians, when it became absolutely necessary, was motivated by the developmental concerns of their respective communities for which they acted as agents in the limited arena of the politics of development.

Transition Politics

The struggles for political reforms occurred initially as a contest between the pro-democracy civil society and the alternative civil society which fought to forestall the overthrow of the PNDC government. The struggle was precipitated by the *coup d'état* against the democratically elected government headed by President Hila Limann, and suspension of the

1979 Constitution simultaneously on 31 December 1981. The pro-democracy civil society almost instantaneously mobilised against the new military government. Its constituent actors called on the military government to return the country immediately to constitutional rule; that is, restore a regime that would be based on the consent of the governed, respect for fundamental human rights and the rule of law. These demands amounted to the removal of the military regime from power. The response from alternative civil society was swift, relentless and devastating.

Hansen (1991:56-57) has distinguished three dimensions of the struggle waged by the alternative civil society in defence of the new military government; namely, (i) the struggle for control over the traditional trades union structures; (ii) the 'struggle against the domination of capital and consequently of imperialism'; and (iii) 'the struggle against the local state and the old political leadership whose structural position as the mediator between imperialism and the broad masses of the people dictated an inevitable conflict; and in a way ... against the petty bourgeois coalition which has dominated politics in Ghana since the time of independence'. These facets of the struggle by the alternative civil society constituted the heart of the struggle for political power, which was for the actors of alternative civil society aimed at defeating the dominant social forces in Ghanaian politics, the beneficiaries of the status quo, so that the military coup could be convert into a popular revolution.

The pro-democracy civil society actors like the Association of Recognised Professional Bodies (ARPB), the Ghana Bar Association, Christian Council of Ghana, and Catholic Bishops Conference employed non-violent forms of political agitation in pursuit of their demands. They sent memoranda to the government, held press conferences, sent delegations to the government to present their case, sent pastoral letters to their congregations (in the case of the two orthodox Christian Churches), denounced the government at the their congresses at the end of which they issued a communiqué setting out a list of democratic demands, and used the private media to actively publicise their demands. Quite often, and especially from 1985 onwards, by which time the GTUC and NUGS had joined the pro-democracy movement, the use of strikes and boycotts to back demands for political reforms became an important method of struggle.

The alternative civil society associations, on the other hand, initially (that is, in 1982-84) showed a striking tendency to embark on rowdy demonstrations; its members engaged in violent acts and open confrontations with the opposing associations; they denounced middle class groups in various sectors of society and their associations, and often destroyed or seized property belonging to members of this class.

From January 1982 till about the end of 1984, the struggle for constitutional rule took the form of a struggle for power, a struggle to overthrow the military regime. Between 1987 and 1992, it became a movement for democratic reforms in which the military regime was a reluctant convert. The rest of the chapter outlines and discusses the various phases through which the movement for multi-party parliamentary democracy passed.

The Pro-Democracy Movement: From Challenge to Defeat

The first phase of the pro-democracy movement was led by the Association of Recognised Professional Bodies (ARPB). Active during this period were also the Ghana Bar Association (GBA) which tended to act independently of the ARPB, the Christian Council of Ghana (CCG), and the Catholic Bishops Conference (CBC). The few private newspapers that had survived the latest military intervention, and operated until about 1984, also joined the protest against the overthrow of the constitutional government which was barely two years and six months old. *The Echo*, *Pioneer*, *Free Press* and the *Catholic Standard* gave unqualified support in this initial phase of the struggle against military rule.

The National Union of Ghana Students (NUGS) and the Ghana Trades Union Congress (GTUC) were not part of this incipient movement for democracy. Throughout 1982 the NUGS, which was then under radical leadership, actively supported the military government. It joined ranks with the anti-government forces when its radical leadership was replaced by a moderate, liberal minded group. By the close of 1982 the honeymoon with the military government was over; thenceforth the student movement became one of the avowed opponents of the new government in particular and military rule in general. Especially from the day the 1983 budget which inaugurated the new government's economic reform policy was announced, the NUGS remained consistently critical of the government. Its statement on the 1983 budget, for example, denounced the government and the direction of its political, economic and social policies. A major feature of the NUGS' opposition to the military government was the nation-wide student protests it organised almost on a regular basis.

The GTUC was also not part of the initial spurt of opposition to the military government. From the very early months of 1982, the leadership of the labour movement had been taken over by the government — first through the Association of Local Unions and later through the defence committees (Yeebo 1991; Hansen 1991:24-90). From 1985 onwards, the leadership of the labour movement also asserted its independence of government. From then on much of its political activity could be described as anti-government. By then organised labour was feeling the adverse effects of the government's economic reform policies; especially labour retrenchment and wage freeze, inflation and the rising cost of living, and the removal of subsidies on social services like health and education. Such policies had had a devastating effect on the quality of life of workers and undermined the political unity and strength of the labour movement as an organised social force. The scale of labour retrenchment, which compounded the unemployment situation in the country, hit the labour movement the hardest (Yeebo 1991:202-217; Gyimah-Boadi/ Essuman-Johnson 1993:200). The response of organised labour was no longer acquiescence to the government, contrary to Herbst (1991:173-192), but sporadic and often concerted struggle against the government's policies. As the government itself became increasingly repressive in response to the growing labour agitations, state-labour relations became increasingly antagonistic (Graham 1989; Ninsin 1989; 1991; Yeebo 1991:218-265).

None of the government's repressive measures intimidated organised labour which rather became more militant and critical of government policies. On 18 February 1985, for example, the GTUC sent a 13-page memorandum to the government which was severely critical of the harsh economic and political regime it had imposed on workers and the nation at large. The leadership of organised labour singled out the government's infringement of the economic, social and political rights of Ghanaians.

Other labour unions expressed their disillusionment with the government and their opposition to its economic and political policies through various methods of civil disobedience.

The anti-government protests of the labour and student movements notwithstanding, the pro-democracy forces had, by the end of 1984, been effectively frustrated and contained by the government leaving the latter triumphant. The failure of the pro-democracy movement to undermine the government's legitimacy, even slightly, was due to several reasons. The civic associations which were engaged in the movement were elite organisations and lacked any significant mass base. A more important reason is that the alternative civil society had been effectively and purposefully mobilised to challenge and intimidate leading individuals and groups engaged in the pro-democracy civil society. Also from early 1982, the PNDC government had established 2 investigating bodies and a public tribunal outside the judiciary: the Citizens Vetting Committee (CVC) under the *Citizens Vetting Committee Law 1982* (PNDCL 1), the National *Investigations Committee* (NIC) under the *National Investigations Committee Law 1982* (PNDCL 2), and the Public Tribunals under the *Public Tribunals Law 1982* (PNDCL 24). These new organs of the Ghanaian state were used to systematically investigate, expose and bring to trial members of the Ghanaian establishment — the political, economic and cultural elites — for alleged crimes against the state.

Despite their obvious excesses, these extra-judicial bodies were widely acclaimed as instruments of revolutionary justice; but their motive was clear: cripple and de-legitimise the social forces of the Ghanaian establishment politically.[7] Furthermore, the alternative civil society pitched the political struggle at the highest level: it waged an intense and most violent class struggle in the history of Ghana against the dominant social forces which had organised the pro-democracy movement. Led by the defence committees and other radical forces, the alternative civil society challenged the hegemony and monopoly of these pro-democracy forces in various subsectors of the economy, administration and politics:[8] for example, in the management and ownership of economic units; in the area of distribution of goods and services; in the control and management of the state, especially economic policy-making; and in political representation as political elites.

These struggles took specific forms such as sending management personnel to go on indefinite leave, suspension, or outright dismissal; taking over industrial production units; investigating management personnel for alleged malpractices like corruption, authoritarian management practices, etc.; taking over distribution of goods and services like rental houses from landlords, determining the selling price of consumer goods — especially food; suspending the General Orders of the civil service; attacking and destroying the temples and meeting places of secret societies like Freemasons and Odd Fellows; and attacking the leadership of the orthodox Christian Churches, as well as chiefs; taking over local councils and, in some cases, traditional councils.

Hence, by the middle of the 1980s the middle class organisations, with the exception of the Ghana Bar Association, had been demoralised and silenced; and their members had lost political credibility and support. For several of its members the dire economic circumstances of the period had also deprived them of valuable material resources by which they could function socially and politically as the leading members of society. Consequently the ARPB, for example, had either disintegrated or become inactive leaving the GBA as the only vocal middle class organisation to agitate for constitutional rule.

The Christian Council of Ghana and the Catholic Bishops Conference had also come under severe attack and, in some cases, physical threats. For example, the mouthpiece of the Catholic Church, *The Standard*, had been banned in late 1985. Such acts of intimidation had forced the Churches to limit their intervention in the politics of the country to the occasional pastoral letters which they circulated among their congregations. During this period, therefore, the agitation for constitutional democracy could not galvanise popular support. In contrast, the government had successfully mobilised enough political support and legitimacy to resist the onslaught of the pro-democracy movement.

Resurgence of Protest

The political situation began to change from 1985. By then the PNDC government's relationship with labour and radical political organisations which had previously been its most loyal allies had become sour and antagonistic: ideologically and politically the two former allies were now at loggerheads. The causes were complex and far-reaching. Hansen

(1991:79-80) explains why the Rawlings government suppressed organised labour, often violently:

> [The] emergence of people's power and the independent actions of workers presented him (Rawlings) with a profound embarrassment. It made his administration vulnerable to the charge of the petty bourgeoisie that it was a government of anarchists, hooligans and never-do-wells, anxious to expropriate the wealth which others had created. ... He [Rawlings] was anxious to reach some accommodation with the petty bourgeoisie in order to consolidate his regime; but he was also aware that so long as people's power held the position it did, there was no way he could entice the petty bourgeoisie into his administration. ...[His] own personal power was not safe. ... Lastly, the structural position which he occupied as presiding (sic) over the consolidation of the neo-colonial state and the structural position of the people's power as a grassroots anti-state movement whose interests could only be meaningfully realised by the liquidation of the neo-colonial state, put him into contradictory and antagonistic relationship with the movement for people's power.

In sum, the activities of the radical social forces in the alternative civil society threatened Rawlings' continued stay in power: he resolved that contradiction by suppressing the organs of people's power — workers and other lower class element who had been organised into militant units as defence committees.

When workers and other radical forces realised that the state which Rawlings headed no longer represented their interest, or at least aspired to do so, they abandoned their earlier political position as 'defenders of the revolution' against the pro-democracy forces and opted for a policy of confronting Rawlings and the 'neo-colonial state' over which he presided on a number of issues. During this period various local unions embarked on sporadic strikes on issues of work, income and democracy (Ninsin 1989, 1991; Yeebo 1991:218-240). The GTUC as the central organ of the labour movement gradually asserted itself and resumed its leadership role. As strikes by organised labour became more frequent,[9] almost every strike assumed the character of anti-state action and became politicised.[10] This turn of events not only firmly put organised labour in the camp of the pro-democracy civil society; the participation of organised labour— with its 17 national unions — in the pro-democracy movement immediately brought about a realignment of political forces in favour of the pro-democracy civil society. The involvement of the GTUC and the student movement — (NUGS) — in the pro-democracy civil society increased the movement's potential for attracting mass support.

The new militancy shown by organised labour and the student movement encouraged a number of smaller civic associations which were overtly political in their aims and objectives— like the New Democratic Movement, African Youth Command and Kwame Nkrumah Revolutionary Guards, to re-enter the political arena. Like organised labour, such radical organisations became engaged in politics again on the side of the pro-democracy movement. For them also the government's authoritarian practices were a source of alienation. Their return to the political arena further increased the potential political capital at the disposal of the pro-democracy movement.

Three major developments in the pro-democracy struggles of this period require special mention. First, organisations representing the lower classes — like the GTUC, NUGS, New Democratic Movement and the Kwame Nkrumah Revolutionary Guards (KNRG) had become the principal actors in the campaign for constitutional rule. This was propitious; because, as pointed out earlier, the middle class professional associations and the two orthodox Christian Church organisations that dominated the pro-democracy movement in its initial stages had apparently been forced by the government's repressive and intimidatory measures to scale down their political activities. Therefore, the defection of these militant organisations to the ranks of the pro-democracy civil society filled a gaping vacuum and infused a new sense of urgency and militancy in the movement. Second, the agitations of organised labour, the student movement, and the radical organisations seriously shook the government's self-confidence and threatened to undermine stability. Third, the defence committees which had given the government considerable political support and legitimacy in its fight against the pro-democracy forces had been depoliticised and deprived of considerable political influence and public support. The cumulative effect of these developments was the increasing vulnerability of the government, and the threat that it could lose the political initiative to its opponents.

In the face of these developments, the PNDC government moved tactically and with dazzling speed to reassert full control over the political situation by announcing the limited political reforms which culminated in the district level elections of 1988/89. In a policy paper entitled *District Political Authority and Modalities for District Level Elections* (The Blue Book), issued by the National Commission for Democracy (NCD) and dated Wednesday, 1 July 1987, the government announced its intention to establish district/local level representative institutions through popular elections. Those intentions were given legal backing in the *Local Government Law 1988* (PNDCL 207).

Consequently, between December 1988 and February 1989, elections were conducted on a no-party basis to choose representatives for the 110 district council units that had been established throughout the country. Notwithstanding the substantial central government control (especially through the District Public Education Committees and District Election Committees which were given direct responsibility for managing the elections), and the no-party character of the elections, the local government reforms marked an important political development which ultimately hastened the transition process. In particular, the reforms exposed the actual motives of the government's democratisation programme as being structurally and ideologically inconsistent with liberal democracy. This knowledge encouraged the pro-democracy civil society to intensify their agitations for such political reforms as would restore the political freedoms of the citizens of the country.

Radicalisation and Expansion of Protest

The government had announced in *The Blue Book* that the new district assemblies that would be established under the reform programme 'were the initial building blocks for the setting up of a national democratic structure'. That statement confirmed the fears of the pro-democracy groups that the government was not keen on returning the country to constitutional democracy. Instead, it was determined to pursue its original populist programme of establishing a kind of grassroots democracy by which the defence committees, before they were reconstituted, would form the bases of any future representative government at the national level. To compound this fear, the government inaugurated a series of controlled public fora from July 1990. Staged under the auspices of the National Commission for Democracy, the fora were alleged to be a means for achieving national consensus on a new democratic order for the country. On the contrary, the fora became closed debating sessions for government supporters — mainly members of the Committee for the Defence of the Revolution, members of the district assemblies, the 31st December Women's Movement, and others.

Contrary to the government's intentions, both the local government reforms which allowed for no-party electoral politics at the sub-national level, and the public fora on the search for true democracy had the opposite effect. They inadvertently created cracks in the tightly controlled political discourse. Various political tendencies could thereby air their views on the politics of the country. The government's critics and opponents exploited the opportunities for debate to criticise the government's economic and political policies as well as demand liberal political reforms.

Three significant developments occurred in the wake of these democratic openings which were influential in precipitating the transition to democracy. Militant and radical political entrepreneurs took advantage of the situation to form a number of militant pro-democracy civic associations. Second, the pro- democracy associations made concerted effort to mobilise broader popular support behind their opposition to the PNDC government. Third, they now showed a greater inclination to form alliances or form a united front against the government. Furthermore, their demands showed greater co-ordination and consistency in pursuit of the goal of achieving mult-party constitutional rule. A few examples will illustrate this positive trend.

For the first time since the early 1980s, the Christian Council of Ghana and the Catholic Bishops Conference took the unusual step of mobilising their congregations behind their demand for a return to constitutional democratic rule in the country. In the last quarter of 1990, the Christian Council, for example, issued a document entitled *The Church and Ghana's Search for a New Democratic System — A Study Material for Christians*. According to the leadership of the CCG, this intervention had been prompted by the lessons learned by its General Secretary during a nation-wide tour to address various Synods and Conferences of member churches on the political situation in the country. That tour, according to the CCG, revealed the need for the Church 'to speak out to bring comfort to its members who, for one reason or the another, had not been able to participate in, or contribute to, the on-going debate... on (this) vital national issue'. The booklet formed the basis for a week of prayer, fasting and discussion by various congregations of member Churches. The response was overwhelming. After a week of prayer and discussion, several congregations of the member churches all over the country submitted a written memorandum which formed the material bases for further discussion at the national level.

A two-week seminar involving representatives of the member Churches, including 12 Heads of Member Churches and 83 leading individuals from the CCG's member Churches, was then organised in Accra on the bases of the memoranda received from their congregations. The result of this nation-wide mobilisation was a memorandum titled *Christian Council Response to Ghana's Search for a New Democratic System* (dated December 1990 and signed by all the 14 Heads of member Churches and 2 leaders of affiliated organisations). The CCG submitted this document to the government as its contribution to the debate on the country's search for true democracy (CCG 1996:32-37).

The memorandum may be summarised as follows: that (1) the PNDC government should take steps to return the country to constitutional rule without further delay; (2) lift the ban on political party activity by the end of January 1991; (3) allow freedom of political association; (4) grant general amnesty to all political prisoners, detainees, exiles and refugees; (5) repeal all laws which constitute curtailment or abuse of fundamental rights and freedoms of the citizen; (6) convene a constitutional assembly by the end of March 1990 to write a new constitution for the country based on respect for human rights and the rule of law. Other demands concerned the structure of state power which they wanted limited and separated in order to safeguard liberty.

The CBC also submitted a memorandum to the government after a similar exercise of nation-wide debates and consultations with the rank and file of its congregations. In its memorandum entitled *The Catholic Church and Ghana's Search for a New Democratic System*, dated February 1991 (CBC 1996:38-53), the CBC demanded (1) the establishment of a representative body at the local, regional and national levels; (2) the promotion of an open society in which the basic freedoms will be safeguarded, and the independence of the judiciary and the press guaranteed; (3) the promotion of good government based on equity, social justice and probity as a necessary ingredient for a stable society; (4) a definite timetable for returning the country to constitutional rule by the end of 1992, and as part of this, the setting up of a constitutional review committee, followed by a constitutional referendum; and (5) repeal of all laws which violate or limit the free enjoyment of fundamental rights and freedoms.

But even before this surge in criticism and pro-democracy demands, the GTUC had submitted a position paper entitled 'The Trade Unions and Democracy in Ghana' to the National Commission on Democracy. The document was dated 17 December 1986. In it the Executive of the GTUC had dismissed the government's 'search for democracy' as:

> indeed diversionary and seeks to direct us to look for democracy in mere forms of government whereas the essence of democracy lies in the creation and existence of political economic conditions that promote the overall material and cultural well-being of the people. We make this observation more so because especially at a time when the country is supposed to be 'searching for democracy', undemocratic policies that impose heavy socio-economic burdens on large sections of the population are being pursued by the government (GTUC 1996:171-174).

The GTUC continued its agitations into the early 1990s. For example, at the end of its 3rd Quadrennial Delegates' Congress held on 16-18 March 1988, it passed a resolution in which it called on the government to respect the fundamental rights of Ghanaians; convene a constitutional conference which would write a new constitution, and submit that constitution to a referendum for approval. It further rejected outright the government's proposal for non-partisan district/local level elections.

The NUGS also continued its criticism of the government's political and economic policies. In the final communiqué issued at the end of the 24th Annual Congress held on 3-7 May 1989, it reiterated its call on the government to respect basic human rights, repeal draconian laws, govern according to the rule of law, and restore constitutional rule. According to the NUGS, they were motivated by the need to 'secure a healthy environment for the full development and realisation of individual, intellectual and physical capabilities of the broad masses of Ghanaians'. The GBA had also intensified its opposition to the regime demanding, as the others had done, a return to constitutional rule, respect for human rights, and the rule of law. As part of its strategy of bringing political pressure on the government, the GBA had further decided to institute a 'Bar Martyrs' Day' to be observed in June of each year to commemorate the murder of 3 judges and a retired army officer which occurred under the PNDC regime in 1982. All these developments brought enormous political and moral pressure on the government.

The most important development that gave the pro-democracy movement its biggest impetus was the formation of the Movement for Freedom and Justice (MFJ). Inaugurated on 1 August 1990, the MFJ was an umbrella organisation grouping leaders of various political persuasion. The strength of the MFJ lay in the fact that as a result of political developments since 1987 when *The Blue Book* was published to usher in the limited political reforms at the local government level, leaders from the major political groupings which had been banned by the PNDC government since 31 December 1981 and were traditional political enemies, could now unite to consolidate their political capital. The political leaders had come from the two major political party traditions— the Convention People's Party and the United Party traditions, as well as political organisations ranging from those of the moderate to the extreme left-wing political orientation. Among them were A. Adu Boahen (Chairman), Johny Hansen (1st Vice Chairman), Ray Kakraba-Quarshie (2nd Vice Chairman), Obeng Manu (National Secretary), Kwesi Pratt, Jnr. (Deputy National Secretary), John Ndebugre (National Organiser), Dan Lartey (National Treasurer). In the press briefing launching this new organisation, the leaders denounced the PNDC government's attempt to foist its own brand of democracy on the nation through a puppet debate which was, above all, characterised by intimidation, intolerance, and exclusion. Among other things, they argued:

> The formation of the MFJ has been precipitated by a number of considerations. The first and most important is, of course, the inauguration of the national debate on the future political structure for the country. While we welcome this initiative on the part of the PNDC, we cannot but express our profound dissatisfaction with the manner in which it has been conducted so far. Naturally, every debate or discussion, if it is real, cannot foreclose the possibility of opposing views. Unfortunately, the current debate has been confined to only those individuals and groups (who are) in favour of the positions officially or unofficially adopted by the PNDC. While it is true that the PNDC has proclaimed officially that it has not decided on any type of political system for the country, it is nonetheless

obvious to even the most simple-minded person that the PNDC is at least opposed to the multi-party system. How else can one explain the overwhelming prominence being given to arguments against the multi-party system in the government-controlled mass media? Clearly the debate has been one-sided against all the norms of justice and the democratic process of arriving at decisions by consensus.

In their rebuttal of official denunciations of the multi-party system of government, the MFJ leaders affirmed that the multi-party system of government provides a more democratic mechanism for involving all the people in coming to grips with the economic problems facing the country.

> *We are ... deeply convinced that only a political system that guarantees the fundamental human rights and political liberties of the people, that enables people of like-minded views freely to associate, and form political parties to contest (political) office, and in which the people elect their own leaders through free and fair elections can be considered truly democratic. That is what the multi-party system is all about* (Italics original).

In pursuit of this goal of multi-party democracy, the MFJ further called on the PNDC government to, among others, repeal all repressive laws, and grant unconditional amnesty to all political detainees, prisoners and exiles (MFJ 1996:10-16).

This was a momentous development in the transition politics; because the coming together of political elites from such diverse political orientations immensely strengthened the political demands of the pro-democracy movement against the government's apparent claim to be the authentic representative of the people, and have exclusive mandate to decide the political future of the country. It was now evident that a political force capable of challenging the government's monopoly of power, and contesting the government's claim to represent the people of Ghana had finally emerged on the political scene. Henceforth, the pro-democracy movement could count on a unified vehicle by which it would bring maximum pressure on the government to liberalise. From the day of inauguration, the MFJ stepped up political agitation through rallies, demonstrations, public lectures, and public statements.[11] The agitations of the MFJ encouraged many more civic organisations to join the struggle for democracy.

Despite these politically strategic advances made by the pro-democracy forces, the PNDC government did not give in to the demands for dialogue about the issues in the transition politics. The government could defy the pro-democracy forces largely because of the swell of support it continued to enjoy from the remnants of the CDRs, the rank and file of the 31st Women's organisation and other social forces which had been successfully organised and incorporated in the alternative civil society; for example, the members of the Mobisquads, Civil Defence organisation, and CIBA. Functionaries of these organisations continued to believe in the validity of the revolutionary mission of Rawlings and his government. The acrimonious exchanges that raged between the government and pro-democracy leaders concerning the politics of retribution should the pro-democracy forces come to power, further strengthened the identification of such functionaries with, and support for, the PNDC government. As a result, they had intensified their mass mobilisation drive for the PNDC government. Another source of support for the government came from the members of the 110 district and metropolitan assemblies and leaders of the Ghana Private Road Transporters Union (GPRTU). These and other — much smaller — clusters of grassroots elites also had developed a stake in the survival of the PNDC government.

Finally, the congregations of the member-churches of the Ghana Pentecostal Council were a potential source of support for the Rawlings government. Even though the clergy and the rank and file of these churches did not canvass open support for the regime, the fact that their churches fraternised regularly with leading members of the government, including Rawlings, was enough to yield substantial legitimacy and support for the government. The populist leadership style of Rawlings himself was a major asset in the transition politics. Wherever he went in the country, especially the countryside, Rawlings was accorded enthusiastic welcome and hailed as leader of the nation. Such pockets of popular support, both latent and active, which lay mainly in the country-side, were vigorously mobilised.

The total sum of these fragments of support far outweighed the support enjoyed by the pro-democracy movement which came largely from the urban areas where the adverse effects of the government's austerity economic policies were felt most. Given the extensive political support which the government enjoyed almost throughout the country, it was easier for it to maintain a firm grip on the transition process through to election day.

Nevertheless the government could not entirely ignore the new wave of pressure from the pro-democracy civil society. Even as it rejected the opposition's demands to negotiate the transition process, it took a number of steps towards constitutional rule. That the government could no longer stem the tide of political protest and demand was revealed in the New Year address of 1 January 1991, delivered on Ghana radio and television by the Head of State and Chairman of the PNDC, Flt Lt. J. J. Rawlings (Ninsin 1966:59-64). After reviewing his government's record of political reform he added:

> [...The] NCD has been requested to present its report by the end of March this year to enable the PNDC convene a broad-based national consultative body which would use the report as well as the 1957, 1960, 1969 and 1979 constitutions and other constitutions, as the basis for further consultation. A group of constitutional experts will also be assembled to assist in setting the constitutional proposals into an appropriate legal framework. We expect that by this time next year, we would have completed steps that will give us a draft constitution. The NCD has also been requested to open the voters register in accordance with the electoral regulations by the end of the year and take the necessary steps towards the programme of issuing identity cards to all citizens of Ghana.

Chairman Rawlings also used the occasion to give a rather casual response to certain criticisms and demands regarding his government's laws, policies and practices on human rights and press freedom. Significantly also, Rawlings showed in his speech how cynical his government was towards the type of constitutional regime which the pro-democracy movement had been agitating for. He observed:

> Our eyes are now dimly set on the final phase of our journey as a provisional government and the road to establishing for Ghana a new constitutional order. But I believe we have learned over the years that a Constitution as a mere legal document is of no real value, however fine the language and however lofty the sentiments, unless it is a true reflection and embodiment of the perceptions and noble aspirations of ordinary Ghanaians. ... *[T]he character of the constitution we envisage cannot be the work of any small group of people. Its contents must, as we have always been insisting, derive from our historical experiences and from the democratic process set in motion on 4 June 1979 and 31st December 1981* (Emphasis added).

The NCD's report (1966:79-97), which was submitted to the government on 25 March 1991, provided additional grounds to compel the shift in the government's position, however slight that was, on whether or not it should move the country towards a multi-party constitutional system of government. The NCD had reported quite clearly and frankly the overwhelming preference among the Ghanaian public for a constitutional order based on multi-party system of government. As the government conceded in its statement accepting the report, 'Government has studied the report and accepts the various views expressed as the embodiment of the aspirations of Ghanaians on the future constitutional order ...' (GG 1996:99). The heart of the matter is that at that point in time the government could not have acted differently. Among others, the response to Chairman Rawlings' new year address in which he announced the inconclusive and limited transition programme was swift, vehement, critical and skeptical (See for example, GBA 1996:65-68; MFJ 1966:69-75), signifying the growing mistrust the government enjoyed among articulate Ghanaians as well as the growing confidence of the pro-democracy forces that they could continue to sustain the pressure on the government. The government had indeed lost considerable political ground as a result of the events of the recent past, especially since the conduct of the public fora on the 'search for true democracy' in Ghana. Hence, in its statement on the NCD report it had felt compelled to also announce the appointment of a 9-member constitutional committee to be chaired by Dr. S. K. B. Asante, former Solicitor-General. The duty of this committee was to prepare the outline of a new constitution for consideration by a consultative assembly. Finally, the government announced a date on which the law establishing the consultative assembly would be published, and when the consultative assembly would start its deliberations on a new constitution for the country. Clearly, the pressure from domestic forces on the government was so high that, as its statement on the NCD report shows, it often could not take a final decision on a matter before announcing it.

The PNDC government announced the measures contained in its statement without consulting the pro-democracy forces. But the mere fact that it had conceded the need for political reforms signalled to the pro-democracy forces that the government's resistance to reform was flagging. The pro-democracy forces therefore intensified their attacks coupled with demands for negotiated reform measures. The MFJ, for example, immediately issued a statement in which it reiterated 'Seven Basic Demands', which in its view constituted the heart of the 'positions and aspirations of the people' which have been made repeatedly since July 5 'through their representative and independent public organisations'. The demands were the lifting of the ban on political party activity, repeal of all repressive laws, release of all political prisoners, amnesty for all political exiles and refugees, dissolution of the PNDC and the NCD and their replacement with independent bodies, an independent and representative constitutional conference, and a constituent assembly. In addition to these, the MFJ denounced the government for not consulting the people's representative organisations and for ignoring their legitimate demands. 'This is DICTATORSHIP not democracy,' it charged. (MFJ 1966:103-110) The GBA's position was identical: but it went further in its statement of 13 May 1991 (GBA 1966:113-116), which was in reaction to the government's statement, to propose the composition of the 'Interim Administration' which the pro-democracy forces wanted established to replace the PNDC government. The CCG and the CBC also issued a joint statement in which they not only reiterated the reservations and demands expressed by the other pro-democracy organisations; they also impugned the government's sincerity for issuing an ordinary public statement on the NCD report instead of a white paper (CCG/CBC 1996:117-118).

The publication of the Constituent Assembly's composition in the *Constituent Assembly Law 1991* (on 31 July 1991) provoked additional storm of criticism and denunciations. The pro-democracy forces accused the government of loading the assembly with its supporters.[12] It was argued that the PNDC government had gone beyond established norms to excavate an unusually large number of civic associations in the informal sector, some non-existent, and given them undeserved representation on the constitution-making body. Second, the government was accused of having given a disproportionately large representation to the CDRs and the 31st December Women's Movement, compared to representation by mainstream professional associations like the Ghana Bar Association. To emphasise their objection in a politically more dramatic form, the GBA and NUGS refused to be represented on that assembly.

The pro-democracy forces responded to such overt attempts to control the progress and content of the transition politics in a more practical manner. They attempted, *vis-à-vis* the government's towering political power, to form many more associations with a view to increasing their political capital so that they could challenge the government much more effectively. Between 26 August 1991 when the Consultative Assembly was inaugurated and the end of April 1992 when the ban on political party activity was lifted, numerous anti-government, pro-democracy, pro-reform associations were launched. The associations which came into existence included the Danquah-Busia Memorial Club, the Great Unity Club, Our Heritage, the Kwame Nkrumah Welfare Society, Kwame Nkrumah Youngsters Club, and the Ex-CPP Group. In due course these and other associations revealed themselves as political clubs representing the two main political traditions in the country — the Danquah-Busia (or United Party), and Nkrumah (or Convention People's Party) political traditions. They had indeed been formed in anticipation of the lifting of the ban on political party activity. On 6 August 1991, eleven pro-democracy civic associations came together to form the Co-ordinating Committee of Democratic Forces (CCDF). Their main aim was to put concerted pressure on the PNDC government to open up the political space and expedite the transition process. The 11 bodies were the Movement for Freedom and Justice, NUGS, Danquah-Busia Memorial Club, the Great Unity Club, Our Heritage, the Ex-CPP Group, Kwame Nkrumah Revolutionary Guards, Kwame Nkrumah Welfare Society, Ashanti Youth Association, Gold Coast Ex-Servicemen's Union, and the New Democratic Movement. Later in the year the United Revolutionary Front joined this coalition.

The pro-government alternative civil society responded to this radicalisation and expansion of the pro-democracy civil society by taking steps to expand their own ranks as well. They also created new civic associations of their own. Among them were the Eagle Club, Friends of the Progressive Decade, Rawlings Fan Club, New Nation Club, Development Club, Development Union and Development Front. They followed this up by also forming an umbrella organisation called United Clubs for Rawlings. These new civic associations strengthened the ranks of the already existing alternative civil society to counteract the activities of the pro-democracy forces: their ultimate goal was to ensure the survival of the Rawlings regime into the constitutional era. When the ban on political activity was lifted and the PNDC formed the National Democratic Congress (NDC), the social forces that had organised or been organised for action in the alternative civil society expressed their preoccupation with the survival of the Rawlings regime in their electioneering slogan: 'NDC for continuity'. It had become clear that the PNDC government could not continue to either suppress the pro-democracy forces or ignore their demands: it had to bow to the inevitable — submit to the will of the people through democratic elections and hand-over the reigns of government to a democratically elected government if it lost.

Outside these two antagonistic civil societies several private citizens had also been awakened from the years of political inertia which characterised the repressive regime of the PNDC. Several of such individuals had sent memoranda to the National Commission for Democracy during its nation-wide search for *true democracy* for the country. A review of the memoranda, which the Commission had received during the second half of 1990, shows a remarkable rebirth of political consciousness on the part of thousands of individual Ghanaians. Apart from the fact that some of the private citizens who submitted memoranda to the Commission made more than one submission, their individual positions put together also revealed a large measure of consensus on the key issues in the transition: like the need for a return to constitutional rule, multi-party politics, limited government, independence of the judiciary, the rule of law, etc.[13] Therefore, the government's decision to concede to the demand for political reforms was pragmatic — an admission of the massive growth in the political pressure for democratic reforms, and also that the emerging consensus regarding the nature of the expected political reforms differed from what the government was trying desperately to sell as *true democracy*. This conjuncture augured well for the transition process. For, even though the government remained firmly in control of the transition politics it meant that it could not substitute its own a democratic society for what had emerged as the national consensus.

These developments were boosted by a dramatic growth in the number of private newspapers, especially during the 1991-92 period. The new generation of private newspapers was different from the previous one. In contrast to the earlier generation of private newspapers most of which had specialised in sports and entertainment news, this new crop of private newspapers — like *The Ghanaian Chronicle, The Ghanaian Voice, The*

Free Press, The Guide, and others joined *The Pioneer* (a veteran crusader against dictators) and the pro-democracy movement to agitate for democratic reforms. The private press became the unofficial mouthpiece of the pro-democracy movement, and played an important role in moving the reform process forward.

Shrinking Civil Society and Democratisation

By the time the Consultative Assembly started its work in August 1991 the transition process had become irreversible. The only obstacle was the mutual mistrust and acrimonious exchanges that characterised the political discourse, as well as the government's stout refusal to negotiate the transition with the pro-democracy forces. These obstacles notwithstanding, the process limped on until the Consultative Assembly completed its work on 31 March 1992; a referendum was held on 28 April 1992; and the ban on party political activity lifted on 15 May 1992.

This period exposed the volatility and fragility of Ghana's existing civil societies. Soon after the ban on party political activity was lifted, the two main contending civil societies which were then expanding exponentially suddenly showed signs of shrinking. A number of civic associations, which had hitherto been active and vociferous in the politics of the transition, disappeared from the political scene: they had either been co-opted into one or the other political party which had sprung to life; or they had metamorphosed as political parties. As a result of this, between the referendum of April 1992 and the presidential and parliamentary elections of November-December 1992, the struggle for power became the primary pre-occupation of leading political entrepreneurs and civil society actors. This process sapped the energy of the existing civil societies and, at the same time, forced them to shrink dramatically in size and vigour: they had been superseded by political parties and party politics. The following are some of the political parties which sprang up just before the presidential elections: Eagle Party, Democratic Republican Party, National Democratic Congress, New Patriotic Party, National Convention Party, National Independence Party, People's Heritage Party, People's National Congress, People's Party for Democracy and Development, Democratic People's Party, New Generation Party, National Justice Party, and National Salvation Party.

The major political parties among these — especially, the National Democratic Congress, Eagle Party, New Patriotic Party, the Peoples Heritage Party, People's National Convention, National Convention Party, and the National Independent Party either grew out of the newly formed civic associations which were active in the two contending civil societies; or the new parties simply absorbed such civic associations. Henceforth, the politics of civil society was overshadowed by the politics of the newly formed political parties.

As a result of these transformations the politics of the country following the legalisation of political parties in April 1992 was dominated by the struggle among political parties for state power. Politics was no longer a struggle for political freedoms, and political parties actively campaigned for the mandate of the electorate to rule rather than contend over the nature and direction of the democratisation process. The formation of political alliances also became the preserve of opposing political parties rather than civil society actors. The definition of the political divide also changed overnight: Ghanaian politics was now defined by a contest between the 'liberal' democrats and the 'popular' or 'true' democrats. Indeed, the disorderly and extremist style of politics which had characterised the beginnings of the pro-democracy movement, with a strong tendency towards violence, seems to have been superseded by politics with civic responsibility. Fragments of extremism and intemperance in political action, language and style from the past decade remained; but they also showed visible signs of decline; though not overnight.

Between April and November 1992 the anti-Rawlings political parties resorted to new political strategies as a means of consolidating their position in the political contest with the PNDC government, especially as the general elections drew nearer. Among the new strategies was the formation of a new umbrella organisation — the *Alliance of Democratic Forces* (ADF). The pro-Rawlings political parties immediately responded with a counter grouping — *The Progressive Alliance*. Second, when this consolidation did not appear to exert the expected impact on the PNDC, the ADF — the anti-Rawlings political alliance — turned to the judicial process in a relentless struggle to level the political play ground for the forthcoming electoral politics.

A good example of this new strategy was the ADF's handling of the dispute over certain provisions of the *Political Parties Law 1992 PNDCL 281*. Rather than resorting to street action, they sought redress through an action at the Supreme Court. Clearly there was an emerging political attitude that preferred the use of peaceful and established rules and procedure to resolve disputes.

In this emerging political culture the activities of the established civic associations — the GBA, GTUC, NUGS, CCB, CBC, the ones which had either spearheaded the pro-democracy movement or helped to radicalise it, merely complemented the efforts of the new exponents of democratic politics — the political parties. Even though the remnants of the pro-democracy civil society still adhered to the original agenda of advocating for democratic rule in the country, the struggle for political power was now at the centre stage of Ghanaian politics. The activities of pro-democracy civil society can best be described as mediatory rather than confrontational.

This resurgent democratic tendency has underpinned intraparty relations since the elections of November-December 1992. There has been a constant search for consensus through dialogue, bargaining, or some activity intended to achieve the same goal among the various parties that are now engaged in the political arena.[14] Political conflict in the post election period has not been as acrimonious and destabilising as the power struggle which occurred during the early 1980s. The rank and file of political parties are gradually learning the virtues of civility in politics. Above all, a large number of private civic associations, whose interest lies mainly in ensuring peaceful and orderly resolution of conflict rather than the pursuit of power or violent conflict, is emerging to intermediate in the political process. Among them are human rights organisations and *democracy clubs*. Their activities are not antagonistic, and go a long way to complement the efforts of the existing pro-democracy civil society actors such as the Catholic Bishops Conference, the Christian Council of Ghana, and the Ghana Bar Association. Even the civic associations which constituted the alternative civil society seem to be outgrowing their anti-democracy habits and tendencies.

Conclusion

In 1991, the government was able to identify about 51 civic associations and bodies representing various social forces which constituted the bases for representation on the Consultative Assembly. The archives of the defunct NCD also has records concerning about 21 bodies that had submitted memoranda to the NCD during the public debate on the direction of government and politics in the country. The vast majority of the associations which were given representation on the Consultative Assembly did not submit any memorandum to the NCD. Nor did they engage in the transition politics in any manner that the NUGS, GBA, CCG and CBC for example, were known to have done. Also, of the 21 or so bodies that submitted proposals to the NCD, the majority did not engage in any formal political action during the crucial period of the transition; and it is most unlikely that they will ever initiate any form of political action, or be heard of, or seen, in the country's political process as conscientious and vociferous exponents of a particular political vision, however vague, of society. As indicated above, most of such civic associations represented social forces which were normally inactive politically; but had been co-opted by the PNDC — and later, NDC — government, were above all, economically weak and could not take autonomy positions in politics. Even though they represented a segment of civil society, they had become instruments of government rather than agents of society in the struggle for political freedom and rule of law. They could therefore not be considered as contributing to the creation of a political society in which the basic rights and freedoms of the citizen, and the rule of law, would be guaranteed. Their contribution to the process of democratising power could only be described as trivial.

The formation of the CIBA soon after the 1992 elections was a powerful signal of the potential direction of Ghanaian politics. It showed that Ghanaian politics could easily relapse into the kind of populist authoritarian democracy which the PNDC had tried in vain to establish.

The events of 13 December 1994 underscores this point. On that day, a group of people embarked on a peaceful march to parliament in protest against the forceful closure of a private FM station — *Radio Eye*. The democratically elected government of the Rawlings party (the NDC) mobilised another group to stage a counter demonstration. The counter demonstrators were described scornfully as 'concerned citizens of Ghana' by one private newspaper;[15] and ironically as 'defenders of democracy' by a state-owned newspaper.[16] The result of those alternative mobilisations was a violent confrontation between the two groups in front of parliament house. Another bloody confrontation, allegedly engineered by the governing party, occurred on 11 May 1995 in Accra.[17] During the massive demonstrations against the imposition of value added tax (VAT) and the high cost of living, which were organised and led by the Alliance For Change (AFC),[18] armed groups attacked the peaceful demonstrators leaving 4 people, including 2 teenagers dead and about 12 others either injured or maimed.

Concurrently, however, another tendency that is supportive of the development of democratic culture and practice is gradually taking root. The primary agents of this pro-democracy tendency are the minority of pro-democracy civil society actors which have established a long tradition of struggle against dictatorship and the abuse of human rights. This small group remains the guardians of democracy and ultimate catalyst to the current democratisation process in the country. Among them are the Ghana Bar Association, National Union of Ghana Students, Catholic Bishops Conference, Christian Council of Ghana, and the Ghana Trades Union Congress. Since 7 January 1992, when a new constitution came into effect and a democratically elected government was sworn into office, a number of small human rights associations and *democracy clubs* have also been formed to swell the ranks of this group. Admittedly these small pro-democracy civic associations have not achieved the longevity and experience necessary for institutionalisation. According to Huntington (1968:12-24), institutionalisation is '... the process by which organisations and procedures acquire value and stability'. The institutionalisation of organisations, rules and procedures results in the achievement of organisational adaptability, complexity, autonomy and coherence. These are important attributes which are necessary for performing the role of political intermediation and any other social functions effectively, and in an orderly and predictable manner. The majority of the pro-democracy civic associations have not become institutionalised yet.

Such limitations notwithstanding, it is important to recognise the intrinsic value of the proliferation of civil associations and, especially, their disposition towards dialogue, peaceful resolution of conflict, the rule of law and protection of the freedoms and rights of the citizen. The fact that these habits are being formed by the leading strata of Ghanaian society suggests a growing awareness of the need to create social structures to combat authoritarian tendencies in Ghanaian politics, and consolidate the democratic order. Arguably, if this trend could be sustained then, with time, the rest of society would become socialised in such democratic habits. To a large extent the survival of democracy in Ghana lies in this constant struggle to rejuvenate and nurture the democratic ethic that lives in Ghanaian society. Indeed, the success of the elaborate constitution which was approved at the referendum of April 1992 hinges on this strong national disposition.

Notes

1. Daily Graphic. Friday 27 May 1994.

2. Yeebo (1991).

3. For an explanation of the decline of the CDRs see Yeebo (Ibid.). Hansen (1991:76-82) explains this as Rawlings' attempt to resolve the contradiction inherent in 'the structural position which he occupied as presiding (sic) over the consolidation of the neo-colonial state...'[p. 80].

4. Refer to 'No Politics by CIBA', *The Ghanaian Democrat*, November 21-27 1994. page 12.

5. See Ninsin (1991:112-115).

6. For a list of such civic associations which were accorded sudden recognition, and then representation at the Consultative Assembly, refer to 'The Register of Consultative Assembly Members 1991/92'. Accra. Because of what the pro-democracy civil society regarded as subtle attempts by the PNDC to control and manipulate the Constituent Assembly, the GBA and the NUGS refused to send representatives to serve on that body.

7. See Oquaye (1993) for a critique of the PNDC government's conception, practice and instruments of 'popular justice'.

8. Hansen (1991:55-90) provides a sophisticated political analysis of the political struggles by the alternative civil society.

9. The number of recorded strikes which had declined sharply soon after the chaos in industrial relations of 1982, a situation that had been precipitated by the PNDC government. The incidence of labour unrest increased again after 1984, when as few as 9 strikes were recorded, to 22 in 1987. Gyimah-Boadi & anr (1993; 206).

10. Refer to Yeebo (Op cit.:202-239) for instances of such worker- government confrontations.

11. For more statements by the Movement for Freedom and Justice (MFJ) see Ninsin (1996).

12. In previous instances the outgoing military government had appointed about 30 per cent of the members of the constitutional assembly to ensure a fair control over its deliberations (Jonah 1991). The PNDC was accused of exceeding this norm.

13. These sentiments were faithfully reported by the national Commission for Democracy in its report to the PNDC government in March 1991.

14. The most recent of such negotiations between the governing party and the opposition parties centred on agreement on the rules and procedures to ensure free and fair electoral practices in the 1996 general elections.

15. 'Radio Eye Gets Support' *The Independent*, Wednesday, December 1994.

16. 'Demonstrators Take to Their Heels' *The Ghanaian Times*, Wednesday, 14 December 1994.

17. It was alleged at the time of this incident that certain elements within the governing party had organised thugs and members of the Association of Committees for the Defence of the Revolution and armed them to attack the peaceful protestors (Abdulai 1995:16). In spite of calls by many pro-democracy civil society actors like the CCG, CBC, GBA as well as some opposition political parties for an independent public enquiry into the incident the government has remained unperturbed; and so the identity of the perpetrators of those acts has not been established.

18. The leaders of the Alliance For Change included Akoto Ampaw, Charles Y. Wereko-Brobby, Nana Akuffo-Addo, and Kwesi Pratt, Jnr. They numbered about nine.

4

Political Parties and the Transition to Multi-Party Politics in Ghana

Kwesi Jonah

This paper examines how different party political traditions responded differently to the demands made on them by the politics of the transition to multi-partyism in 1991-92. It is argued that to understand the role of parties in this transition process it is not enough to study the parties as parties but as parties with the rich political traditions in which they are embedded and which have both functional and dysfunctional consequences for their identities and organisational unity. In this paper, therefore, the term *political party* is used with reference to both the party as a distinct political organisation, and the party as an institution that embodies a specific political tradition.

This paper argues that after a long period of military rule political parties can, and indeed do, rise to the occasion and effectively meet the challenges of multi-party politics because of the existence of a rich party political tradition. Tradition in this case reinforces the capacity of political parties to stand up to the tasks of multi-party politics. Tradition, however is not always an asset. It is sometimes a political liability, and tensions do arise between the needs and requirements of the political transition process and the nature or character of a party political tradition. In such a situation party traditions project different and even divergent responses to the demands of the democratisation process. Three party political traditions may be identified: the Danquah-Busia, Kwame Nkrumah, and Rawlings political traditions.

Briefly, three different responses emanated from the three party political traditions existing in Ghana at the time of the 1991/92 transition. The Danquah-Busia tradition projected a model characterised by unilineal and unilevel progression in which apart from a few defections, the essential unity with which the party had started, remained unimpaired to the end despite internal tensions. The Kwame Nkrumah tradition, on the other hand, demonstrated a pattern characterised by fission in which several centrifugal political forces finally emerged as autonomous political actors. There was also the Rawlings-populist tradition representing a model of political fusion in which several political actors, some of which were bitterly opposed to each other, gravitated towards a single centripetal force and were ultimately able to stick together politically. To fully appreciate the force of these traditions it is essential to know how the party tradition evolved in Ghana.

Evolution of Party Traditions

After World War II Ghana became the first country in sub-Saharan Africa to gain political independence. The emergence of the party marked the terminal stage of a three-phase evolutionary process. Anti-colonial nationalism in Ghana began around the end of the nineteenth and early twentieth century when the Aborigines Rights Protection Society (ARPS) comprising chiefs and lawyers and the National Congress of British West Africa (NCBWA) were founded (Kimble 1963). By the 1930's the second phase of the long journey towards the development of political parties had been reached. Political organisation this time took place under the aegis of the elite dominated Youth Associations whose members were youth in mind rather than in age (Apter 1963). The thrust of their activities was to keep the spirit of nationalism alive by discussing pragmatic measures by which to promote national development. One of the most distinguished leaders of the Youth Associations was Dr. J.B. Danquah who was to become even more prominent in Ghana's post World War II politics.

The end of World War II marked the beginning of an epoch when political activity and organisation ceased to be the exclusive preserve of the elites (Padmore 1953). The interest of wider sections of the population especially urban workers, demobilised soldiers and cocoa farmers came into sharp conflict with the interest of the colonial power structure. The country's body politic was by then seething with mass discontent. In those conditions a political organisation of a new type, possessing the appropriate mass-oriented leadership, was required to galvanise the masses into the correct political action (Austin 1964). The first post World War II movement, the United Gold Coast Convention

(UGCC) led by J.B. Danquah lawyer, philosopher, politician and member of the Kibi royal family, sprang up in 1947; but it did not meet these requirements apparently because it was the organisation of lawyers, businessmen and other professionals. For example, its financier was 'Paa' (George) Grant a prominent and wealthy timber merchant of Sekondi (Fitch and Oppenheimer 1966). These lawyers and businessmen, unable to devote full time to party organisation, invited Kwame Nkrumah to be the General Secretary of the UGCC.

Having been involved in the organisation of the Pan-African Congresses and the West African students union in the UK, Nkrumah was particularly suitable for the job. Right from the outset he knew the difficulties of accepting to work in an organisation dominated by businessmen and lawyers but was prepared to come to 'logger heads' with them if working with these elites proved to be impossible (Nkrumah 1957). The outbreak of anti-colonial riots in 1948 brought into sharp relief the ideological and political contradictions between Nkrumah and the rest of the conservative UGCC leadership (Austin 1964). As a consequence, Nkrumah's supporters within the Committee of Youth Organisations (CYO) which he had established inside the UGCC compelled him to break away to form the first mass political organisation in the country, the Convention Peoples Party (CPP) (Austin 1976).

The transition from a nationalist political activity almost entirely dominated by the intelligentsia or educated elites to one in which the mass of the people dictated the pace and momentum of national politics is what produced an enduring polarisation in the internal politics of the country. The CPP or Nkrumah tradition dominated the politics of Ghana from 1951 to 1966 while the Danquah-Busia tradition produced its first government from 1969 to 1972. Apart from a short spell during which the Nkrumah tradition recaptured power in 1979-81, the military has become the main ruling 'party' in Ghana. The prolonged military involvement in Ghana's politics created the view among leading members of the two main political traditions that military intervention is the principal obstacle to democratic politics in the country. Accordingly military regimes tend to be viewed as a common enemy.

Party Tradition:
A New Perspective in Ghanaian Political Studies

Scholarly works on Ghanaian political parties have been skewed, in terms of interest and attention, in favour of the nationalist movements, the UGCC, CPP, NLM, UP, Northern Peoples Party and the Togoland Congress. Few have spared time and thought for the political parties of the post-Nkrumah period in Ghana's politics. This imbalance in scholarly writings on political parties has meant that only a few general aspects of Ghana's political parties have been the focus of past studies. At one level there have been in-depth studies into the origin, structures, role, function, strategies and organisational skills of political parties.[1] At another level scholars have examined the ideological orientation and social bases of political parties. Studies of this category have emphasised the class, ethnic and regional bases of support of the parties.[2] Only a few studies have been devoted to the party system and its impact on the evolution of a plural democratic political system.[3]

These and other conceptual formulations of political parties in the past, no doubt, served the purposes for which they were intended. But they do not adequately respond to the problems posed by the democratisation process and, in particular, the capacity of parties to promote and propel a young and fragile multi-party democratic system forward. To answer this question a new approach to the understanding of parties is required.

To appreciate the potential of Ghanaian political parties to make an effective contribution to multi-party democracy, scholars will have to analytically draw a distinction between *the political party as party and the political party as tradition*. The two complement and reinforce each other. A political party is the bone and flesh of the party political tradition; it exists to ensure the continuity of this tradition, while the party tradition on the other hand is the deeper life and soul of the party. The party and its tradition, however, do sometimes come into conflict with each other when tradition blocks the necessary steps and actions required by a party to push the democratic process forward. I would argue that at the current conjuncture in Ghana's political evolution the functions of political parties extend beyond traditional ones of recruitment, socialisation, among others, to include nurturing, sustaining and strengthening democracy. Party political traditions should enable the parties to perform these new challenges effectively.

Unlike the party, the party political tradition is a body of symbols, myths, ideas, ideals, ideologies, philosophies and concrete political achievements associated with a national political hero and a political party in the history of the country. The party political tradition is characterised by personification, indivisibility, indissolubility and invariable leadership. Personification refers to the tendency of a party political tradition to be symbolised by its founding father or fathers. Indivisibility means that a party tradition cannot be divided. There can only be a multiplication of divisions within it.

A party tradition is indissoluble, in that it enjoys a more or less perpetual continuity and cannot be legislated out of existence. If a legislation declares a party tradition illegal the latter continues a vibrant existence in conditions of splendid semi-clandestinity or open defiance. For example, the banning of the Convention People's Party in 1969 resulted in the formation of the National Alliance of Liberals and later the People's Popular Party. In the same vein, the founding father of the tradition, the hero whose name is synonymous with the tradition is the recognised and indisputable leader of the tradition. A rejection of his leadership and everything he represents amounts to a rejection of the tradition itself.

These essential attributes of the party political tradition have some implied consequences for both the party and the political culture of the society. In specific terms it implies idealisation or even over-idealisation of the tradition, the institutionalisation of the party political culture and the increasing tendency towards fragmentation of parties within a tradition over time. The fragmentation assumes an alternating pattern moving from one tradition to the other over a period. Moreover, the more recently a tradition produced an elected government the higher the risk of fragmentation if it stays out of power for a while. A tradition with a living hero who still controls the levers of state patronage is the least likely to suffer serious fragmentation. The hero welds the fractions together by a combination of charisma and the power of patronage.

The party political tradition serves two principal purposes. It is a source of legitimation for political parties and party leadership and the basis of socialisation and recruitment. The tradition confers on the party two principal types of legitimation, normative or philosophical and empirical. Normative or philosophical legitimation refers to the set of ideological or philosophical postulates that guide the programme of the original or mother party of the tradition and its other parties or hero rather than concrete achievements. This may be socialism, Pan-Africanism, anti-colonialism, liberal democracy, individual liberty, human rights, private enterprise and so on. Empirical legitimation on the other hand, refers to the concrete achievements associated with the founding father or fathers and the mother party or parties of the tradition. Apart from party political activity, what has kept the party political tradition going in Ghana is a complex network of personal friendships and mutual support in the form of funerals, birthday parties, weddings and other social activities. 'Funeral politics' or 'political funerals' is now a popular political strategy employed by the various political traditions, especially during periods of military rule, to maintain their existence.

Main Party Traditions in Ghana's History

The party political tradition and its impact is recognised by both scholars and leading politicians in Ghana. The Ghanaian historian Adu Boahen, a recent NPP Presidential candidate, when explaining the electoral defeat of the Gbedemah-led NAL in 1969 pointed out that 'many people identified NAL with the CPP'.[4] Writing about the same period Naomi Chazan recognised that Ghanaians believed in an unbroken continuity between the victorious Progress Party and antecedent political organisations such as the UGCC, NLM and the United Party.[5] Adu Boahen observed again that the PNP won the 1979 elections on account of the fact that the PNP 'being the successor of the CPP, that is to say Nkrumah's Party, it gained from the enviable legacy which the party left behind' (Boahen 1988). These observations by the Ghanaian historian complement Naomi Chazan's view that the PNP which won the elections of 1979 'was unabashedly constructed on the remnants of the old CPP organisation' while the vanquished PFP 'was the self-proclaimed successor of the Progress Party. Its founding members read like a list of Busia's inner circle' (Chazan 1983).

Continuity of party political tradition has become an article of faith among Ghanaian politicians who accept not only their party political tradition as legitimate and desirable but as having a highly influential weight in their political calculations and affiliations. For Ghanaian politicians the party political tradition is real, good and should be maintained. Hence, Mr. J.A. Kuffuor, one of the Presidential aspirants of the NPP during the 1992 elections could argue that the party political tradition signifies multi-partyism and is honourable. As he once quite emphatically explained:

> The Danquah-Busia and Nkrumah traditions are both time-tested and honourable. They have attracted to their respective sides, sons and daughters of the nation whose over-riding concern is seeking by their respective means what they consider to be the nation's highest good...[6]

One of his rivals and competitors for the NPP Presidential nomination, Safo-Adu confirmed the force of party political tradition when he stated in an interview that 'Politics is history and you cannot easily dismiss past leaders ... It's not so much their faces but the contributions they have made. It's the maintenance of tradition'.[7] From another camp, General E.A. Erskine, renowned UN Middle East peacekeeping soldier and Presidential candidate of PHP in the 1992 elections, stated with conviction that 'I do not believe that Ghanaians can forget the CPP and PP and those parties which pioneered Ghana to independence. Even if they are banned by a government instrument they will function under other guises'.[8]

A strong party political tradition gives hope and assurance that a multiparty culture exists in seed form which can, and does germinate at the appropriate time. A military coup d'état may ban political activity for a long time. Once the ban on political parties is lifted parties very quickly spring back into action and establish backward linkages with their respective traditions. Traditions die hard and are positive for democratic political practice. Tradition could also be counter-productive. It could, and in 1992 did indeed, block essential political alliances for the formation of larger, more viable and highly competitive political coalitions among traditional opponents for ensuring electoral victory.

In 1992, though the two main political traditions were both against military rule and coups, traditional antagonism between them prevented joint action to form a united front against the pro-Rawlings coalition. As we shall see, initial co-operation between the two party traditions was not transformed into an alliance or political coalition.

Today two main party traditions are recognised in Ghanaian politics. The Danquah-Busia tradition is associated with such past political parties as the UGCC, NLM, UP, Northern People Party (NPP) PP and PFP. The New Patriotic Party (NPP) is the direct descendant of this tradition. Among the well-known political ideals and principles associated with this tradition are sovereignty and liberty of the individual, multi-party democracy, rule of law, free market and private enterprise and initiative.[9]

The Nkrumah tradition is associated with the CPP, NAL and the PNP and has historically been identified with socialism, Pan- Africanism, anti-imperialism and active state involvement in the economy. It is strongly believed that a Rawlings tradition has now been established in Ghanaian politics drawing its support from each of the old established traditions and organised around the vague principles of probity and accountability, and participatory democracy at the grassroots.

In spite of the common opposition of the Danquah-Busia and Nkrumah traditions to the newly established Rawlings tradition, they could not produce a united front to challenge their 'common enemy'. Tradition embodies not only past failures and achievements but also conflicts and antagonisms which constrain the capacity to face present challenges. Attitudes of the Danquah-Busia and Nkrumahist politicians toward the coup of 24 February 1966 that toppled the Nkrumah government, for instance, are sharply opposed. To the Danquah-Busia group 'it was the most justifiable coup in the history of Ghana' and 'the greatest thing that happened in the country'. To the Nkrumahist group 'the cowardly *coup d'etat* of 24th February, 1966 put a break on Ghana's forward march and marked the beginning of a long dark period in Africa's quest for freedom, unity and progress'. Some hard feelings arising from the 24 February 1966 coup are still fresh in peoples minds.

In 1969 leading politicians of the Nkrumah regime were barred for ten years from holding any public office. This disqualification stopped Imoru Egala, a founding father of the PNP from becoming a presidential candidate in 1979. He roped in his nephew, Dr. Limann, to take his place. Indeed, some West African immigrants in Ghana who have acquired the vote support the CPP tradition but are vehemently opposed to any merger or alliance with the Danquah-Busia Party which they still associate with the expulsion of aliens in 1969. This is why the numerous calls on the two-party traditions to come together against the pro-Rawlings clubs and parties, came to nothing. On the other hand it was relatively easy for the comparatively young Rawlings tradition to strike very successful electoral alliances.

Rawlings Revolution and Multi-Party Politics

When Rawlings and his PNDC came to power on 31 December 1981, it was not envisaged that political parties would have a place in the country's political process again (Hansen 1987). Indications were that revolutionary political structures, in particular the PDC's and WDC's would be nurtured and developed into a future political system not based on parties (Shillington 1992). This notwithstanding, political parties could once again emerge after ten years of suppression.

Independent of the will of the PNDC and its opponents, Ghana's political system between 1982 and 1992 passed through a very familiar and well established three-stage evolution before political parties were allowed. The first stage was the formation of PDC's and WDC's in 1982. The task of co-ordinating these structures was assigned to the Interim National Co-ordinating Committee and later the National Defence Council. Before long, however, even the revolutionary leadership became fed up with the many hasty, ill-conceived undisciplined and anarchic actions of the defence committees. The co-ordinating bodies also became centres of power struggle between different supporters of the revolution, especially the JFM and the NDM. Consequently, they were quickly brought under direct political control in 1984 and a ministry was set up to exercise oversight functions over them. The role of the structures was depoliticised and the name changed to CDR.

The second stage before the emergence of political parties was the establishment of District Assemblies in 1988. The decision to establish District Assemblies was taken as early as 1982, the first year of the revolution but had nothing revolutionary about it. Mr. J.A. Kuffuor, who was the Secretary of Local Government at the time, has explained that as an admirer of the late Prime Minister K.A. Busia and a member of the Progress Party, his source of inspiration was the Local Government Act (1971) which was passed by the Busia government.[10] Opposition by revolutionary cadres left the Local Government reforms unimplemented for six years. The change from a non-representative participatory political structure to a representative district assembly system signalled a shift in the support base of the PNDC from urban to the rural areas where most of the 110 Assemblies were located (Ninsin 1989).

The third stage was the announcement by the PNDC on 10 May 1991 that political parties, free and independent judiciary and an elected President and National Assembly would be part of the evolving constitutional arrangements for Ghana. This was the government's official response to the NCD report, 'Evolving A True Democracy'. Approximately one year later on 18 May 1992, the ban on party political activity was lifted and political parties began to register with the Interim National Electoral Commission (INEC). A substantial part of the pressure to allow party political activity had emanated from within; mainly from groups such as the Movement for Freedom and Justice, the Bar Association, National Union of Ghana Students, the Catholic Bishops Conference and the Christian Council of Ghana.[11]

Response of the Traditions to the Lifting of the Ban

Long before the government decided to allow political parties, members of existing party political traditions had come to the conclusion that the PNDC government was cheating them by monopolising the political space through continued suppression of party political activity. Immediately before the ban on party political activity was lifted, the only political movement available to the party traditions was the Movement for Freedom and Justice which was handicapped by lack of resources and constant police harassment. The MFJ was not even invited to participate in the regional fora on 'Evolving A True Democracy'.

The response of the party political traditions was to begin to reorganise in anticipation of the lifting of the ban by forming political parties under the guise of social clubs. The evolution of parties followed three distinct patterns. The first was typified by the Danquah-Busia Club of the New Patriotic Party (NPP) which followed a unilevel, unilineal course in which the Party moved from the club stage to the party stage while keeping its unity intact. The unity of the Danquah-Busia tradition during the 1991/92 transition had deep roots in ideological, historical, and class factors. While the founding fathers of the tradition are no longer alive to hold their followers together, the ideological underpinnings of the tradition, especially free market and private enterprise, the rule of law, liberal democracy and individual liberty have remained current and valid. Common attachment to these values serves as a greater source of strength and cohesion for its adherents. Above all, history has also taught them to remain united and firm. For example, the Danquah-Busia camp contains a large number of businessmen and professionals who were the main target of political attacks during the Rawlings-led 'house-cleaning' crusade of 1979 and the 'revolution' of 1982-92. Consequently, its members are further united by their determination to reverse that humiliation which was meted out to them by the Rawlings regime.

One characteristic of this model of party evolution is that the leaders of the emerging party were known from the club stage of the process. On Saturday, 14 March 1992, two clear months before the lifting of the ban on party political activity, the six presidential aspirants of the yet to be formed party were introduced at the inauguration of a branch of the club at Koforidua.[12] Also from the formation of the Danquah-Busia Club on 23rd February 1991 to the inauguration of the party on 2 June 1992, it was clear that the inner circle of the party was closed to persons who were not traditional Danquah-Busia followers. Accordingly, two prominent non-traditional members of the club, Dr. John Bilson and Mr. Sam Boateng left in protest to join one of the Nkrumahist groups. Mr. Kwaku Baah, who had always been a leading member of the tradition later followed for the same reason.[13]

The second model was provided by the Kwame Nkrumah tradition which started as a collection of clubs — e.g., Our Heritage, Kwame Nkrumah Welfare Society, National Co- ordinating Committee of Nkrumahists and Kwame Nkrumah Youngsters Club. In the transition to the party stage these splinter clubs could not overcome their state of fragmentation. This tendency stemmed largely from the objective conditions in which they found themselves at the beginning of the 1990's. First, since the founding father of the tradition passed away, no outstanding personality had emerged to unify his followers. Through persuasion, personal charm and kindness, Imoru Egala was able to keep together Nkrumah's followers throughout the military rule of 1972-79 and organise them for victory in the 1979 elections. His death in 1980 deprived this party political tradition of a unifying force. Second, the ideologies of anti-colonialism, Pan-Africanism and Socialism which gave them a unique identity and strength in the early years of independence had by the 1990's lost their hold on the mass of Nkrumah's followers. To make things worse for the Nkrumah tradition, the young militants who could have been its field organisers had been attracted by the Rawlings revolution to join ranks with the Rawlings crowd — as members of the defence committees, civil defence organisation, June Fourth Movement, 31st December Movement, etc. Those militants remained with Rawlings when he declared his intention to engage in civilian politics. They constituted the core of what has become the Rawlings tradition.

Within the Nkrumah tradition the transition from club to party stage manifested itself not so much in internal changes as in further fragmentation and realignment across political traditions. The first and most important change is that the National Co-ordinating Committee of Nkrumahists (NCCN) led by Rev. Kwaku Boateng and John Tettegah, instead of uniting the various factions, teamed up with Roland Atta Kesson's Kwame Nkrumah Youngsters Club (KNYC) to produce the National Convention Party (NCP). When Rev. Kwaku Boateng failed to secure the presidential nomination, he quit and denounced the alliance with the NDC whose presidential candidate was Jerry Rawlings.

The second and more profound of the subsequent fission was represented by Dr. Hila Limann's formation of his own Party, the Peoples National Convention (PNC). Former President Limann started at the club stage as a member of Our Heritage knowing fully well that the old established CPP members in KNWS had no regard whatsoever for him. They rejected his Nkrumahist credentials and always held the view that Limann was imposed on the PNP by his uncle Imoru Egala. After a brief stint with Our Heritage, Limann discovered that he was equally unwelcome among the young Nkrumahists. What made him unacceptable was his insistence that as the former President he should automatically be the Presidential candidate of any group he joined and that his status should take precedence over democratic processes. Since the majority of members could not agree with him, Limann quit Our Heritage to form his own party. The stage was then set for the process of fragmentation to persist.

The Nkrumah tradition further showed signs of decline both in relation to its past and compared to the Danquah-Busia tradition. The lively ideological conflicts between right and left CPP followers of the 1960's and even the debate between socialists of the KNRG and the right-wing of the PNP had all given way to trivial personality conflicts centred around Botsio, Gbedemah, Limann and others. Compared to the Danquah-Busia tradition, the former had lost the benefit of a vigorous internal democracy. Hence, its inability to contain conflicts within its ranks.

By the November 1992 elections, therefore, the Nkrumah.tradition had produced four registered political parties: The National Convention Party (NCP) which was a product of the NCCN and KNYC, the Peoples National Convention (PNC) with Limann as leader, a breakaway from Our Heritage; the Peoples Heritage Party (PHP) which came out of Our Heritage Political Club and the National Independence Party (NIP) constituted by the remnants of KNWS after the founding father Kojo Botsio and some old CPP stalwarts who started it had left. Even K.A. Gbedemah who joined late had to leave the group in the end.

In contrast to these two models, the Rawlings tradition was the outcome of a deliberate attempt to construct a new coalition of social forces using young militants from the Nkrumah tradition in combination with young aspiring middle class business men and women. In 1991-92, approximately eight groups initiated actions, some of which were closely related and others quite independent, to ensure that Rawlings would be elected president under the 1992 Constitutional rule. Among these clubs were the Eagle Club, Friends of the Progressive Decade, Rawlings Fan Club, Development Club, Development Union, Development Front, New Nation Club, and the Front Club. Many of these were small, localised organisations and did not have any national structure. The Eagle was the only one that pretended to be national, and in the process earned for itself a big name and powerful attacks which it did not really deserve.

With the notable exception of the Eagle Club, some of these bodies joined together to form the United Clubs for Rawlings, UNICRAWL, which was expected to function as an umbrella organisation for the clubs of the Rawlings tradition. The most striking feature of these pro-Rawlings clubs was that their membership and initiatives derived from the grassroots supporters and admirers of Rawlings. They were mostly revolutionary cadres, members of the CDR, CDO, June Fourth Movement and 31st December Women's Movement. They formed the core of the masses who felt that they had gained very little material benefit from more than a decade of loyal and dedicated service to the Rawlings revolution and stood in danger of being dumped under constitutional rule. Their involvement in the clubs was intended to assure them of, at least, a toe-hold in the Fourth Republic rather than supreme admiration for Rawlings.

Meanwhile, those who were opposed to these grassroots supporters of Rawlings, but were also determined to ensure the continuity of the Rawlings regime, had organised separately into what later became the National Democratic Congress (NDC) which was also interested in sponsoring Rawlings for election as president of Ghana. The name most closely associated with the rise of this middle class professional and business group is Obed Asamoah. Eventually the majority of Rawlings supporters gathered in the NDC. In the meantime, two minor political parties — the National Convention Party (NCP) and Eagle Party had been formed to support the Rawlings election project. Eventually, these teamed up to form an electoral alliance with the NDC to affirm the evolution of the Rawlings party political tradition into a full-fledged political party.

During the period of fission and fusion associated with the evolution of these three models of party political traditions into actual political parties, all other parties not attached to any distinct political tradition, were ultimately doomed to political extinction or disintegration. The New Generation Alliance (NGA) led by Mr. Harry Sawyerr split into two. One half led by Mr. Sam Okudzeto a renowned lawyer joined the NPP while Mr. Harry Sawyerr, and a few other NGA members made their way into the NDC. Sawyerr was later rewarded with the Ministry of Education portfolio and the post of Deputy Chairman of the NDC. Other small parties which faced a familiar fate included the Democratic Peoples Party (DPP), Ghana Democratic Republican Party (GDRP), and the National Justice Party (NJP) which simply died a natural death.

Polarisation and Dualisation of the Party System

Side by side with the fusion and fission processes that were going on within individual party traditions the emerging party system was also undergoing a process of polarisation into two broad camps and reduction into a *de facto* two-party system. This was an unconscious re-arrangement for appropriating the limited political space available. The political parties tended to see themselves as fighting a two way contest between the *democratic forces* and the rest — that is, all the pro-PNDC parties of the 'Progressive Alliance' comprising the NDC, NCP and Eagle Party.

This polarisation dates back to the club stage in the evolution of political parties, sometime in August 1990 when the leading opponents of the PNDC got together to form the MFJ. The majority of the founding members of the MFJ, whose main aim was to demand constitutional rule based on a multi-party system of government were also the leading members of the opposition parties which finally materialised. For example, Professor Adu Boahen, Ray Kakraba Quarshie, Obeng Manu and Owusu Gyimah joined the NPP; Johnny Hansen joined the PHP while Dan Lartey joined the NIP. The various members of the MFJ subsequently formed different political clubs based on their party political traditions. To bring all these 'opposition' clubs together Adu Boahen initiated the formation of a new movement — the Co-ordinating Committee of Democratic Forces (CCDF) in August 1991 soon after his return from a lecture tour of American Universities.[14] His aim was 'to pool together all forces opposed to the PNDC'.[15] Even though eleven pro-democracy forces joined,[16] namely, the MFJ, Danquah-Busia Club, Our Heritage, Great Unity Club, Ex PP Group, Asante Youth Association, NUGS and the KNWS. The Gold Coast Ex-Servicemen Union, KNRG and NDM, the CCDF was also not very successful in posing an effective challenge to the PNDC. Its main impact was to deepen the polarisation of the political arena into the pro-PNDC group and its opponents.

The formation of political parties did not end the process of polarisation. Eleven parties had registered with the INEC by August 1992. The political parties are National Convention Party (NCP), National Democratic Congress (NDC), Peoples National Convention (PNC) Peoples Heritage Party (PHP), New Patriotic Party (NPP), National Independence Party (NIP), New Generation Alliance (NGA), Democratic Peoples Party (DPP) Ghana Democratic Republican Party (GDRP) and National Justice Party (NJP).[17] Only two, the National Salvation Party (NSP)[18] and Peoples Party for Development and Democracy (PPDP) did not register; and indeed the NSP died soon after announcing its formation. An Alliance of Democratic Forces (ADF) was formed which included seven of the registered political parties opposed to the PNDC.[19] The nucleus of the ADF was the group of politicians who took the Interim National Electoral Commission (INEC) to court over the Political Parties Law 1992, contending that restrictions on the choice of name, emblem and slogan constituted a violation of their freedom of association. Among these politicians were K.A. Gbedemah, B.J. Da Rocha, Dr. Hilla Limann, Prof. A. Adu Boahen, Mr. Kojo Botsio, Dr. Kwame Safo-Adu, Alhaji Mohammed Farl and Mr. Bawa Dy-Yakah.[20]

Alongside the emergence of two broad opposing camps, the ADF and pro-Rawlings group, was also the development of a *de facto* two-party instead of a multi-party system. The technical definition of a two party system is that, regardless of the number of parties in existence, only two possess the political capability to win an election and form a government. Ghana's political system is characterised by an inherent tendency toward a two party system because of its persistent reliance on the 'first-past-the-post' system. The politics of the transition, especially during 1991-92, has confirmed what appears to be a permanent characteristic of Ghanaian politics; namely, the existence of a *de facto* two-party system. The main indicator was the Presidential election results which gave nearly 90 per cent of the votes cast to the NDC and NPP Presidential candidates. Even before the elections some leading 'opposition' figures had advocated the merging of the Nkrumah and Danquah-Busia traditions in the form of a temporary electoral alliance to defeat the pro-Rawlings alliance [21] and re-establish the traditional two party system.[22] As the political campaign gathered momentum it became even clearer that the NDC and the NPP were the only political parties possessing a substantial presence in every part of the country as well as the political strength to win elections and form a government.

Elections and the Boycott

If the gradual dichotomization represents a re-arrangement among parties for the effective sharing of political space already monopolised by Jerry Rawlings, the basis for self-exclusion from the political arena was laid even before the elections. It is interesting that fundamental policy differences among parties was negligible. No party was prepared to challenge the basic market-oriented economic strategy of development adopted by the PNDC under the Structural Adjustment Programme. The NDC pledged to continue policies of the PNDC which conformed with the aspirations of the people, in particular, the strategy of development, participatory democracy and rural development[23] while the NPP offered its own version of continuity. The party promised to continue where Busia's government left off: promote free enterprise, rural development and individual liberty. For them Rawlings had simply been implementing policies started by Busia during the Second Republic.[24] According to Mr. J.A. Kuffuor 'Busia's twenty-seven months tenure in government proves beyond doubt how reliable his prophetic vision was and could still be. His policies and laws can be said to form the foundations of most of the laws and policies now passing as the economic recovery programmes, co-operation with the IMF, World Bank ..., promotion of the private sector as the main engine of economic growth'.[25]

In spite of essential similarity in policy outlook or lack of fundamental differences among them, and especially the two main parties— the NDC and NPP, had constructed an image of the self and the other party which could only heighten political tension and ruin mutual trust. Official statements and public pronouncements of leading members of the main parties tended to portray their opponents as the devil incarnate and themselves as immaculate angels. In an official statement released to the press after the lifting of the ban on party political activity, the Danquah-Busia Club which had just announced the formation of the 'Progress Party' described the PNDC as a government of 'human rights abuses' made up of 'unprincipled faithless and greedy men'.[26] Prof. Adu Boahen who eventually became the Presidential candidate called the PNDC 'brutal' and 'blood-minded'.[27] By implication, the NPP and its leading members were associated with only the loftiest ideals and political behaviour.

On the NDC side the Presidential candidate is reported in *The Stolen Verdict* to have once said that he would not hand over to rogues and thieves, an oblique reference to the NPP and its leaders. The NDC and its leaders on the other hand had 'integrity'. To make matters worse none of the leading Presidential candidates anticipated a possible defeat. Each was sure to win 'hands down'.[28] In these conditions none of the other parties and candidates was prepared to accept the massive electoral victory of the NDC candidate, Jerry Rawlings, especially given the many imperfections of the electoral system and some of the malpractice announced on election day. Soon after the presidential elections the, losing parties announced a boycott of the parliamentary elections at a joint rally held at Kumasi in November.[29] The NPP even threatened to dismiss any of its parliamentary candidates who would stand as independent candidates.[30]

Adjusting to Self-Exclusion

Withdrawal from the Parliamentary elections was the most effective way in which the parties could exclude themselves from the central political platform in the new constitutional order. The right to vote against objectionable legislation was completely forfeited and the chance to put up a staunch opposition to unacceptable policies of the executive was allowed to slip. Alternative strategies had to be devised to enhance the political effectiveness of the opposition, to get the government to listen to them, to influence government policy and prevent the creation by default of a *de facto* single-party state.

The first strategy was an attempt by the four defeated parties — the NPP, NIP, PNC and PHP — to stick together and take joint actions such as the rally at Kumasi Abbey Park where they announced their withdrawal from the parliamentary elections. This was followed by a meeting between the opposition parties and high-powered government delegation which included all the powerful people in government apart from the President-elect.[31] The objective of that meeting was to devise ways of reintegrating the opposition into the political processes of the Fourth Republic. The National House of Chiefs and the Religious bodies, Christian and Muslim alike all assisted in these efforts; but to no avail. Early in 1993, the defeated parties — NPP, NIP, PNC and PHP — came up with an Inter-Party Co-ordinating Committee and promised the nation a 'shadow Cabinet' outside Parliament, to monitor the activities of the government to ensure that they were within the framework of the constitution.[32] They appealed to the government to consult them on major national issues and urged their supporters to accept the NDC government and post-election situation for the sake of peace.

These collective moves did not produce much positive response, an indication that reintegration into the democratic political process could not be achieved in any other way than by direct participation in competitive elections. The parties therefore began individual efforts to enhance their political effectiveness. The Nkrumahist front, to end its two-year fragmentation, began a series of unity talks to unify their ranks.

A technical committee was established comprising representatives of the Nkrumahist parties such as the PPDD, PHP, PNC and NIP and other groups such as the Concerned Nkrumahist Forum and Nkrumahist Unity Caucus. Though Dr. Hilla Limann's PNC refused to be part of this reunification effort most of his leading members deserted him and joined the unity talks. Among the leading people involved in the talks were J.K. Tamakloe, B.K. Nketiah, S.S. Baffour-Awuah, Kwesi Armah, Dr. and Mrs. Chinebuah, Kankam Da Costa, Dr. Edmund Delle, Mike Eghan and Kojo Armah.[33] At the end of the talks the formation of a new united Nkrumahist Party — the Peoples Convention Party (PCP) was announced. Some serious Nkrumahists, after a brief involvement, cast doubts on the capacity of the new Party to maintain its unity and the Nkrumahist political and ideological legacy.

The NPP effort to strengthen itself has both internal and external dimensions. Externally the NPP entered into dialogue with the NDC government. This attempt to do business with the government divided the party into pro-dialogue and anti-dialogue members,[34] and alienated the NPP from the other opposition parties.[35] The party therefore had to unofficially abandon its dialogue with the government.

Even before abandoning the dialogue the NPP had found a more effective way of re-inserting itself into the political process by extending the political arena to the judiciary which consequently became a theatre of political struggle. In several constitutional cases NPP successfully obtained a favourable Supreme Court ruling. Some of these are that no police permit was required for the holding of demonstrations; the Ghana Broadcasting Corporation should accord the political parties equal coverage; 31st December can no longer be commemorated as a public holiday; the NDC government could not use District Assemblies as constituted before constitutional rule to elect the District Chief Executives. The effect of these and the other rulings of the Supreme Court was to establish clearly that the NPP while not in Parliament, still possessed the capacity to influence or check the political conduct of government. It was as if the NPP was telling the NDC 'You got us at the polls; we've got you in court'.

The internal response to the exclusion from parliament was more likely to affect the unity and cohesion of the NPP. There was, for example, a struggle within the party to establish alternative centres of control over constituencies. In the Ashanti region a Parliamentary Candidates Association was inaugurated on the 21 August 1993 to strengthen the position of those parliamentary candidates who missed the chance to contest the last election because of their parties' decision not to participate.[36] Mr. S.K. Boafo, the Interim Chairman of the Association explained that the aim was to re-organise the party on a constituency basis and not to challenge the leadership of the Party. Two months later, the constituency secretaries of the party came up with their own association.[37]

On 2 October 1994, the NPP launched yet another internal association, The Patriotic Club, at Kumasi. The new association announced at its first meeting in Kumasi that 'the aim of the club is to constitute ourselves into a militant movement and take the NPP to the remotest parts of the country'. Among prominent party members invited were Dr. Wayo Seini, a lecturer at the University of Ghana who is a known critic of Prof. Adu Boahen, the Party's former Presidential candidate, Dr. Dsane-Selby, the closest rival of Adu-Boahen for the Party's Presidential candidate and Dr. Wereko-Brobbey, chairman of the club. These leading members of the Party were allegedly opposed to Dr. Donkor-Fordwor, former Chairman of African Development Bank, Chairman of Ashanti region branch of the NPP and a close ally and supporter of Prof. Adu Boahen to whom most members of the new club were opposed.

This made the NPP, probably the most saturated party as far as the number of internal associations is concerned. Already in existence were the Women's Wing, the Youth Wing, Business Executives and the Young Executive Forum. The Young Executive Forum has been described as 'a group of young upwardly mobile cellular-phone-clutching business executives and professionals who provided substantial financial backing for Prof. Adu Boahen's 1992 Presidential bid'.[38]

Towards 1996 Elections

Two issues that are critical to success in the 1996 Presidential elections are the nature of the internal conflicts of each party and the capacity of each party to retain its present social basis of support and broaden it before 1996. It was clear from the 1992 presidential election results that some of the parties, especially those of the Nkrumah tradition —PCP and

PNC — enjoyed a rather limited national following. It was most likely that only a miracle could enhance their electoral chances. The PNC, in particular, lost most of its leaders and supporters who do not come from the northern part of the country. The only option open to it was to align itself with the PCP or the NPP or be part of a broader alliance of opposition parties.

The PCP gained substantially from the near collapse of the Limann-led PNC. However, the so-called unity excludes the Nkrumahists who have joined the Rawlings camp and Limann's followers in the northern regions of Ghana. Besides, the persistent media reports that the PCP has been infiltrated by the NDC government is not likely to make the party appealing to those looking for an alternative to the NDC. Not only is the party seriously cash strapped, insiders are worried about the lack of any ideological or philosophical connection with Nkrumah. What is emphasised is Nkrumah's developmental achievements not the philosophy and ideals that inspired those achievements. Accordingly, some parties to the unity talks, especially the PPDD led by Kwesi Pratt, continue to maintain a separate existence from the PCP. Internally it is reported that the power struggle for the Presidential nomination has already began even though the party is only now struggling to establish itself throughout the country.

The NPP faces a very serious financial crisis.[39] The gloomy financial picture painted by Mr. Hackman Owusu Agyeman, National Treasurer at the Annual Delegates Conference of 19 and 20 December 1993 does not seem to have changed in 1994.[40] More important, however, is the conflict within the party — that is, between the 'constitutionalists' who support the position of the party's national chairman, B. J. Da Rocha, that the Presidential candidate of the party is not its leader and those who consider Adu Boahen both as leader and presidential candidate for the 1996 Presidential polls.[41] Of equal importance is the persistent conflict within the party between the economic nationalists led by Dr. Jones Ofori-Atta and the laissez-faire capitalists led by K.A. Pianim. The conflict has manifested itself as a struggle over the PNDC's divestiture programme, between those who support it and those who view it as 'an inordinate act of betrayal of national interest'.[42] The conflict is both deep-seated and completely bound up with the tradition of the party. The party's virile internal democratic life can withstand these and other minor conflicts.

What is crucial to its electoral success is its ability to retain its present support base in the industrial towns of Sekondi-Takoradi, Kumasi, Obuasi, Accra and Tema (Jonah 1994).

The lines of conflict within the NDC are many. There is first the conflict between the original PNDC members (and Secretaries) and those who joined the NDC without prior involvement with the PNDC. The original PNDC officials benefited enormously from the distribution of government posts and have shown greater resilience in retaining their positions in government than others. There is also some dissatisfaction among cadres who have not yet been resettled. Many cadres have been found jobs in various commissions and public service organisations; but many more are yet to be rewarded for their services to the 'revolution' or compensated for their sacrifices. There is also the problem of holding together the Progressive Alliance of the NDC, NCP and Eagle. Though the contribution of the NCP and Eagle Party to NDC electoral success is minimal, the psychological value of the alliance is immeasurably great.

Since the time of the Parliamentary elections, however, there has been signs of NDC-NCP tension. Some individual members of the NCP who lost in the Parliamentary elections became convinced that the circumstances of their defeat strongly indicated that opposition charges of rigging in the Presidential elections should not have been ignored so easily. In the absence of a strong opposition party, some NCP MPs have tried to play that role in Parliament resulting in sporadic brushes with some of their NDC colleagues on the floor of the House. Some NCP members are still not satisfied with the inequitable distribution of the spoils of the Alliance's electoral victory. Even more important, they are disgruntled about the alleged anti-Nkrumah posture of Rawlings. They are embarrassed about their continued separation from the mainstream Nkrumahist party, and desperately want to quit the Progressive Alliance and join the other Nkrumahists.

Conclusion

We have argued that in the Ghanaian political process party political tradition is an inextricable component of the country's political culture and an important variable in the transition. During the 1991-92 period of the current transition politics, each party political tradition charted its own direction in the arduous and tortuous journey to multi-partyism. The principal outcome of all these complex processes was the emergence of a political order that was polarised into two principal antagonistic camps, pro-Rawlings and anti-Rawlings, and two powerful political opponents the NDC and the NPP. As the country moves toward the 1996 elections these processes will continue but in different forms and under new conditions. With the initial phase of the transition process over all the party political traditions are re-assessing their strategies in order to enhance their position and role in the country's politics. This re-assessment combined with conflicts within and between parties is giving rise to interestingly new processes which will in the end confirm the established patterns of a two-camp, two-party political system.

Several elements of these new processes may be noted. First, there have been defections from the NPP to the NDC and from the NDC to the NPP and other smaller parties like the PPDD. Second, there have also been break-a-ways from some major parties. The most spectacular example is the breakaway of Nana Addo Aikins, former Chairman of Appeals Tribunal under the PNDC, from the NDC to form his own party, The National Front. There are moves among the opposition parties to form new alliances to challenge the pro-Rawlings parties of The Progressive Alliance at the 1996 elections. Discussions are going on at various levels; individual and group, official and unofficial; between the NPP on the one hand and the PCP and PNC on the other. These delicate and subtle constructions in the country's political arena are significant in that they represent moves towards a more effective sharing of political space by the emerging multi-party actors all of whom are keen to consolidate their presence in the country's political process.

Notes

1. See for example, Coleman and Rosberg (1964).

2. Examples of such studies are Fitch and Oppenheimer (1966), and Ninsin (1985).

3. Example, Kraus, J. 'Political Change Conflict and Discontent in Ghana', in Philip Foster and Aristide Zolberg (ed.) *Ghana and Ivory Coast*, University of Chicago Press, Chicago 1991, p.33-71.

4. See Adu-Boahen, A., *The Ghanaian Sphinx*. Accra: Ghana Academy of Sciences, 1988.

5. See Chazan (1983).

6. Ref: 'J. A. Kuffuor, A Presidential Hopeful' *Uhuru*. Vol. 4, No. 1, 1992.

7. See 'Interview with Safo-Adu' (by Kojo Yankah and Kwesi Yankah) *Uhuru*. Vol. 4, No.4, 1994.

8. General Erskine, 'Political Aspirant or Victim of Speculation', *Uhuru* Vol. 3, No.3, 1991.

9. 'Danquah-Busia Manifesto', *Uhuru* Vol. 4, No. 1, 1992.

10. 'J.A. Kuffuor a Presidential Hopeful', *Uhuru* Vol.4, No.1, 1992.

11. See Ninsin, K. A., 'Civic Associations and the Transition to Democracy' (in this volume) for a discussion of the contributions made by civil society actors like the Christian Council of Ghana, Catholic Bishops Conference and the Ghana Bar Association to the movement for democracy during the 1990-92 period.

12. 'Race for the Presidency Begins for the UP and CPP' *Pioneer*, Monday, March 16, 1992, p.1.

13. See 'Dr. John Bilson Joins Nkrumah's Front' *Pioneer*, April 7, 1992. Also, John Bilson 'Why I left Danquah-Busia Club', *Pioneer*, June 2, 1992.

14. Ref: A. Adu Boahen, 'I'll Beat Rawlings Hands Down', *Uhuru* Vol.4, No.5, 1992.

15. *Week-End*. Vol.3 No.58 8-14 August, 1991.

16. S.Y. Mpiani; 'We Need a United Political Front', *Pioneer*, June 3, 1993.

17. Refer to *NCD Annual Report*, 1992, p.16.

18. 'Another Political Party', *Pioneer*, July 10, 1992. The leader of the National Salvation Party was Evangelist Ernest Pianim.

19. 'Seven Parties on Opening of Voters Register', *Pioneer*, July 10, 1992.

20. 'Politicians Take INEC to Court', *Pioneer*, May 18, 1992.

21. 'United Front to Save Ghana', *Pioneer*, July 14, 1992.

22. S.Y. Mpiani; 'We Need a United Front to Save the Nation', *Pioneer*, June 3, 1992.

23. See 'The National Democratic Congress (NDC)', *Uhuru*, Vol.4, No.6, 1992.

24. 'Danquah-Busia Manifesto', *Uhuru*, Vol.4, No.1, 1992.

25. Statement by Danquah-Busia Club, *Pioneer*, May 25, 1992.

26. *Ibid.*

27. Adu Boahen; 'I'll Beat Rawlings Hands Down', *Uhuru*, Vol.4, No.5, 1992.

28. *Ibid.*

29. 'Yennto' NPP Declares at Rally at Kumasi Abbey Park', *Pioneer*, December 1, 1992. Also 'PNC National Executive Took a Decision to Withdraw their Participation from Parliamentary Elections', *Pioneer*, Nov. 25, 1992.

30. *Pioneer.* Monday, November 30, 1992 reported that NPP Presidential candidate A. Adu Boahen had warned that NPP Parliamentary candidates who would stand as independent candidates would be dismissed from the party.

31. 'After Long Fracas; Government, Opposition Now in Dialogue', *Pioneer*, November 26, 1992.

32. 'Opposition to Form Shadow Cabinet',*Pioneer* Monday, January 11, 1993.

33. 'Nkrumahist Unity Talks: Forward Ever Backward Never', *Uhuru* Vol.5, No.7, 1993.

34. Obeng Manu; 'NPP Doing Business with NDC! They are Partners in Crime', *Pioneer*, August 25, 1993.

35. Limann, 'We're Not Party to any Dialogue', *Pioneer*, Nov.26, 1993.

36. 'NPP Parliamentary Candidates Association',*Pioneer*, August 23, 1993, p.4.

37. 'Mammoth Rally, Quarshigah Shakes Kumasi', *Pioneer*, Monday, Oct. 19, 1993,

38. 'NPP Elects New Leaders', *The Ghanaian Chronicle*, Vol.3, No.60, June 2-5, 1994.

39. *The Statesman* Vol.2, No.32, Dec. 1993.

40. *Weekly Insight*, Vol.1, No.48, 10-16 August 1994.

41. 'NPP Will be Tough' *The Statesman*, Vol.3, No.10, August 1994.

42. See a detailed report about the Annual Delegates Conference in *The Statesman*, Vol.2, No.31, Dec. 19, 1993.

5

State Organisations in the Transition to Constitutional Democracy

Gilbert Keith Bluwey

Introduction

State organisations provide the basic medium through which government programmes are translated into concrete actions (Dotse 1990). In periods of transition to constitutionalism, the pre-eminence of state organisations as primary facilitators becomes both obvious and pronounced (Bratton and van de Walle 1992). As a rule, the basic challenge which a government presiding over a transition must overcome is how to ensure the legitimacy of the transition programme: that is to say, how to ensure that all political groups agree that the transition programmes, laws and regulations, as well as the machinery and the persons chosen to administer it are acceptable. This basic challenge becomes crucial when, as in the Ghana transition of 1991-93, the incumbent regime was also interested in succeeding itself.

In addressing this basic challenge, governments invariably and for good reason, assume direct control and make extensive use of the permanent state bureaucracy often supplemented by a few additional creations specifically meant to facilitate the transition. The reasons are obvious: first, the permanent state bureaucracy has a tradition of political neutrality; second, the internal workings of rational organisations tend to insulate them against external controls and enable them to maintain a good degree of autonomy in their operations. These organisational attributes tend to commend state organisations to competing political groups as competent and acceptable (legitimate) facilitators of political transitions (Bratton and van de Walle 1992).

In the transition which produced an elected government on 7 January 1993, the government of the Provisional National Defence Council (PNDC) made extensive use of the permanent state bureaucracy and also created other organs specifically to facilitate the transition. The Civil Service bureaucracy was by far the most important of such actors in the transition. The Ministry of Information served as the organ for public political education. It published leaflets, hand-bills and even booklets on the transition programme and on key issues of relevance to it. The national radio and television services and state newspapers were all used to educate the public on the transition. They were assisted in all this by the Ministry of Employment, Mobilisation and Social Welfare. The Ministry of the Interior, in collaboration with the office of the Attorney-General, churned out the laws and regulations which guided the transition process. The Ministry of Local Government was the central source of ideas and programme facilitation. The Judiciary and the Police Service also played their traditional roles, howbeit, in support of the transition. While the police ensured public order, the courts tried erring individuals and groups, and pronounced on legal points of disagreement between competing groups of power-seekers.

There is no general agreement on the composition of the group of state organisations specifically established to facilitate the transition. This disagreement derives from dispute over the starting point of the transition. Those who accept the claim of the PNDC that its assumption of power was not a mere *coup d'état* but the beginning of a transition from a fraudulent to true democracy (Rawlings 1 January 1982) would include the National Commission for Democracy (NCD) and District/ Metropolitan Assemblies among state organisations specifically established to facilitate the transition. On the other hand, those who deny this claim insist that the series of ten regional forums which were launched at Sunyani in July 1990, marked the starting-point of the transition process. According to the latter view, the NCD and the District/Metropolitan Assemblies were, in fact, meant to pre-empt the growing demand for movement towards a return to constitutional democracy (Bluwey 1993).

This study takes the view that no objective analysis of the transition can ignore the significant roles played by the NCD and the Assemblies. The two organisations have therefore been studied as establishments specifically meant to facilitate the transition along with the Regional Forums, the Committee of Experts, the Consultative Assembly, the Interim National Electoral Commission and the Transition Committee. It also focuses on certain organs which were created by the 1992 Constitution — what I choose to call democracy commissions — with the specific mandate to nurture democracy in Ghana. Although the democracy commissions played no role in the transition, it is obvious that the overall success of the democratic enterprise in Ghana would depend very much on their effectiveness. It is therefore necessary to evaluate their constitutional strengths and weaknesses in order to anticipate future trends with a fair degree of certainty. The democracy commissions are the Council of State, the Media Commission and the Commission on Human Rights and Administrative Justice. These special institutions are expected to supplement the powers of the Judiciary, Parliament and the National Electoral Commission in promoting democracy in Ghana.

In sum, this paper tries to identify the various ways in which state organisations either facilitated or hindered the transition. It addresses the critical issue of how far administrative agencies like the Ministry of Local Government, the Police, or the District/Metropolitan Assemblies were, or were not used as instruments of partisan politics by the government during the transition. The second objective is to examine the nature and extent of executive control prescribed by the constitution over those organisations specifically created to nurture democracy. This is because the success or failure of the democratic enterprise in Ghana would, more than any other factor, depend on the attitude of the government towards these organisations.

The first section deals with the state organisations which were clearly active in the transition; namely: the PNDC; the Ministries of Local Government; Employment, Mobilisation and Social Welfare; Information, Interior (with emphasis on the police); the National Commission for Democracy; the District/Metropolitan Assemblies and the Regional Forums; the Committee of Experts; the Consultative Assembly; the Interim National Electoral Commission (INEC) and the Transition Committee. The second part focuses on the Executive, Parliament and Judiciary; the Council of State; the Media Commission; and the Commission on Human Rights and Administrative Justice.

State Organisations During the Transition

A total of eight state organisations were actively involved in the transition and would be discussed in this section. They are as follows:

i) *The Provisional National Defence Council (PNDC)*

The PNDC was the executive organ of state. It was the supreme policy-making body and all decisions and directives on matters of state either emanated from it or carried the weight of its authority. In principle, the PNDC made every decision after full deliberation and by consensus. However, insinuations by highly-placed people during interviews indicated that the Chairman almost invariably acted alone and the full Council rarely met.

The PNDC shared its executive functions with a junior partner called, the Committee of Secretaries. The Secretaries were the political heads of the state ministries and were appointed by, and remained responsible to, the PNDC. The pre-eminence of the Council over the Committee was emphasised first, by the presence of a senior member of the Council as chairman of the Committee. In addition, each member of the Council had supervisory responsibility over a group of ministries and was responsible for presenting policy papers to the Council on behalf of the ministry or ministries under his supervision. As the supreme policy-making and legislative authority of state, the PNDC was also the source of policy initiatives for the transition. It synthesised and gave practical effect to civil pressures for the transition. It created such special organs as the District/Metropolitan Assemblies and the National Commission for Democracy (NCD) and sanctioned the holding of Regional Forums to prepare the nation for the transition. By its establishment proclamation (PNDC Decree I, 1982), the PNDC committed itself to the eventual emergence of 'true' democracy in Ghana. Chairman Rawlings, as indeed all PNDC functionaries, persistently thundered exaltations to the lower classes and urged them to become active in politics and thereby 'take your destiny into your own hands' (Hansen 1991). The PNDC demonstrated a clear disposition towards the transition especially after the Regional Forums although, as argued below, the process was to be on its own terms.

The Committee of Secretaries was the policy-executing arm of the PNDC. It was a cabinet without policy-making powers although it is probable that it reviewed policy and made recommendations to the PNDC. The initial attempt to ensure regional and gender representation in its ranks seemed to have been abandoned as several Secretaries and Deputy Secretaries failed to keep up with the tide of the 'revolution'. A good many Secretaries and Deputy Secretaries however proved to be ardent PNDC devotees and were accordingly rewarded by the post-transition (P)NDC government with promotions or retention at their previous posts.

As the author of the policy leading to the transition, the PNDC also assumed direction and control to ensure its consummation. It decided on the programme, appointed and determined the remuneration of the personnel of the organisations which were specifically created for the transition and promulgated laws and regulations for the various stages of the transition. It also appropriated funds and equipment required for the programme. The PNDC has been criticised for doing all these with little or no form of consultation with other political groups in the country.

The criticisms have been made in the full knowledge that the intention of Chairman Rawlings to seek the presidency had never been in doubt. The critics complained that while the *Political Parties Law (PNDCL 263)* for example, made no provision for state assistance to political parties, it did not impose any restrictions on the use of state property by government functionaries, including the PNDC Chairman for their electioneering campaign. The law also omitted provision for the state press, including the sole radio and television net-work, to operate independently of the Ministry of Information and the PNDC. Because of these and other reservations about the PNDC's control of the transition process, the private newspapers which were launched from about August 1991 to the eve of the elections, were inundated with calls for a national conference to prepare a neutral and acceptable programme for the transition.

The most vexatious issue and the one that almost wrecked the parliamentary elections and made all the political parties other than the NDC and its allies reject the validity of the presidential election was the voters' register. Against vehement protest by opposition groups, the

PNDC directed the INEC to use the 1988 voters' register for the presidential and parliamentary elections of 1992. As reported in the *Daily Graphic* and *Ghanaian Times* of 20 June 1992, the government argued that time and money were in short supply for carrying out a fresh nation-wide registration of voters.

The Alliance of Democratic Forces (ADF) which was a condominium of all political parties other than the PNDC and its allies in the Progressive Alliance, countered that time indeed was needed for free, fair and acceptable elections to be conducted. It urged the PNDC to suspend its unilaterally proclaimed transition programme and to convene a national conference to prepare a 'genuinely national programme for the transition' (*Daily Graphic and Ghanaian Times* 11 February 1992).

In general, the PNDC appeared to have exerted a little more than merely providing the broad framework of policy direction for the benefit of the organisations involved in the transition. An important factor which worked in favour of the PNDC in this regard was finance. None of the organisations had any independent source of finance. Since they all depended on government subvention even for stationery and remuneration, it was easy for the PNDC to dictate programmes for each of them. The Accountant-General could, for example, only authorise a subvention for a regional forum if he received authorisation from the appropriate PNDC Secretary. He would not do so upon a request from the Chairman or Secretary of the NCD. Perhaps, a decree authorising funding in respect of transition activities from a consolidated fund would have removed the organisations concerned from the direct financial control of the PNDC.

On the whole, the PNDC remained the sole author and absolute controller of the programme for the transition. In a general sort of way, it exerted control over the behaviour of the various organisations — although some, such as the Regional Forums and the Consultative Assembly (see below) did assert a good degree of autonomy in their internal workings and in the making of decisions.

The crucial point is that in the absence of a constitution, no organisation, agency or group could raise legal challenges to the will of the PNDC — the government. Coupled with its antipathy towards consultation with political groups outside its own fold, the PNDC was openly dictatorial in its handling of the transition.

ii) Three Key Ministries: The Police, Military and Judiciary

Every state establishment probably played a role in the transition. The Ministry of Finance and Economic Planning for example, provided the funds, the Ministry of Education pulled teachers and pupils out of their classrooms to organise public education rallies and parades and the Ministry of Works provided technical services for the open-air rallies. However, only three of the ministries and three other state establishments would receive mention here for their towering role in facilitating the transition.

The Ministries of Local Government, of Information and of Employment, Mobilisation and Social Welfare, were the combined instruments through which the PNDC conducted the transition. While the Ministry of Justice churned out the decrees and the Interior ministry regulated the conduct of competing political groups and individual politicians, the three ministries I have mentioned produced the modalities for the implementation of the decrees related to the transition. They were the organisations that reached out to the people and supervised the actions of officials assigned to implement the transition.

As state ministries, each of them was responsible to the PNDC and was expected to execute faithfully and at all times every responsibility assigned to it, including ensuring the success of the transition programme. The three individuals who headed these ministries were carefully chosen. Each belonged to the genre of incipient Marxist cells which were widely believed to have engineered the PNDC 'revolution'. Kwamena Ahwoi, the Secretary for Local Government, was an outspoken anti-establishment member of the Faculty of Law at the University of Ghana. He was a popular speaker on student platforms and was widely believed to have been a member of the Marxist cells at the University that allegedly engineered the *coup d'état*. Totobi Kwakye, the Secretary for Information was a radical student-leader and widely believed to have been the organiser of Marxist cells for students at the University of Cape Coast. The Secretary for Mobilisation and Employment, S. D. Boateng was one of the original core of activists who toured the country to organise the Committees for the Defence of the Revolution (CDRs).

Each of these three Secretaries exhibited exceptional commitment and dedication to the success of the transition. But there is no doubt that they did so not merely as PNDC Secretaries but more as PNDC activists. Therefore, as far as the three ministries they headed were concerned, there could be no talk of organisational autonomy and neutrality. They were the PNDC itself in action. The records also show that the three Secretaries and the Secretary to the NCD were members of the campaign committee of the National Democratic Congress (NDC) — the political party sponsored by PNDC. Therefore, it cannot be gainsaid that the PNDC could not concede operational autonomy to the three ministries that were central to the determination and execution of the transition programme.

The Police

Responsibility for internal order rested with the Police. In the absence of constitutional guarantees of individual freedom, the Police could turn into a law unto themselves. Besides, under existing laws, police permit was required for the holding of public rallies, processions and for organising any public gathering. The political parties law also restricted public gatherings, publications and individual utterances of a political nature only to registered political parties and their accredited agents. There were also laws that protected the PNDC and its functionaries from public criticism.

These laws operated at a time when the whole country was a beehive of political activity, and several private newspapers (many of which were noted more for their scurrilous attacks on public officers than the substance of their messages) proliferated, at least in Accra, Kumasi, Cape Coast and Sekondi-Takoradi. To the credit of the Inspector-General of Police and the Attorney-General's Department, virtually no notice was taken of these violations of the law. Various meetings took place often ending in parades through busy streets without police interference. The sum of the evidence therefore is that the Police enjoyed a reasonable degree of autonomy in dealing with political groups up to about a month before the presidential election. As argued below, during the one month before the election, it was quite evident that the police had come under the thumb of some invisible hand.

The Ghana Armed Forces

In normal times, Ghana's Armed Forces are expected to remain neutral of partisan politics. Individual military personnel may have political views and party preferences but they are not permitted to join party groups or show open party affiliation as long as they are in uniform or are in the barracks. This tradition was broken on 4 June 1979, when the men of the other ranks mutinied, overthrew the government and formed the Armed Forces Revolutionary Council (AFRC). The attempt by the short-lived government of the Peoples' National Party (PNP 1979-81) to restore the tradition of military neutrality in politics was again aborted by the coup d'état that brought the PNDC to power on 31 December 1981. Throughout the eleven years of PNDC rule, the military, particularly the other ranks, got too closely identified with the incumbent government. Military personnel held ministerial posts, and served in the diplomatic corps.

Key financial institutions like the Customs, Excise and Preventive Service (CEPS), the Ghana Ports and Harbours Authority (GPHA) and the Ghana Airways Corporation (GAC) were headed by men seconded from the military. The other ranks were not left out in the sharing of the spoils of office. The military hierarchy was expanded to include a position for the head of the Other Ranks — the Forces Sergeant-Major. Several non-commissioned officers were also seconded to key state enterprises as security co-ordinators and even as members of management boards. Others took up positions as District Secretaries and as officials of the National Commission for Democracy in the Districts and Regions. Others were seconded to the Regional and District branches of the Ghana Private Road Transport Union (GPRTU) as co-ordinators and drill instructors. Thus, on the eve of the transition, the Ghana Armed Forces had developed high stakes in the future of the incumbent government.

The commanders used every opportunity for a public appearance to profess the support of the military for the transition as well as to profess loyalty to the PNDC and its chairman. It is significant that PNDC officials along with NDC leaders visited the various military barracks and addressed the service men on the transition in general and also about the candidates contesting the presidency. However, none of the other parties ever made an appearance at any barracks.

It is significant also that contrary to the demand of other parties, military personnel were not permitted to travel out of their stations to vote. Indeed, military leave was cancelled a week to the presidential election (even though there was no evidence of tension in the country at that time) and military personnel were made to vote only in booths erected at the barracks. The sum of all this is that although the military could not be seen to have been used by the PNDC to promote its fortunes at the polls, at least the top brass knew where their hearts were and took measures to ensure the satisfaction of their heart's desire.

The Judiciary

In general, an independent judiciary is considered a basic condition for democracy. The PNDC adverted to this in principle. In practice however, the PNDC clearly preferred revolutionary justice — speedy trials and maximum penalty. The PNDC therefore set up two types of revolutionary courts early in its tenure of office. A Citizens' Vetting Committee (CVC) composed of revolutionary cadres with no legal or police training investigated and brought charges against individuals and business enterprises suspected of evading the law in any form. A CVC could exact penalty from a guilty party and close the case. Alternatively, the party could be sent for trial at a Peoples' Tribunal. A tribunal consisted of between five and seven members including a chairman who usually had legal education. Orthodox rules of court were not strictly observed, but an accused person could be represented by counsel. The PNDC seconded lawyers from the Attorney-General's Department to handle the government's case against accused persons. In the very beginning, there was no appeal against the decision of a tribunal although a guilty person particularly those that faced capital punishment could appeal to the PNDC chairman for pardon. Later however, a national appeals tribunal was instituted to review cases from regional tribunals.

The infusion of 'revolutionary courts' in the judicial system had the effect of sapping the courage of judges of the regular courts. In general, they tended to be cautious in handling cases of a political nature. They almost invariably declared their courts incompetent to hear political cases and cases involving abuse of human rights by agents of the state. Thus, although the controlling hands of the PNDC over the courts could not be obvious, the superior courts could not produce any landmark decision to illustrate judicial courage and independence from the executive.

iii) The National Commission for Democracy (NCD), the District/Metropolitan Assemblies, Regional Forums and the Committee of Experts

The establishment of the NCD marked the first instalment in the series of measures which the PNDC had to take in fulfilment of its promise to evolve a true democracy for Ghana. The promise was contained in that part of its maiden statement to the nation which read: '...it is necessary ... that a machinery should be established... for the due establishment of true democracy in Ghana' (PNDC Establishment Proclamation 1981:*PNDC Law I*).

Early in 1982, *PNDC Law 42* established the NCD. Section 32 of this law laid down the NCD's mandate as follows:

a) to disseminate within the society, awareness of the objectives of the revolutionary transformation of society being embarked upon by the PNDC in the interest of real democracy;

b) to assess for the information of government, the limitations to the achievement of true democracy arising from the existing inequalities between different strata of the population and make recommendations for redressing these inequalities; and

c) to formulate for the consideration of government a programme for a more effective realisation of true democracy in Ghana.

The mandate envisaged a long process of research and social engineering whose main instrument would be the NCD. In his public pronouncements, Chairman Rawlings persistently depicted a decadent social, economic and political order which was in need of a revolutionary overhaul. Rawlings complained about outmoded customs based on false values which diverted the nation's perspectives from high achievement motivations to indulgence in frivolities. He decried the growing official corruption and incompetent management which had become the hall-mark of official behaviour and had consequently eroded public confidence in all facets of economic policy. The pluralist political system had been abused and battered out of any semblance of a democratic polity. He depicted the franchise (in Marxist terms) as a fraud meant to deceive the ordinary citizen into believing that he could effectively review the mandate of the rulers at least once every four years (Hansen 1989; Yeebo 1991; Yankah 1991).

The NCD was thus set on a revolutionary mission although its membership did not reflect any assurance of commitment to a revolution. The 15-member Commission included a retired judge, a core of retired military and police personnel and civil servants, and two traditional rulers. E.A. Haizel, then Director of the Institute of Adult Education at the University of Ghana, became Secretary to the Commission. In 1984, Justice Daniel F. Annan, Vice-Chairman of the PNDC became chairman of the Commission. That was probably to make the Commission reflect the PNDC's stamp of authority more clearly in the public minds.

A cursory look at the activities sponsored by the Commission throughout its life shows that its mind was set on a gradual, systematic progress towards reform along-side a systematic nurturing of the culture of mass political participation. There is no record, for example, of a programme for preparing the nation for a revolution through the recruitment of cadres and the creation of cells. That was probably left to the Workers' Defence Committees (WDCs) and the Peoples' Defence Committees (PDCs) directed by the Office of the Political Counsellor of the Defence Committees.

In the first four years of its establishment, the NCD sponsored workshops, seminars and public lectures in close collaboration with the Institute of Adult Education to promote public debate on evolving a new political order for Ghana. It made the government provide financial support for the Institute's annual New Year Schools and the discussion forums organised by branches of the Peoples' Educational Association throughout the country. The following sampling of topics addressed at various forums sponsored by the Commission illustrate its preference for political reform through evolution as against revolution:

a) 'Ghana in Search of a Stable Democracy' (New Year School, 1984)

b) 'The Military and Politics in Ghana' (New Year School, 1986)

c) 'Organised Labour and the Free Enterprise System In Ghana' (A public lecture at the Awudome Residential College, 1985)

d) 'Politics Without Political Parties' (A public lecture at the Workers' College, Accra, 1985)

The NCD also made extensive use of the national news media to promote political awareness and participation. It sponsored feature articles to encourage group debate on national issues. It also sponsored discussions and debates over national radio and television for the same purposes.

There is no evidence that the NCD had its own programme by which it would determine when the nation was ready for the first concrete steps towards 'true' democratic rule. Besides, since it depended entirely on government subvention for its operations, it could operate only within the framework approved by the PNDC. This probably explains the undue delay first, in announcing the modalities for the district level elections and the equally long hold-up on the next steps towards establishing representative structures at the national level. It was clear from the very beginning that the PNDC was in no hurry to relinquish power. Hansen (1989) suggests that a Leninist revolution was clearly envisaged and the WDCs and PDCs were meant to be the nucleus of a Leninist vanguard party of the future. I am inclined to think that the NCD was born out of wed-lock. It was meant to assuage the fears of the conservative elite (traditional and religious leaders, the learned professions and business leaders) during the period when the revolutionary cadres were being recruited and trained for the ultimate onslaught. The launching of a programme for elected local government bodies in 1987 was therefore a reversal of policy by the PNDC. It was a response exacted by the IMF/World Bank conditionalities for economic reform. And the capitulation of Marxist-socialism to market principles and political pluralism as signalled by the disintegration of the Soviet Union in 1990, pushed the pendulum back in favour of political reform. Ghana's transition to constitutional democracy, based on pluralist principles, was not envisaged by the PNDC at its assumption of power. Indeed, the PNDC was a most reluctant convert to political pluralism and market principles. It was the changed conditions of the international political economy and the economic circumstances of Ghana rather than the will of the PNDC that made the transition possible.

The NCD took the first concrete step towards the re-establishment of representative democracy in Ghana on 1 July 1987. On that day, the NCD launched a booklet entitled, *District Political Authority and Modalities for District Level Elections* (Accra: Government Printer, 1987). Popularly known as *The Blue Book*, it set out to establish representative institutions of government at the local levels under a policy of graduated development of representative institutions from the local, through regional, to the national level. Section 1.4, of *The Blue Book* declared:

> In order to democratise state power and advance participatory democracy and collective decision-making at the grassroots, there is need to set up decentralised political and administrative authorities with elected representatives of the people. The decentralised authorities will be the bodies exercising state power as the people's local government.

The PNDC Chairman launched *The Blue Book* at a durbar of the Armed Forces, Police, Prisons and Revolutionary Cadres at the Elwak Stadium in Accra on 1 July 1987. Soon after that event, the NCD launched a nation-wide campaign for the registration of voters. It also conducted the elections that were subsequently held to the District/Metropolitan Assemblies. The NCD thus added the registration of voters and the administration of elections to its task of political education.

At the end of the first quarter of 1989, all the 110 District/Metropolitan Assemblies had been inaugurated. But if the PNDC expected the inauguration of the Assemblies to defuse the growing agitation for a return to constitutional rule, it was sadly mistaken. The inaugurations, on the contrary, accentuated the pro-democracy demands. Indeed, opposition to the Assemblies was overwhelming from the very beginning. In addition to challenges to specific short-comings in the composition and powers of the Assemblies, the opponents dismissed the idea as merely a device to unduly prolong the return to constitutional rule. A good number of people, adherents of anti-PNDC views, refused to register and so to vote at the subsequent elections. The registration was therefore not critically monitored to preclude the possibility of fake names appearing on the register of voters. This is why political parties, other than the NDC, called for a fresh registration of voters on the eve of the 1992 general elections.

The District/Metropolitan Assemblies, almost unanimously, set out to resist further advance towards constitutional rule. Several Assemblies, notably those in the Brong/Ahafo region passed resolutions asking the PNDC to halt the advance to constitutional rule so that the Assemblies 'would find their feet and stabilise as seed-beds of true democracy in

Ghana' (*Daily Graphic* and *Ghanaian Times* 29 January 1990). Although it cannot be conclusively demonstrated that those resolutions were instigated by the PNDC through its Regional and District Secretaries and Zonal Organisers of the CDRs, they were consistent with the public pronouncements of Chairman Rawlings. It may therefore be argued that the PNDC and its adherents wished that constitutional evolution beyond the Assemblies be held up indefinitely.

On 20 July 1990, the PNDC chairman, J.J. Rawlings, launched the first of a series of ten regional forums for the presentation of ideas to the NCD on a new constitution for Ghana. It must be noted that although both the NCD and the PNDC insist that the regional forums were part of the modalities drawn up by the NCD and approved by the PNDC for synthesising public opinion for a new constitution, the records point to the contrary. The records of the NCD make no mention of such deliberations. Impeccable confidential sources have disclosed that the idea of the forums and the launching in Sunyani were the product of a fortuitous combination of intuition and other events. Chairman Rawlings was scheduled to visit Sunyani to address the speech day of the local secondary school and inspect government projects in the municipality. A few days to the day, the thought of adding touch to the visit to make it a high national event was conceived and adopted by three Secretaries close to the Chairman. The Chairman was therefore to meet with all Assembly members in the region. The speech-writers decided to send a call to Ghanaians from all walk of life to join in a national evaluation of the performance of the Assemblies. The state news media subsequently made the call to appear as if a PNDC party would visit every regional capital to receive memoranda on the performance of the Assemblies. At Kumasi, which was the next stop, petitioners seized the opportunity to call for civil rule and even proposed a new constitution. From then on, the theme changed from one of evaluating the performance of the Assemblies, to various proposals for a new constitution. In reality therefore, the NCD was dragged out of its 'do-nothing' dungeon to 'collect and collate views on a new constitution for Ghana'. Public opinion was therefore the real owner of the regional forums and not the NCD. Several individuals and groups made presentations to the regional forums. The atmosphere at the forums was often changed and partisan. There was no evidence of intimidation or harassment.

On 25 March 1991, the NCD made public the summary of the views presented at the ten regional forums along with its own recommendations in a report entitled, *Evolving a True Democracy*. Against the widely known preference of Chairman Rawlings and the PNDC, for example, the Commission recommended a return to multi-party politics and the exclusion of the military from partisan politics.

The PNDC accepted the report and accordingly promulgated *PNDC Law 259* by which it set up the Committee of Experts to draft a constitution for the Fourth Republic of Ghana. The law required specifically that the draft constitution should provide for:

a) an Executive president to be elected on the basis of universal adult suffrage;

b) a Prime Minister who must command a majority in the legislature— which also should consist of a single chamber; and

c) a decentralised system of national administration based on a non-partisan district/metropolitan assembly system with development as its objective, including revenue-sharing clauses.

The still skeptical public raised no objection to the composition of the Committee of Experts. The chairman Dr. S.K.B. Asante, had once been the Solicitor-General in the Attorney-General's Department. Of the three persons drawn from academia, only one had attained the rank of senior lecturer. There was an elementary school teacher, a trade union leader, a traditional ruler and a petty-trader. Since none of them had attained national prominence in politics or in their various vocations, the nation simply staked its future on the slim chance that something surprisingly good might come out of the Committee's deliberations.

The report of the Committee was presented to the government in the form of a draft constitution with a memorandum to explain the reasoning behind its proposals. In sum, the draft constitution included almost all the known ideas preferred by Chairman Rawlings and members of the PNDC on a new constitution for Ghana. It provided for a dual executive consisting of an elected President and a Prime Minister who may not belong to the single legislative chamber but who must command its majority support. It provided for direct participation in politics by the military, police, civil servants and traditional rulers. Furthermore, it provided that local government bodies would be composed partly of members who would be elected on a non-partisan basis. Above all, it provided that representation in the national legislature be based not on individual franchise but on occupational and social groups. Its thesis was that Ghana 'need not re-invent the wheel' (of familiar democratic structures?).

As expected, the draft constitution sparked off such bitter controversy throughout the country as had never been the case before. Indeed, it may be said that the one great (and perhaps the sole) contribution which the Committee of Experts made to the transition was that its proposals aroused justifiable anger within informed political circles and prompted several eminent groups to seek representation in the Consultative Assembly.

This is however, not to suggest that the Committee laboured under the thumb of the PNDC. Indeed, none of the respondents to my enquiries suggested even remotely that the Committee came under pressure from anywhere in its work. The conclusion, therefore, is that although the Committee sounded as if it was merely the mouth-piece of the PNDC, its conclusions reflected the political preferences of its membership. They were innovative without being realistic and their idealism was unappreciated by their fellow citizens.

iv) Consultative Assembly

Following the Committee of Expert's Report, the government established a Consultative Assembly to draft a definitive constitution that would, subject to a nationwide referendum, usher in the Fourth Republic. *PNDC Law 253* which established the Consultative Assembly provided for a 200-member body. Public reaction was swift and hostile especially regarding the Assembly's powers and composition of the consultative Assembly. For example, the Assembly was composed of representatives of economic and other social groups recognised by the PNDC. These included hitherto non-political associations such as those of butchers, hair-dressers, in-land canoe fishermen, fish-mongers, drinking-bar owners and chop-bar owners; etc. Indeed, many of these economic groups had no national organisation. It was feared that the PNDC would use its incumbency to hand-pick representatives for such virtually shadow groups. The allocation of seats was also thought to favour the revolutionary organs unduly. The CDRs, for instance, had 10 seats while the National Council of Women and Development, which was controlled by the 31st December Women's Movement, also got 10 seats. At the same time, organisations such as the Ghana Bar Association, the University Teachers Association of Ghana, the National Union of Ghana Students, the Christian Council and the Catholic Bishops Conference, were allocated just one seat each. That transparently disproportionate distribution of seats aroused fears that the PNDC intended to pack the Assembly with its adherents for the possible advantage of entrenching its pet ideas in the constitution. The third point was the denial of immunity from prosecution to the members of the Assembly. Articles 14(1) of the law stated that 'nothing in sub-section 1 and 2 above shall be deemed to relieve any person from any action or proceedings to which he would otherwise have been liable if this section had not been enacted, in respect of anything said or done by him against the Head of State and Chairman of the PNDC, or any member o the PNDC or a Secretary'.

Finally, opponents of the law objected to the provision that denied the Assembly the ultimate right to promulgate the constitution. Under the law, the Assembly would submit its final draft of the constitution to the PNDC which had the power to amend it. The final version would then be put to the nation in a referendum.

Alternatively, the opponents of the law proposed a Constituent Assembly composed of persons directly elected by universal adult franchise as a way to eliminate the appearance of discrimination in the allocation of seats in favour of pro-PNDC groups. Second, once elected, the Assembly should have the power to promulgate the constitution since it would be more representative of the nation than the PNDC. It was held that a referendum would not provide a fair chance to the people to assess the constitution as would a chamber composed of directly elected representatives who also would be in regular touch with the people through the press and other channels of political communication. Finally, opponents of the law insisted that full immunity from prosecution be accorded members of the Assembly.

When the PNDC chose to ignore these various demands, the opponents of the law sought a court injunction against the government. The suit was thrown out with costs to the plaintiffs. The groups made several unsuccessful attempts to discuss the issues with the government at the conference table. When it became clear that the PNDC would proceed with the transition only on its own terms, the Ghana Bar Association and the National Union of Ghana Students announced a boycott of the Consultative Assembly.

In spite of the misgivings of the GBA, the NUGS and the generality of the intellectual community of Ghana (as evidenced by columns in several of the private newspapers), the Consultative Assembly rose admirably to the occasion. Indeed, it could be said that with the singular exception of one controversial clause (the Transitional Provisions) which it adopted, the Assembly asserted its independence of the PNDC.

Newspaper reports indicate that the PNDC Chairman was at one stage so shocked by the Assembly's refusal to be tele-guided from the Castle that he allegedly accused its members of having 'lost touch with reality'. The point was that in spite of the GBA boycott, several lawyers and eminent jurists were elected to the Assembly by many of the associations that were given representation. Besides, many of the 10 CDR regional representatives, were not just the rag-tag of blunt revolutionary cadres, but experienced professionals, former parliamentarians and lawyers.

Furthermore, the University Teachers Association of Ghana, other recognised professional bodies, the National House of Chiefs and the Association of Ghana Industries (AGI) took up their seats through very competent representatives. On the whole, the Assembly exhibited clear independence of the PNDC and produced a constitution which was very different from the draft presented to it by the Committee of Experts. The only aspect of the work of the Consultative Assembly which cast a dark shadow of doubt on its integrity was the adoption of the First Schedule of Transitional Provisions which granted blanket indemnity to every functionary of the PNDC in any action or decision he or she might have taken during the 11 years of that government.

v) Interim National Electoral Commission (INEC)

The Interim National Electoral Commission was established under the *PNDC Law 271*. It was charged with primary responsibility for the administration, regulation, control and oversight of the electoral process including the registration and discipline of political parties. It had eleven members, and was headed by an Executive Chairman, Justice Joshua Ofori-Boateng, an Appeal Court Judge who was assisted by two deputies namely, Nana Oduro Numapau, a chartered accountant (responsible for finance and administration) and Dr. Kwadwo Afari-Djan, a Research Fellow at the Institute of African Studies, University of Ghana, Legon (responsible for operations). The other eight members including, a woman, were also outstanding national figures.

The *Political Parties Law 1992 (PNDC Law 281)* made INEC the sole authority for registering political parties as well as discipline and restrain political parties which might infringe the electoral law and regulations. Decisions of INEC could be appealed in the first instance to the Appeal Court and then to the Supreme Court of Ghana. A respected legal opinion sums up the extensive rule-making, enforcement, investigative and adjudicating powers of INEC as follows:

> INEC also serves as the national clearing-house for information on elections and political parties.... It is the principal repository of the numerous reports, statements and declarations which political parties are required to file in respect of their sponsors, officials, members and finances. It thus has record-keeping and disclosure functions as well. It is given the power to make those records available to the public (Kumado 1993:50).

But unlike its predecessors in previous transitions, the INEC had no police powers to order the arrest and prosecution of persons who harassed political opponents. This handicap also undercut its credibility in areas where police complicity made it possible for pro-NDC groups to deface the posters of their opponents. In Berekum, for example, the local NPP office was ransacked in broad day-light. Witnesses identified the predators but the police took no action. When the NPP leaders then turned to the local INEC officials for protection and redress, they were told that INEC was powerless to help them.

Part of INEC's problems may be traced to the acrimonious relations between the PNDC, on the one hand, and all the leading political parties, on the other hand. Contrary to precedence from two previous transitions, the PNDC had refused to talk to other political groups on issues relating to the transition. Among other things, the PNDC appointed the INEC, formulated the electoral laws and decreed the entire transition without any form of consultation with other political groups. At one stage, the

Alliance of Democratic Forces (ADF), which was the grouping of all political parties other than the (P)NDC and its two allied parties, made an unsuccessful attempt to seek a court injunction against the transition programme.

In addition to their demand for consultation on major decisions affecting the transition, the ADF asked for fresh registration of voters. It contended that the five-year old electoral register was compiled under conditions which did not favour proper scrutiny. A fresh registration would therefore enable a more reliable voters register to be produced. The government dismissed this and every other demand of the ADF, including a demand to meet at the conference table.

The appointment of the INEC without consultation with the ADF and in a climate of acrimony between the PNDC and other political groups immediately cast a cloud of suspicion and distrust in ADF circles over the Commission. INEC's position was made worse by some of its officials who went out of their way to defend, on grounds of paucity of funds and time, the PNDC's refusal to conduct a fresh registration of voters (*Daily Graphic* 17 May 1992).

Despite all that, when the curtain finally came down on the 1992 elections, the opinions of international observers prevailed: the elections were declared free and fair. The first implication of that verdict was that the INEC was not used by the PNDC to its advantage. On the face of it, it is a fair verdict. It is however doubtful whether a clear appearance of INEC independence of the PNDC prevailed during the transition. One may also deduce from that verdict that there were only minimal and therefore tolerable short-comings in the conduct of the elections. But a situation such as occurred in Kumasi where the PNDC District Secretary was allowed to use her car to collect ballot boxes to a central counting station without the supervision of the agents of the other parties was certain to raise genuine suspicion.

vi) Transition Committee

This committee of fifteen members was set up by an executive instrument soon after the elections. Its mandate was to advise government on the details of the law and protocol regarding the transfer of power from the PNDC to the elected government of the NDC. It was also expected to screen the president's nominees for appointment to high offices of state and take them through security clearance.

The establishment of the committee was warmly received throughout the country. Press editorials and private commentators thought the committee should reach out to the Alliance of Democratic Forces and perhaps produce an all-party government of national unity. In a spirited editorial, the *Ghanaian Chronicle* suggested that the committee be expanded to include representatives of the Christian and Muslim communities, traditional rulers and professional bodies. It added that the Transition Committee should deal with such issues as the grant of unconditional amnesty to all Ghanaians in exile, the restoration of confiscated properties to their original owners, and compensation for those who lost their parents and relations in the heady days of the PNDC revolution. Nothing came out of these very well-meaning propositions. Indeed, nothing was heard further about the committee and its work. Its inauguration picture which appeared on the national television and on the front pages of the state-owned newspapers is the only record of its life.

These were the state organisations which facilitated the transition. We would now consider those organisations that were created by the 1992 constitution to nurture the democratic enterprise in Ghana.

State Organisations in the Post-1992 Era

i) The Political Horizon Since the Inauguration

The high point of the transition politics was the formal transfer of power from the PNDC to the elected government of the National Democratic Congress (NDC) which took place at the Black Star Square, Accra, on 7 January 1993. Leaders of five out of the eight registered political parties were absent from the ceremonies. Those five parties had also boycotted the elections to the first parliament of the fourth republic.

The boycott produced one of the two peculiarities of the 1993 transition: it produced a virtual one-party parliament. The Eagle Party and the National Convention Party had formed an alliance with the National Democratic Congress under the name, The Progressive Alliance. It was The Progressive Alliance that sponsored Jerry Rawlings (NDC) and Nkenssen Arkaah (NCP) as presidential and vice-presidential candidates, respectively. Thus, although three different political parties were seen to have contested the parliamentary elections, the reality was a charade of competitive elections performed by off-shoots of the same family-tree. The first parliament of the Fourth Republic therefore lacked an essential ingredient of a pluralist polity: a multi-party parliament composed of government supporters, and other parties genuinely opposed to the political views of the former.

The other peculiarity was the participation of the incumbent coup-regime in the contest for succession to power in the fourth republic. In both 1969 and 1979, the incumbent coup-regimes refrained from participating in the competition for succession. The transitions of 1969 and 1979, which were supervised by the National Liberation Council and the Armed Forces Revolutionary Council, respectively, were therefore smooth and generally free from acrimony. The successor government in each case also enjoyed considerable legitimacy. The first government of the fourth republic was, on the contrary, born out of bitter controversy and its inauguration was a distinctly partisan affair.

These peculiarities have affected the tenor of politics in the post-transition era with quite serious implications for the survival of the fourth attempt at pluralist democratic politics. First, the absence from parliament of the opposition parties meant that they would have a negligible impact on public policy. They could, and do address petitions to parliament and its committees as well as use the pages of the private press to whip up public opposition to specific government measures. But their absence from parliament definitely denied them (and the nation) the extensive opportunities which a parliamentary opposition in a democracy could utilise to good advantage. The consequences of this self-imposed handicap has the potential of driving frustrated opposition extremists into violence which may disrupt the already fragile peace in the country.

Second, the PNDC government, angered by the refusal of the opposition parties to concede defeat gracefully has also refused to be magnanimous in victory. It has refused to take the opposition into confidence and has made appointments to the Council of State and the special commissions created by the 1992 constitution including the National Electoral Commission, without any form of consultation with the opposition parties. In other words, the NDC government has refused to abandon its acrimonious attitude of the pre-election era towards the opposition parties. The result is that pressing issues such as revision of the electoral register, issuing of photo-identity cards to voters, and other issues regarding the administration of elections still remained unresolved. Yet these matters had to be dealt with in good time so that agreed solutions could be implemented before the 1996 general elections.

In sum, the political playing field has remained uneven with its attendant bumpy rides which give occasional hiccups and threats of a crisis. The urgent need was for government and opposition to meet to level the playing field in good time for a smooth take-off towards the 1996 general elections.

ii) The Constitution and the Principal Organs of State

The 1992 constitution recreated the main principles of pluralist democracy and in particular the principles of representative government; viz., separation of powers, checks and balances and the home-grown principle of executive consultation with 'the old man' for advice and the counsel of wisdom through the Council of State.

First, the constitution reiterated the principle much cherished in Ghana, that only the elected representatives of the people, or persons approved by the elected parliament can serve in top executive positions of state, and in the legislature. Second, the principle of the separation of powers, checks and balances received renewed emphasis in the 1992 constitution. The traditional separation in personnel and functions between the judiciary on the one hand, and the executive and legislature on the other, was maintained. There was however a fusion between the executive and legislative personnel. The president and the vice-president remain outside the legislature and neither the executive nor the legislature can terminate the tenure of the other. However, unlike previous constitutions, Article 78(1) now requires that the executive and the legislature share ministerial posts with the latter taking a majority (more than half) of such posts. Ministers of State who are not members of parliament and the Vice-President may however take part in its deliberations but may not vote (Article 111).

Third, the constitution kept faith with the tradition inherited from Britain that politicians, especially elected executives must be compelled to seek the counsel of eminent citizens who are transparently neutral of partisan politics. The constitution therefore established a Council of State, composed of 25 eminent persons, drawn from critical areas of national life to offer advice to the president in the discharge of his constitutional duties (Articles 89, 90, 91 and 92).

Finally, the constitution created three special commissions for the purpose of enhancing and protecting democracy and political pluralism in Ghana. The Media Commission is to ensure the independence of the state media from direct executive control and generally enhance freedom of the press (Articles 166, 167). The Commission of Human Rights and Administrative Justice is to maintain a vigilant watch against the abuse of the rights of citizens especially those vulnerable to indifference or outright abuse by the agents of state (Articles 216 to 230). Finally, the National Commission for Civic Education, is to promote political consciousness in the citizens through various means of public education (Articles 231-239). These are what I call democracy commissions. The ultimate hope is that together with the entrenched principle of judicial independence, autonomous parliament, and a responsible executive, these commissions would enhance and make pluralist democracy the core of Ghana's political culture.

Obviously, much will depend on how far the first two or three governments dedicate themselves to this lofty goal. I am less than convinced that the NDC government intends to pursue pluralist democratic policies. First, the appointments to the Council of State and the democracy commissions which are to be made directly by the President seem to have gone to card-carrying members of either the NDC or its partners in the Progressive Alliance. Admittedly, this should not render the appointees pliant to the executive will. However, in the prevailing climate of profound suspicion among the various political parties and within the political elites generally, even the slightest semblance of a non-partisan composition of these commissions would have enhanced their legitimacy.

The second reason is even more compelling. The government has so far done nothing to ensure the financial autonomy of Parliament, the Council of State and the democracy commissions. Their salaries and allowances were announced only recently. Furthermore, despite a clear constitutional injunction on the matter, the budgets of these bodies were yet to be guaranteed against governmental interference. The result was that stipends, and even basic equipment required for their operation were subject to the approval of the Minister of Finance and Economic Planning. Members of Parliament and those on the commissions confirmed that they were usually under pressure to conform and be 'good boys in order to be recognised'. Of particular concern in this regard was the practice of the chairman and members of the Council of State being used as if they were members of the NDC or an extension of the NDC government. The chairman and members were regularly sent on errands to represent the president at purely political functions where they read out partisan political messages on behalf of the president. Furthermore, although proceedings of the Council are required to be in camera (Article 92:3), the chairman and members frequently declared publicly their position on issues deliberated upon by the Council. In such circumstances where its non-partisan advisory stature was daily being compromised, its efficacy as a counselling and restraining voice on the president was bound to remain very much in doubt.

Conclusion

It is obvious from the preceding discussion that the overall success of the transition to constitutional rule owed much to the effectiveness of several state organisations in fulfilling the roles that had been assigned to them. Foremost among them were the regular civil service departments and state ministries. The Ministry of Local Government, for example, acted as the research and overall supervisory ministry for the entire operation. It played a pivotal role in the organisation of the regional fora and in constituting the Consultative Assembly. Indeed, interviews conducted for this paper disclosed that the Minister of Local Government was the chairman and executive director of the sub-committee of PNDC Secretaries that was specifically assigned to supervise the transition process. The organs of state created specifically to manage the transition process were equally effective in the execution of their roles. The national Commission for Democracy, the Committee of Experts, the Consultative Assembly and the Interim Electoral Commission exhibited a high degree of competence which none of the various external observers failed to note. In spite of these commendations, several allegations of incompetence and partiality were levelled against the state organisations, the more important of which we have already discussed.

The behaviour of those state organs was predictable in the political circumstances of the moment. First, the PNDC did not envisage returning the country to a pluralist democracy when it established the National Commission for Democracy in 1982. Its heart was clearly after a populist no-party system with the CDRs, and later on the district assemblies as the basic structure of a so-called representative government of popular or grassroots democracy. This antipathy towards liberal democratic political institutions and processes permeated the attitude of the PNDC government towards the opposition in particular and the transition process in general. That undemocratic attitude also influenced and underpinned the behaviour of the state and quasi-state organisations in the management of the transition to constitutional rule.

Much of this seem to be changing since the inauguration of the Fourth Republic under the 1992 Constitution on 3 January 1993. The attitude of the NDC government of Rawlings towards democratic institutions and practice appear to be improving as it gains greater self-confidence and survival stake in the system. There seems to be a growing tendency to act by the rules, especially the Constitution. Its attitude towards state and quasi-state organs is consequently becoming one of benign indifference instead of trying to impose strict control over their behaviour. This change has been reflected in the behaviour of several state and quasi-state organs in the run-up to the 1996 elections. For example, the National Electoral Commission, which came up for considerable criticism regarding its administration of the 1992 elections, has taken steps to negotiate agreement with the major political parties on the rules and procedure that would govern the 1996 elections thereby removing one of the major grievances of the opposition political parties, restoring confidence in the entire electoral machinery, and creating the necessary grounds for the conduct of free and fair elections. Therefore, the prospect for Ghana's democratic enterprise no longer rest precariously on a foundation of undemocratic attitudes, behaviour and norms of those who were entrusted with the task of shaping the outcome of the transition process. It now rests on a growing circle of civic conscious public institutions which are daily demonstrating a higher commitment to the public good.

6

Transition to Democracy and Control over Ghana's Military and Security Establishments

Robin Luckham

Decomposition of Military Institutions in Authoritarian States

Democratisation is normally initiated outside the state, through the struggles of groups in civil society, or in response to international pressures, like those exerted on Ghana and other African states under the rubric of 'political conditionality'. Yet hegemonic or institutional crises within authoritarian regimes and their military and repressive apparatuses also play a central role. Authoritarian regimes neither have to be popular nor legitimate to survive. They require compliance rather than consent.

But compliance has to be organised. Regimes have to invest in the means of physical coercion and in the military and police establishments which deploy them. They must be able to control the latter, and this can be just as difficult for authoritarian as for democratic governments. Typically, they supplement brute military force with other means of organising compliance, including political surveillance, intelligence networks, patronage, and control of the media. They usually put forward ideological rationales for repression, for instance in terms of 'national security' or 'development', attempting to convince powerful interests, like business elites or the civilian bureaucracy, that even if they lack legitimacy, at least they are effective in managing the economy, or assuring political stability; and they can seldom do any of these things without access to crucial external resources, such as investment, credit, aid, military assistance and arms.

The stereotypical view that authoritarian regimes are 'strong' or 'hard' and that their military and security establishments are cohesive and fully in control is seldom, if ever, correct. Yet, their latent weakness does not usually become apparent until the ruling group's monopoly of violence and its capacity to assure continued compliance comes into question. Once this happens, cracks rapidly open in the edifice of power, political forces acquire space in which to organise and demonstrate that they can get away with disobedience, and regimes rapidly look more fragile. Thus, the crucial issue is how they arrive at, or are pushed into such moments of crisis; and in what circumstances their capacity to repress becomes insufficient to rescue them. Even if the impetus for change usually comes from outside the state, the structure, composition, conflicts and inner weaknesses of authoritarian power blocs and their military structures influence how and when crises occur, and whether the outcome is transition to democracy, or some other result, such as state collapse, or reconsolidation of dictatorship. Hence, it is essential to consider a number of institutional variations in these structures and how they can affect the democratisation process.

(i) To start with, by no means all authoritarian regimes are military in origin. Nor indeed have all 'military' regimes been equally military. The latter range from personal military dictatorships; to military juntas ruling on behalf of the military hierarchy; to military-based cliques or 'parties' (like the Free Officers in Egypt, or the Dergue in Ethiopia); to 'revolutionary' or populist regimes instituted by rebellions of junior officers or men in the ranks (as in Burkina Faso or Ghana). To make things even more confusing, there are many regimes of military origin — like those of Nasser in Egypt, Mobutu in Zaire and arguably, Rawlings in Ghana — that reinvent themselves as 'civilian' governments. Indeed, until recently changes from military rule to 'institutionalised' authoritarianism were far more common than transitions to democracy.

(ii) Authoritarian regimes differ enormously in the capacity to secure compliance, ranging from those with large and powerful repressive apparatuses, like Egypt, South Africa, Algeria or possibly Nigeria, to those with far weaker coercive structures like the majority of countries in Sub-Saharan Africa. To be sure, these coercive structures are not absolute barriers to democracy, yet they can make the struggle for the latter more protracted, as well as enabling military and security bureaucracies to insist on the retention of professional privileges and elements of a national security state after the transfer of power.

(iii) Divisions often tend to develop within the dominant blocs of authoritarian regimes, for instance, between elite groups whose power base is the regime itself, the military as an institution; and the state's repressive and surveillance machinery (what Stepan 1988, Chapter 2 calls the 'security community'). The balance among these groups depends partly on whether the regime is civilian or military. But military governments are not necessarily in full control of their own armed forces (i.e., 'the military as institution' does not necessarily support 'the military as government').

This is a frequent fault-line (and source of counter-coups) in authoritarian regimes. It can also create the political space for democratisation, for instance by (a) encouraging authoritarian regimes to liberalise to pre-empt the emergence of open splits in the armed forces; (b) bringing to the fore officers who believe the military establishment's professional interests are best served by withdrawal from politics; and (c) in the more extreme cases, resulting in 'democratic' or 'revolutionary' coups.

(iv) Hence, to conceive of 'the' military as if it were corporately united and solid in support of military or authoritarian rule can be seriously misleading. Whether in reality it holds together or falls apart, makes a major difference to the ability of authoritarian regimes to weather crises, to continue to set the agenda when disengaging, and indeed, once the decision has been taken to disengage, to see the transition to democracy through to a successful conclusion.

(v) For these reasons the micropolitics of military and security bureaucracies is crucial. To the uninformed observer, they might seem the antithesis of democratic participation, being hierarchies and systems of command, in which power flows downwards from the top. Yet in practice, the theoretically subordinated lower ranks can also accumulate a considerable amount of de facto power in their own right (Luckham 1994) and it is this which creates a social basis for left-wing coups and radical or populist military regimes, as in Ethiopia, Burkina Faso or Ghana.

(vi) Military establishments often embody conflicting views of professionalism, for instance between traditional 'non-political' professional ideologies, and the 'new professionalism' of internal security that arose during the Cold War period (Stepan 1973): the former emphasising military subordination to the civil power, and the latter embracing more inclusive conceptions of national security, that envisage greater participation in government by the military and security bureaucracies.

(vii) In addition to the military as such, other state security bureaucracies, like intelligence services, presidential guards, special or 'general service' units, paramilitaries, gendarmeries and armed police, often carry out much of the routine business of political control and surveillance. In some authoritarian regimes — particularly those of 'civilian' origin — their influence rivals or even eclipses that of the regular armed forces. Nor are their activities always purely repressive. They have sometimes come to play a more hegemonic role: for instance, orchestrating the press and media, sponsoring the formation of government political parties and representative structures, or even attempting to orchestrate transitions to democratic rule, as in South Korea (Luckham 1995) or, arguably Ghana.

(viii) The fact that military and security establishments are often entangled in global and regional alliance systems, and depend on external resources (weapons systems, technologies of repression, military training and assistance, and even direct backing by foreign troops) often influences their political behaviour. Until the mid 1980s, such international military ties often in practice enhanced the influence of military establishments and buttressed authoritarian rule. But in contrast, foreign military support for African and other Third World governments has declined sharply since the end of the Cold War; and has increasingly been tied to various forms of democracy promotion. Nevertheless, recent international changes have had a far from uniform impact. As a general rule it is palpably more difficult for military and security establishments to oppose democratisation. Yet in some African states the disappearance of external support has precipitated the fracturing of military establishments and of entire state structures: i.e. the end of the Cold War has opened spaces not only for democracy, but also for state collapse and civil war.

Consolidating Democratic Control

In Ghana, as we shall see, the transition has been pacted by the outgoing PNDC regime; but whether the outcome is a genuine transition to multi-party democratic rule, or to a controlled, 'hard democracy' or *democradura* (as Latin Americans would term it) remains very much a matter for controversy. As in other democratising countries, a great deal turns on the process of consolidation after the transfer of power to an elected government. For, even in countries where transitions to democracy have finally taken place, military and security establishments remain formidably equipped to block further political change, or even to reintervene if they believe their privileges and former policies (like market-oriented economic reforms) are threatened. Once acquired, their taste for power, habits of repression and practices of surveillance are not lightly surrendered. Bringing and keeping them under democratic accountability and civilian control — with the emphasis equally on democratic accountability and civilian control — is a task of Sisyphus, that requires that the following five groups of issues be addressed.

(i) The first and most obvious questions is how the military can be prevented from intervening in the first place or reintervening, or from using the threat to do so to shape the new political order in accordance with its interests. Clearly this is not a problem that can easily be resolved by constitutional and legal bans against coups. Much of the answer lies beyond military establishments themselves: in democratic institutions that function effectively and remain legitimate; in an active civil society in which social and political forces remain strong enough to deter military intervention; in economies that grow and redistribute resources so as to minimise discontent and conflict; and in an international environment that supports democratic institutions. But even the more prosperous Third World democracies cannot entirely discount the possibility of military intervention during periods of political upheaval; all the more so in the great majority of African countries, where the issue is how to construct democracy and control the military in far less propitious conditions.

Nevertheless, a sizeable minority of African countries have never experienced military rule (e.g., Botswana, Côte d'Ivoire, Senegal, Tanzania, Zambia or Zimbabwe). Those who have tried to explain military non-intervention in such countries (Goldsworthy 1981 and 1986; Decalo 1989 and 1991) have come up with long lists of factors that may be individually plausible, but scarcely add up to a parsimonious general explanation (Luckham 1994). Moreover, not all the techniques of civilian control they enumerate — such as bribing the armed forces with higher salaries and more weapons, giving officers access to the spoils of office, ethnic manipulation of appointments and promotions, penetration of the officer corps by the intelligence services and the ruling party, or the use of parallel security structures to counterbalance the regular Armed Forces — can be considered conducive to democracy. Often they simply stabilise one variety or another of civilian autocracy. Hence, even if civilian rule is a necessary condition for the consolidation of democracy, it is by no means sufficient.

(ii) A second set of problems relates to the prerogatives and structure of military bureaucracies themselves. The relationship between democracy and military professionalism is difficult enough in advanced democracies. In countries emerging from authoritarian rule it tends to be yet more contradictory. Dangers come from two directions. In countries like Algeria or Nigeria, the Armed Forces have taken advantage of their control of the state to push forward the boundaries of professional autonomy.

However, there have also been risks in too little as well as too much professionalism, especially in the factionalism and indiscipline that has become endemic in many African armies, which can all to easily become a threat to incoming democratic governments. Indeed in Sub-Saharan Africa, almost all the 'returns to civilian rule' before the recent round of transitions were aborted, mostly by factional coups or by revolts originating in the ranks[1] (as in Ghana in 1981).

(iii) Military establishments tend to acquire new political as well as professional prerogatives under authoritarian rule (column 2 of Figure 1), that they are often reluctant to relinquish. In some new democracies, Faustian bargains have been struck, under which military and security establishments have been permitted to retain powers to police the political order, and to continue to act as virtual states within the state. But elsewhere, incoming democratic governments have attempted to compress the military's privileges into the professional sphere of competence, against resistance from the military elites most deeply implicated in the 'military as government', but not necessarily from the entire military profession. Indeed, sometimes members of the officer corps themselves may oppose further political involvement, either because they have not shared in its perks, or because they believe it diminishes their professional competence.

Figure 1: Prerogatives of Military and Security Establishments

1. Military Professional Prerogatives	2. Military Political Prerogatives	3. Prerogatives of Security Bureaucracies	4. Authoritarian Residues in State and Regime
No overall Defence Ministry.	Active duty officers in Cabinet.	Peak intelligence agencies insulated from political control by civilian executive.	Perpetuation of national security state/ideology
De facto command by service chiefs, not the civilian executive.	Active and retired officers in many government posts.	Lack of routine parliamentary oversight of intelligence matters.	Heavy burden of military spending.
Absence of routine legislative hearings on defence/military matters.	AF in command of police or gendarmerie units.	Continued existence of special security agencies.	Resort to states of emergency during crisis.
Armed Forces (AF) still control top military appointments.	AF in control of national intelligence agencies.	Continued existence of paramilitaries and terror squads.	Secrecy paramount in defence and security affairs.
AF set standards for appointments and promotions	AF have autonomous role in internal security operations/surveillance of dissent.	Special courts/legal procedures for security matters.	Absence of parliamentary/media debate of defence and security issues.
Substantial AF control over military organisation, doctrine, education and reform.	AF maintain independent links with sympathetic political groups/parties.	Security bureaucracies exempt from judicial scrutiny in regard to human rights abuses.	Extensive corporate ties between military, security state and economic elites.
AF effectively control own budgets, procurement and force levels.	AF have access to independent sources of finance.	Intelligence agencies involved in efforts to manipulate media and public opinion.	Weak legal and political protections against human rights abuses.
Military insulated from civil society and governed by different standards (e.g. in regard to labour rights).	Military participation in 'strategic' economic activities including defence industries.	Extensive covert links between security bureaucracies and foreign powers.	
Military personnel largely exempt from civilian justice.	Active duty or retired officers manage many state enterprises.		
	AF keep independent links with external suppliers of arms/military assistance.		

Sources: Adapted from Pion-Berlin (1992), Stepan (1988, Chapter 7) and Zaverucha (1993).

(iv) Further issues arise in relation to the influence and prerogatives of the shadowy security bureaucracies, which provide the state's capacity for internal surveillance and repression (column 3 in Figure 1). The immense influence these can acquire under authoritarian regimes, rivalling and sometimes outshadowing that of the Armed Forces, also gives them leverage under the incoming civilian governments. Unlike the military, they cannot stage coups, but they can make life extremely difficult for incoming governments.

(v) The final set of issues relates to the political behaviour and commitment to democracy of the new governments themselves (column 4 of Figure 1). The fact that they are formally civilian and elected, does not necessarily make them democratic. Many of the new governments now being installed in Africa and the Third World more generally are 'restricted' (Rueschemeyer and Stephens 1992), 'exclusionary' (Remmer 1985-6), 'low intensity' (Gills *et al.*, 1993) or 'delegative' (O'Donnel 1994) versions of democracy. Some, like the present government of President Rawlings in Ghana, are the direct successors of outgoing authoritarian regimes, and the beneficiaries of the latter's manipulation of the political process. In others, the existing ruling parties may have been initiated by the old regime, been financed by its intelligence agencies, or have become vehicles for the political ambitions of retired officers. Even when not thus beholden to their predecessors, democratically elected Presidents or Prime Ministers have on many occasions declared states of emergency, suspended rights, dismissed legislatures, locked up opponents and called the military and police out in their support. In other words, the dangers of regression toward authoritarianism within a formally democratic shell may be as great as, and certainly more insidious and difficult to detect than, those of direct military reintervention.

Hence, the government's capacity to control powerful, non-accountable security bureaucracies remains a major danger to democracy even in nominally 'democratic' polities. This is why it is vital that there be established procedures for democratic accountability with respect to the military and security establishments, not merely civilian control. Such procedures can include parliamentary oversight of defence and security bureaucracies (e.g., through committees of the legislature), parliamentary and legal oversight over the activities of intelligence agencies, appointment of 'ombudspersons' or similar bodies to enquire into abuses by governments and their security bureaucracies, open press and media debate concerning military and security issues, freedom of information, except where the latter genuinely clashes directly with national security, and redefinition of the state security within tight limits, that do not include protection of the privileges of the government of the day, or of the ruling elite. In other words, democratisation requires a systematic reduction of many of the military's professional prerogatives and of most, if not all, of its political prerogatives. It equally requires special powers of security and intelligence agencies, and of many other authoritarian residues entrenched at the heart of the state. The list is comprehensive, and covers matters given too little attention in advanced democracies, let alone in the fragile democracies of the Third World.

Military Aspects of Ghana's Transition

Democracy, Military Rule and State Collapse, 1957-1981

Ghana's present transition to democracy is only the latest in no less than four ventures into democracy: the 1957 post-independence government headed by Kwame Nkrumah; two aborted democratic restorations in 1969-72 and 1979-81 (the Busia and Limann governments); and the self-transformation since 1993 of the former Provisional National Defence Council (PNDC) headed by Flight-Lieutenant (now President) Jerry Rawlings into the elected government of the Fourth Republic, armed with all the formal attributes of parliamentary democracy. The obverse side of the story has been frequent regressions to authoritarian rule: under Nkrumah between 1961 and 1966; three standard-issue military governments 1966-69, 1972-78, and 1978-91 and the two 'revolutionary' military regimes of 1979 and 1981-93.

All this reinforces the need for caution in attaching labels and consequences to regimes (Figure 2). Not only were the content and extent of democracy under each of Ghana's 'democratic' governments far from the same. The country's military regimes have also differed from each other in almost every significant respect. The National Liberation Council (NLC) of 1966-9 as a classic junta of senior soldiers, committed from the start to returning power to civilians after dismantling the legacy of Nkrumah. The National Redemption Council (NRC) which seized power in 1972 also began as a junta. Its head, Colonel (later General) Acheampong, purportedly transformed it — in the form of the Supreme Military Council (SMC) — into the most hierarchical and 'military' of

Ghana's regimes; but in practice it degenerated into an ineffective and corrupt personal autocracy. The Akuffo (SMC II) government was a weak junta of Acheampong's former colleagues, whose main goal was to withdraw from power, whilst retaining as much as possible of the military elite's accumulated wealth and privileges. The Armed Forces Revolutionary Council (AFRC) that overthrew it in 1979 and tore down the military hierarchy, was a committee of junior officers and NCOs, chaired by Flight Lieutenant Rawlings, who saw their role as purely short-term and 'corrective'. Its revolutionary descendant, the PNDC, which took power under Rawlings in 1981, included civilians as well as soldiers, especially disclaimed being a 'military' regime, and undertook to reverse Ghana's economic and political decline.

Nor does Ghana's post-independence history permit facile genera-lisations concerning developmental dictatorship (or indeed democracy), or concerning military regimes as the enforcers of capitalist interests. Having set out in the late 1950s with a prosperous agricultural economy generating surpluses for investment in infrastructure and industry by an interventionist state, Ghana became a graveyard for almost every variety of developmental orthodoxy. It was ruled by socialist and conservative civilian governments and by radical as well as right-wing military regimes. Before it became an IMF/World Bank structural adjustment 'success story' in the 1980s, it had tried out almost every conceivable economic strategy: state socialism under Nkrumah, market-oriented reform under the NLC and Busia; economic 'self-reliance' (or macro-economic populism) under Acheampong; and a quickly abandoned experiment in grassroots socialism in 1982 during the first few months of the Rawlings revolution. Behind these diverse political and economic experiments, there occurred a long-run decline. Between 1960 and the early 1980s, Ghana became an African paradigm of the 'development of underdevelopment'. GDP per head at constant prices declined at an average annual rate of 1.2 per cent between 1960 and 1966, 2.0 per cent between 1972 and 1979 and 5.3 per cent between 1979 and 1981 (Ahiakpor 1991:598-9).[2] And the decline was as much political as economic. Not only was Ghana one of the most unstable and coup-prone countries in the African continent prior to 1981 (Ravenhill 1980; Luckham 1985). Economic decline was reinforced by a slow breakdown in state institutions, and erosion of their capacity to manage development (Chazan 1983). This did not simply reduce the state's ability to get things done, it undermined its ability to reproduce itself, i.e. to maintain its revenue base, control the means of coercion and assure a modicum of political stability.

Two interrelated aspects of this erosion of the state were crucial for civilian-military relations. First, the inability of successive governments, whether civilian or military, to count on the loyalty of their armed forces, and hence stabilise their own political existence. Second, the breakdown of command and control in the military establishment, fatally reducing its ability to act as a professional disciplined body and to carry out its basic security functions. The reasons for this breakdown have been documented in detail by Hutchful (1979 and 1993) and Baynham (1988 and 1984-85): inheritance of rigid colonial military structures; the accelerated promotions of the post-independence era; the consequent dislocation of military careers and lines of command; increasing antagonism between officers and different rank levels, and between officers and subaltern groups at the bottom of the hierarchy (i.e., NCOs and men in the ranks); and ethnic and regional antagonisms (not, however, as acute as in some other African armies).

These institutional dislocations were magnified by the efforts of successive governments to manipulate the armed forces politically, together with the military's own interventions in politics. Their most visible manifestation was military intervention, including not only five successful coups, but many more coup attempts. None was staged by the military command as such; instead groups of officers or of soldiers in the ranks acted on their own initiative, the organisers came from ever descending levels of the hierarchy: senior and middle-ranking officers in 1966; middle-ranking officer (Lt. Colonels and Majors) in 1972; junior officers and men in the ranks in 1979 and in 1981.[3] At the same time there was a steady erosion of the boundaries between military institutions and civil society, so that in 1979 and 1981 soldiers and junior officers acted not only in their military capacities, but also expressed the rage of subaltern groups throughout Ghanaian society against the venal elites they blamed for the country's decline.

Figure 2: Ghana: A Political and Economic Profile, 1957-1994

Dates	Government	Type	Economic Policies	Control of the Military
1957-66	K. Nkrumah, Convention Peoples Party (CPP)	Presidential style democracy, becoming (by 1964) single-party	State socialist, protectionist, high public expenditure	Divide and rule, reliance on parallel security structures
1966-69	National Liberation Council (NLC)	Military junta, preparing return to constitutional rule	Renounced socialism; economic liberalisation and austerity	Return to professionalism
1969-72	K. A. Busia, Progress Party (PP)	Multi-party parliamentary democracy	Continued liberalisation with elements of economic nationalism	Professionalism with some political and ethnic manipulation
1972-75	Col. (later Gen.) I. K. Acheampong, National Redemption	Military junta	Protectionist, reversed Busia's devaluation, 'self reliance'	Increasingly based on personal patronage. Tensions middle-ranks/senior officers
1975-78	Gen. I. K. Acheampong Supreme Military Council (SMC)	Military dictatorship	Protectionist and increasingly kleptocratic	Patronage and corruption prevalent. Armed Forces (AF) discipline suffered
1978-79	Gen. F.W.K. Akuffo (SMC II)	Military junta preparing return to constitutional rule	No real change from above	No real change from above, military falling apart
1979	Flt. Lt. J.J. Rawlings, Armed Forces Revolutionary Council (AFRC)	Revolutionary committee of junior officers/NCOs	Anti-corruption, tightening of economic controls	Final collapse of discipline; 'health purge' of officer corps by AFRC
1979-81	H. Limann, Peoples National Party (PNP)	Presidential-style multi-party democracy	Failure to abandon protectionism or to implement proposed liberalisation. Economy in tail-spin	reprofessionalisation thwarted by continued politicisation and dissent in ranks
1981-83	Flt. Lt. J.J. Rawlings, Provisional National Defence Council (PNDC)	Revolutionary/populist military dictatorship	Radical/grassroots economic programme fails to halt collapse of economy	Formation of Armed Forces Defence Committees (AFDCs) in ranks; but partial restoration of hierarchy
1983-93	Flt. Lt. J.J. Rawlings, PNDC	Populist military dictatorship	Stabilisation and structural adjustment under market-oriented Economic Recovery Programme (ERP)	Slow reprofessionalisation of AF, but continued reliance on AFDCs and on parallel security structures
1993	President J.J. Rawlings National Democratic Congress (NDC)	Presidential and single-party dominant multi-party democracy	Continuation of ERP, but pressures to relax fiscal discipline	Emphasis on professionalism; but de facto retention of parallel security structures

Military regimes were as much at risk from coups as civilian governments. Indeed, to describe any of the country's authoritarian governments prior to the advent of Rawlings as 'developmental dictatorships' would be highly misleading. Quite simply, most of them were not sufficiently interested in development, and were too weak and inefficient to dictate. As the economy declined, government revenues fell disastrously, both in real terms, and as a proportion of a shrinking national product, from 16 per cent of GNP in 1974 to 5.6 per cent by 1982. Military and police spending declined also, with Ghana joining a select group of African countries (including Uganda under Amin, Zaire under Mobutu) where predatory military dictatorships mismanaged the economy so badly that even the surpluses disposable for military expenditure shrank (Luckham 1985). In practical terms this meant that military wages and salaries, like all bureaucratic remunerations, ceased to be enough to live on: the military elite could perhaps survive or even prosper through predatory accumulation, but ordinary soldiers and policemen were unable to feed their families, except by moonlighting, trading or engaging in various forms of extortion and banditry.

The military establishment was finally broken apart by a revolt from the ranks on 4 June 1979, which brought to power the Armed Forces Revolutionary Council (AFRC), a revolutionary committee of junior officers and NCOs, under the chairmanship of Flight Lieutenant Jerry Rawlings. This carried out what Rawlings called a 'health purge' (Folson 1993:78) in the government and armed forces, intended to retrieve the latter's tarnished reputation and restore a degree of public accountability. This culminated in secret trials of members of the military elite, eight of whom (including three former military Heads of State) were executed. The AFRC allowed scheduled national elections to go ahead, and handed over power to a civilian government headed by Dr. Hilla Limann in September 1979. But the Armed Forces remained in turmoil, worsened by the government's clumsy attempts to neutralise Rawlings and his associates. At the same time, the government was too weak to take the difficult decisions (including devaluation of the currency) needed to reverse the collapse of the economy. Both the government and its military command simply fell apart when Rawlings and a tiny band of some 35 serving and former soldiers moved against them on 31 December 1981.

Populist Authoritarianism and Structural Adjustment

Rawlings' 'second coming' at the end of 1981 is when the standard narrative of Ghana's 'success story' normally begins (Callaghy 1990). It tells how he came to power committed to 'nothing less than a revolution, something that would transform the social and economic power of the country', (Rawlings' broadcast of 1 January 1982, cited by Folson 1993:79) how his pragmatic economic advisers then persuaded him to change economic course, negotiate with the IMF and the World Bank and implement an Economic Recovery Programme (ERP) to stabilise and structurally adjust the economy; and how, to impose these changes, he broke with the revolutionary Left, brought the mass or 'revolutionary organs' under central control, curbed the trades unions, and turned to coercive and corporatist methods of political management.

This characterisation is broadly accurate, but does not fully explain the 'foundational logic' of the regime: why it made this momentous shift in strategy; and how, having done so, it managed to carry it through with a success that had eluded earlier governments. Part of the explanation is to be found in Rawlings' and the PNDC's contradictory relations to the military establishment and the two 'revolutions' inside it in 1979 and 1981. As we have seen, the latter were both institutional rebellions by the ranks against the command structure and armed uprisings against the ruling elite by military revolutionaries claiming to act on behalf of Ghana's 'popular sectors'. They swept away not only the corrupt SMC military dictatorship, but also the liberal democracy of the 1979-81 Third Republic, contending that the latter had merely introduced 'a new constitution of slavery' for the 'productive majority' of the population. (Rawlings' broadcast of 5 January 1982, cited by Ahiakpor 1991:588). Rawlings himself emerged (not unlike other military populists, such as Peron in Argentina) as the charismatic interlocutor of these subaltern groups, both inside and outside the armed forces. In his first broadcast after the 31 December 1981 revolution, he asserted that he was not staging a coup, but restoring power to the people; and he has continued to deny ever since that the AFRC and PNDC were 'military' governments (Hutchful 1987). Moreover, he initiated attempts to build popular foundations for the regime, by calling for the formation of the Peoples' and Workers' Defence Committees (PDCs and WDCs), which sprang up all over the country during the early months of 1982.

Yet from the outset he also pursued a more narrowly military and etatist agenda, dictated by the changing calculus of power. He moved as quickly as he could to restore command and control in the armed forces and the police, under officers many of whom had initially been arrested by men in the ranks. Whilst he endorsed the formation of Armed Forces Defence Committees (AFDCs) alongside the mass organisations emerging in civil society, he intervened to block radical proposals for military reform, such as men in the ranks participating in the selection of officers. He co-opted two senior military men (earlier retired by Limann) as his Chief of Defence Staff and Army Commander, and made the former a member of the PNDC.[4] He also insisted on retaining the British and Commonwealth military training teams at Ghana's Armed Forces Staff College and Military Academy.

The decisive break with the radicals came in late 1982, when the three most prominent left-wing members of the PNDC (two ex-NCOs and a former student leader) and other activists were arrested or forced into exile after an attempted coup. The immediate occasion for this was the shift in economic strategy, itself inseparable from the regime's efforts to reconsolidate state and military power. Rawlings backed the Secretary of Finance and Economic Planning, Dr. Kwesi Botchwey, and the Economic Policy Review Committee, who insisted on negotiating a stabilisation programme direct with the IMF, in preference to the proposals of more radical advisers, to negotiate with the IMF, whilst attempting to fit stabilisation into a less market-driven framework (Hansen 1991, Chapter 5).

Rather than cutting the overall size of the state, the Economic Recovery Programme (ERP) restored its revenue base, and substantially increased public expenditures, which grew as a share of an expanding domestic product, from only 6-7 per cent of GDP in 1982-3, to 13-14 per cent by 1986-7, despite large-scale job-shedding in an overmanned public sector. Part of this increase took the form of higher defence spending, which grew some 6 per cent annually in real terms during 1982-8, with defence development expenditure (on arms and equipment) rising even faster, at 44 per cent annually in the same period (Fosu 1993:50-52)[5].

A crucial corollary of the ERP's restoration of the state's strength, and of its capacity to coerce, was the reimposition of labour discipline. The

IMF and the World Bank made little secret of their view that the WDCs and trade unions should be brought to heel, their experiments in workers' control terminated and labour unrest brought under control (Haynes 1991a:450). The PNDC skilfully combined divide-and-rule tactics among workers' organisations with outright repression, including bans on strikes, deployment of armed security personnel to control protesting workers, and detention of ring-leaders. The result, as Gyimah-Boadi and Essuman-Johnson (1993:205-6) observe was that 'while under the Busia, Akuffo and Limann governments, economic policies featuring wage freezes, price increases and especially devaluation had been met by a wave of strikes (79 strikes were recorded in 1971 under Busia, 80 in 1978 under Akuffo and 66 in 1980 under Limann), only an average of 16 strikes were recorded between 1983 and 1989, when a more thorough and consistent version of such policies were being pursued'.

Hence, there is at least a prima facie case that the consolidation of a strong authoritarian state under Rawlings and the re-starting of capitalist growth in the economy were mutually and causally interlinked. Yet this leaves one little the wiser about why the PNDC alone among Ghana's authoritarian governments was effective: not just in managing the economy, but also in enforcing political stability, in redisciplining the armed forces and in reinventing itself in 1993 as a 'democratic' government. A number of outside observers (Callaghy 1990; Chazan 1989; Jeffries 1993) attribute these successes to the political steadiness, managerial competence and economic skills of Rawlings and his small group of advisers. Here at least was a Ghanaian government that 'got its policies right'. A more cynical view is that international financial institutions and donors needed an African 'success story' and were prepared to provide the large-scale injections of finance to back it. If so, their choice of a radical military regime to deliver success was remarkable, all the more since the latter did not deviate significantly from the non-aligned and Pan-Africanist foreign policy of its predecessors (Boafo-Arthur 1993), supported Libya at the UN and OAU, continued to receive assistance from Cuba and Eastern Europe (notably to train its para-military and security services), and continued to have poor relations with the United States (which temporarily terminated its aid programme in 1985, after four US diplomats were expelled following the exposure of a CIA network (Boafo-Arthur 1993:149).

In sum, what needs to be explained is what made the Rawlings/PNDC government a developmental dictatorship, or an 'adjusted state' (Green 1991:70), in marked contrast to the patrimonial authoritarianism of many other African regimes. A crucial, but contradictory, factor was its distinctive populism, which partly survived its alleged betrayal of the revolution that brought it to power. Though most of the Left saw the ERP as a betrayal of the PNDC's original mandate, there remained, as Ahiakpor (1991:584) suggests, a 'considerable consistency' behind Rawlings's search for means to alleviate the plight of the poor in Ghana, and this explains why he decided to alter course so significantly after the original repressions of the market only made matters worse (in 1982-83) than they had been previously'.

Admittedly once he chose this course, poverty alleviation took second place to the requirements of structural adjustment and market efficiency, and how far the poor, and which groups among them, have actually benefited, has remained a matter of controversy (Green 1988). In a 1990/91 survey of urban attitudes, Jeffries found that, despite believing that their own real incomes had declined during the preceding five years, most of the sample thought that the country's and their own economic plight would have been worse without the ERP: a tribute not just to their 'bourgeois economic realism', but also to Rawlings' ability (rightly or wrongly) to persuade at least some of the populace that, in the words of a respondent, 'he always puts the interest of the country first' (Jeffries 1992:215 and 218).[6]

Rawlings' populist-authoritarian style also influenced how he handled another central structural problem: that his regime was of military origin, but did not enjoy full support from the professional military establishment during much of its period of rule. Some other African military rulers facing this dilemma (including the Acheampong regime in Ghana) have attempted to control the armed forces by patrimonialising them, giving them opportunities to enrich themselves through the state. Rawlings, in contrast, insisted on an institutional separation between the armed forces and the PNDC government of which he was Chairman, and which included more civilians than soldiers.[7] He kept his original rank of Flight Lieutenant, and delegated operational control of the armed forces to the General Officer Commanding (GOC). The military and police establishments were removed from the purview of the PNDC in late

1982, and made directly answerable (via their commanders) to Rawlings, his Head of Security, Kojo Tsikata (in charge of the Bureau of National Investigation — BNI), and the National Security Council.

The regime also turned its attention to re-professionalising the military establishment. It needed simultaneously to re-establish its authority over a traumatised and hostile officer corps; and to restore discipline among radicals in the AFDCs and lower ranks. Not only was each of these goals problematic in itself, they also potentially conflicted, as, once the officers were back in control of their men, they might be tempted to move against the government. Rawlings' solution (described in fascinating detail by Hutchful 1993) was to put his GOC, Lt.-General Quainoo, in charge of re-equipping and re-professionalising the Armed Forces, but to keep the AFDCs (or Armed Forces Committees for the Defence of the Revolution — AFCDRs) as they became in 1984), and integrate them into the formal military structure. The most prominent political activists in the ranks were purged, and soldiers who remained rebellious were disciplined.

The Boys Company, a training company for young recruits, mostly sons of soldiers, in which many military radicals had started their careers, was disbanded. The AFCDRs class character was diluted by opening them to officers as well as the ranks; and by cutting their links with civilian mass organisations, whose personnel were banned from barracks. Their functions were also redefined, making them mainly consultative and advisory bodies, reporting to the commanders of military units and managed by the Armed Forces Sergeant Major (a newly created position) and other senior NCOs. A counterrevolution was thus carried out within the armed forces, so as to restore the former command structure. All the same, Rawlings insisted on retaining the AFCDRs, against the advice of his senior commanders. Not only were they a safeguard against coups, since officers could not draw weapons, nor move troops, without alerting them. They arguably contributed to increased morale by reducing the social distance between officers and men, a feature commented on when Ghanaian units served in peacekeeping forces elsewhere in Africa. But above all, they remained an important focal point for Rawlings' own populist- authoritarian leadership within the armed forces.

Rawlings relied on a small cadre of politicised officers, NCOs and security personnel to watch over the military hierarchy. Through their efforts the PNDC built up a formidable array of special military and paramilitary units and security organisations, including the BNI (the former Special Branch, topped up with an additional layer of Rawlings appointees), the Forces Reserve Battalion (the so called 'commandos', composed of a Special Forces Unit and a Presidential Security Unit), and the Civil Defence Organisation (CDO) with its vigilante Mobisquads and militias. They were not dissimilar to the parallel security structures Nkrumah attempted to establish in the 1960s, including the National Security Service and the President's Own Guard Regiment (Baynham 1985). But whereas the regular forces frustrated Nkrumah's efforts to bypass them by staging a coup in 1966, under the PNDC the professional military establishment was too divided and demoralised to act pre-emptively.

The purpose of these reorganisations was not just to stabilise the regime against coups, but also to control civilian dissent. In this there was some continuity from the regime's early and more radical phase, from which much of the government's repressive legislation (like PNDC Law 4 of 1982 on 'Preventive Custody') dated, and when human rights abuses had been aggravated by the PNDC's inability to control the revolutionary excesses of its supporters (Gyimah-Boadi and Rothchild 1982; Haynes 1991b). As Rawlings consolidated his authority, the machinery of repression was brought under firmer political direction. The investigatory or quasi-judicial bodies that had probed illegal acquisition of wealth and abuse of power (like the Citizen's Vetting Committees, the National Investigations Commission and Public Tribunals) were slowly allowed to fall into disuse, or were used to silence political opponents. The secret services (notably the BNI) were expanded, and surveillance of potential dissenters was stepped up. The judiciary was intimidated, or circumvented by extra-judicial bodies like the Special Military Tribunal, which investigated and prosecuted alleged security offenses by civilians as well as soldiers.

The Path From 'True' to Liberal Bourgeois Democracy

Whilst there is little doubt that the PNDC regime was repressive, deploying force both to stabilise its rule and to push through the ERP, it never entirely abandoned its original populist project. Flight Lieutenant Rawlings continued to hold himself out as a democrat and a man of the people (albeit in a manner more reminiscent of Rousseau than of John Stuart Mill); by emphasising that he did not envisage 'a democracy with a hollow political content but one rooted in our economic realities' (Rawlings 1986:80). However, his attitude to democracy was shot through with contradictions. Having staged the 1979 and 1981 revolutions on behalf of 'the people', he clipped the wings of the mass organisations, and scorned radical solutions to the country's economic difficulties as 'populist nonsense', in effect making GDP growth the touchstone of the general will. He complained about the 'culture of silence' surrounding the government, yet refused to engage in serious dialogue with his critics (Boahen 1989:54). Nevertheless, he commanded enough public support to create his own political machine, orchestrate the regime's transition to a multi-party democracy in 1993, and secure his own election as President.

In the process, Rawlings' vision of 'true' or popular democracy was transformed significantly. The mass organisations were purged after the break with the Left in late 1982. In 1984, their national directorate (the National Defence Committee) was disbanded and the PDCs and WDCs were reorganised as 'Committees for the Defence of the Revolution' (CDRs). At the same time, the regime began to redefine its original conception of 'the people': forming corporatist ties with a wide range of groups in civil society (chiefs, women, businessmen, unions, etc.), which did not always belong to the 'masses' in whose name it had carried out the 31 December revolution. It did so selectively: giving political and financial backing to groups supporting it (like the 31st December Women's Movement, the Association of Local Unions, the Ghana Road Transporters Union and some of the Pentecostal churches); downgrading more neutral bodies (like the National Council for Women and Development, or the Ghana Manufacturers Association); intimidating those that were critical (such as the TUC, the Association of Recognised Professional Bodies and the Ghana Bar Association); and heavily censoring the press and broadcast media.

In late 1984, it put its democratisation strategy in the hands of the National Commission for Democracy (NCD), headed by a former judge, Justice D.F. Annan, who also became Vice-Chairman of the PNDC. The emphasis shifted to rebuilding popular participation through a series of reforms in local and regional government, leading to a grassroots-based

'Ghanaian form of democracy' at the national level, and allowing the PNDC to harness its latent support in rural areas amongst farmers who were the supposed beneficiaries of economic reform and increased export crop producer prices (Green 1991:74-5). Elections for partly elected, partly nominated District Assemblies were held in 1988-89, contested by individuals, not political parties, which remained banned, and there seemed little prospect of the PNDC moving beyond this limited opening of the political system to allow its authority to be challenged in multi-party elections.

But a transition to liberal democracy was precisely what it conceded a year or two later, in July 1990 authorising the NCD to hold regional forums on a democratic constitution; and in April 1991 agreeing to the latter's recommendation that such a constitution should provide for multi-party elections, despite Rawlings' frequently-stated preference for a no-party form of government. The finished document which emerged from the Consultative Assembly, composed in roughly equal parts of members elected by District Assemblies and 'established organisations',[8] together with government nominees, was not very much different from the 1979 Constitution overturned by Rawlings in 1981: envisaging an executive president, a legislature chosen through multi-party elections, separation of powers, a bill of rights and an independent judiciary. Little remained of Rawlings' original aspirations for a more 'Ghanaian' constitutional framework. Nor was the political position of the Armed Forces entrenched, except in a constitutional provision (under Article 210) that allocated them a vaguely defined role in national development. However, the PNDC pushed through Transitional Provisions just before the Assembly concluded its deliberations, giving past and present members of the government comprehensive immunity from prosecution for their actions in the 1979 and 1981 revolutions and during their period in office.

Why did the PNDC change its mind and embrace Western-style liberal democracy? The end of the Cold War, the 'good government' agenda of international financial institutions and the advocacy of multi-party democracy by Western donors (notably the UK) all played their part.[9] Yet domestic political and economic considerations were also crucial (Jeffries and Thomas 1993:336) including the social and economic stresses generated by the ERP, continued doubts about the sustainability of economic recovery, and growing protests from a range of civil society groups that the regime had never been able entirely to suppress. The latter, notably the established churches under the Christian Council of Ghana and the Catholic Bishops' Conference, and the Ghana Bar Association, had begun to breach the 'culture of silence' before regional forums were held on constitutional reform in 1990. Thereafter, the pro-democracy movement emerged into the open, with the formation of the Movement for Freedom and Justice (MFJ), bringing together politicians from all the major political parties of Ghana's first three Republics.

The protests organised by this emergent opposition were neither violent nor large enough in scale to fully explain the regime's change of mind. However, they emboldened the NCD, the constitutional drafting committee and the Consultative Assembly to be more independent than anyone had expected them to be. Furthermore, there were divisions of opinion within the PNDC, some of whose influential members (who reportedly included Justice Annan, the chairman of the NDC, and Kojo Tsikata, the security chief) feared that a no-party constitution might encounter the same hostile public reaction as General Acheampong's 'union government' proposals in 1977-78; and calculated that the PNDC could stay ahead of the game and use its formidable political machine to assure victory in contested elections.

Another possible element in the PNDC's calculations was that it could not necessarily count on the indefinite loyalty of the military and security establishments. Since it was not a regime of the military hierarchy as a whole, it could not discount the possibility that elements in the officer corps might move against it. There had been major coup attempts in 1982 and 1983, and a number of subsequent plots, for which over 60 soldiers and civilians had been shot or imprisoned since 1982. The most recent (in 1989) allegedly involved Major Quashigah, formerly the head of Military Police and Chief of Staff at PNDC headquarters, and others, 'in activities that could have compromised the state' (ARB 26(10), 15 November 1989) revealing potential splits in the regime's military constituency. An uncontrolled democratisation resulting from a military revolt or a civilian uprising, as in Benin, Mali or the Congo Republic, would certainly have exposed members of the regime to retribution for the deaths, torture and detention inflicted on their opponents.

Having taken the basic decision to proceed with a multi-party constitution, Rawlings and his advisers were better placed to capitalise on their political assets. They soon recaptured the political initiative from the opposition, by taking over many of the latter's reform proposals; dismantling parts of the PNDC's repressive legislation, including the decrees relating to suspension of habeas corpus, detention and newspaper registration; and pressing ahead with the new constitution and the 1992 elections. Rawlings decision to stand for President seems to have been informed by two interlinked calculations: first (based on informal sounding up and down the country by his advisers), that he had a good chance of organising a victory; and second, that if he did not stand, the National Democratic Congress (NDC) formed to defend the regime's interests, risked losing at the polls.

In the event, Rawlings won the presidential election by a comfortable majority of 58 per cent of the vote, compared with 30 per cent cast for his nearest rival, Professor Adu Boahen, standing on the opposition New Patriotic Party (NPP) ticket. The four main opposition parties immediately challenged this result, alleging voting irregularities and intimidation of their supporters; and then proceeded to boycott the subsequent parliamentary elections (temporarily postponed whilst the government, the diplomatic community and international observer teams tried to persuade them to take part) claiming they feared 'acts of intimidation and harassment' by agents of the PNDC, including commandos, para-military personnel and the BNI (ARB 29(12) December 1-3, 1992:10816). Their non-participation guaranteed the NDC an overwhelming majority of 189 out of 200 parliamentary seats, the remaining 11 seats going to other pro-Rawlings parties and independents. The Western donors, fearing according to the Financial Times, 'that at the very least a defeat of Flt. Lt. Rawlings would cause a period of economic policy insecurity', (ARB 29 (11) November 1992:10782) endorsed the results, whilst continuing to express concern about the absence of a parliamentary opposition.[10]

The reasons why Rawlings and the NDC won the election so decisively remain controversial (New Patriotic Party 1993; Jeffries and Thomas 1993:349-54). The opposition contends it was robbed of victory by electoral fraud, although Commonwealth and Carter Centre observers monitoring the elections did not consider that this took place on a large enough scale to affect the result. Perhaps more important than actual fraud was the PNDC's ability to dictate the scheduling of the democratisation process and the elections, its decision to proceed on the basis of a flawed and incomplete electoral roll; manipulation of electoral procedures; Rawlings' ability to campaign unofficially several months before the opposition was permitted to do so; use of official resources, such as government transport, in the NDC's campaigning; use of government patronage to influence local opinion-makers; and widespread deployment of the CDRs and paramilitaries to intimidate wavering voters.[11]

Rawlings' majority was cumulatively enhanced by these advantages of incumbency. Whether he would have lost without them is harder to say. He campaigned effectively, and made full use of his popular appeal, especially among rural voters. He was also able to claim some credit for the ERP, all the more as the opposition parties did not propose serious alternatives to it. Moreover, the PNDC could count on the political support-structures established during its period in office— the CDRs and other 'revolutionary organs', the 31st December Women's Movement, and, via District Secretaries, sections of the local government machinery — to bring in the vote. The new political machine Rawlings and his supporters had brought into existence broke long-established political duopoly of the libertarian conservative Danquah-Busia bloc and the more radical Nkrumah-ist bloc for the first time since the 1950s. Rawlings also profited from the opposition's failure to turn the MFJ, or the Alliance of Democratic Forces (ADF) as it later became, into a coalition partly putting forward a single opposition presidential candidate. It became split between the NPP representing the Danquah-Busia political tendency, and four other parties, all claiming the mantle of Nkrumah's CPP. The PNDC played on these divisions, whilst simultaneously advancing its own claim to CPP credentials, notably by co-opting a fifth Nkrumah-ist party, the National Convention Party (NCP), to which some of its prominent supporters (like Kojo Tsikata) belonged, into an electoral alliance with the NDC. Moreover, it seems the opposition parties made a major tactical error in refusing to participate in the parliamentary elections, in which they might conceivably have gained a larger share of the vote, as Rawlings' personal popularity arguably exceeded that of the NDC.[12]

Negotiating Civilian Control over the Military and Security Establishments

Both the NCD's 1991 report on *Evolving a True Democracy* and the subsequent Committee of Expert's *Proposals for a Draft Constitution of Ghana*, turned their attention to 'the prospect of military intervention in the constitutional order and the possibility of instituting devices to prevent such intervention' (Committee of Experts 1991:178). The regional seminars which preceded the former veered between the extremes of scrapping the military as an institution altogether, putting it 'through a comprehensive orientation programme after a return to civilian rule so as to respect the sanctity of a constitutional government'; and recognising that:

> the military has now become a major power bloc and is therefore a de facto political constituency. Future systems of government should therefore shift from the traditional civil-military co-operation which emphasised the traditional military role of defence to civil-military integration which emphasises the indispensability of the military in the political administration of the country (executive summary of the seminars in National Commission for Democracy 1991:84).

Both reports, however, emphasised that elected governments themselves had been partly responsible for their own downfall through acts:

> which may be regarded as subversive of the very constitutional order. Whether it be arbitrary detention, arbitrary dismissals of public servants, wilful disregard of basic human rights, etc., such acts... sowed seeds of instability which ended up in the whole constitution being set aside (National Commission for Democracy 1991:53).
>
> Hence, whilst not wanting to be 'so presumptuous as to prescribe a deterrent, the military coups'... that 'stability is best arrived at by a constitutional order which so genuinely reflects the interests of the ordinary man or woman that it cannot be summarily set inside without provoking the wrath of the people' (Committee of Experts 1991:180).

But in the end, one of the most striking features of the 1990-3 constitutional debates was how little detailed discussion there was of possible change in the institutional structure of the Armed Forces and other security services, and of arrangements to control them. Whilst Armed Forces representatives (both officers and ranks) sat in the Consultative Assembly, they were few in number, appointed rather than elected and were given no mandate by their military 'constituency'. Little organised debate of the issues took place in the latter — except at a division in the Burma Camp, at which soldiers shouted their representatives down, when the latter asked for guidance on proposals to take before the Consultative Assembly. Almost all the discussion at the Assembly took place in committees, and the constitutional provisions relating to the Armed Forces that emerged from it were neither controversial, nor involved dramatic change in existing arrangements.

The Constitution of the Fourth Republic established (under Chapter 17) an Armed Forces Council, chaired by the Vice-President, with overall responsibility for appointments,[13] promotions, discipline and budgeting; though operational control of the Armed Forces was given to the Chief of Defence Staff, in turn accountable to the President (in his capacity as Commander in Chief) through the Minister of Defence. The Ministry of Defence was to remain 'civilian' and institutionally distinct from the Armed Forces (as it had been under the PNDC, whose outgoing Secretary for Defence, Alhaji Mahama Idrissu, became Minister after the 1993 elections). Broader integration of defence, public order, intelligence, diplomatic and external economic policy became the responsibility (under Articles 83-4) of the National Security Council, chaired by the President and serviced by the Secretary to the Cabinet.

The military establishments and the PNDC regime's desire that 'the security services must be seen as part of the larger community and not relegated to some artificial political vacuum' (remarks by Flt. Lt. Rawlings after Ghana Armed Forces route march, 31 December 1990, reprinted in Rawlings 1990:108) was acknowledged under Article 210, which specifies that in addition to their defence role, the Armed Forces shall be equipped and maintained for, 'such other functions for the development of Ghana as the President shall determine'. But as one of the military representatives[14] put it, although the Armed Forces were to be 'integrated into the main stream of Ghanaian life', through their developmental role, they would be:

> completely divorced from the political arena [Hear, hear!]... the glaring absence of any article or clause permitting members of the Armed Forces to actively participate in politics is also a clear manifestation of the constitution-makers speaking the will of the people (Proceedings of the Consultative Assembly, No. 63, 28 January 1992:1750).

The Constitution's provision for the appointment of a Warrant Officer to Armed Forces Council was its sole recognition of the military populism that had driven the June 4th and December 31st revolutions. Far from making defence the 'concern of the entire population', expanding the activities of the 'mass organisations as active peoples organisations for peoples safety and accountability' and instituting civil defence and compulsory military training, as originally proposed in *Evolving a True Democracy* (National Commission for Democracy 1991:42-3), the Constitution dis-established both military and civilian CDRs and other mass organisations, by removing their eligibility for state funding.

Nor did it focus in much detail on democratic (as opposed to government) control of the military and security establishments, including parliamentary oversight, press and public debate and greater public accountability and transparency in the defence sector. To some degree, this was because other provisions of the Constitution covered such matters. Parliament, for instance, was empowered to appoint its own standing committees, and indeed established a Standing Committee on Defence and the Interior not long after it began its sessions. However, even the senior military figures to whom the author spoke after the transition deplored the absence of public debate; indeed sharing more concern about its absence than many civilian politicians.

In sum, the 1992 Constitution changed very little in existing civil-military arrangements, basing itself very largely on the provisions of earlier Constitutions. As in these previous constitutional documents, much of the emphasis was on executive authority over a politically 'neutral' military establishment. To the more professional elements in the officer corps, indeed, return to constitutional rule was an opportunity 'to use the constitution and its structures to fashion out a change to a modern force, one that is disciplined, adequately supplied with modern equipment and management systems, appropriately trained and exercised' (the Chief of Defence Staff, Air Marshal A.H.K. Dumashie interviewed in *Afnews*, No.81, January-June 1984).

Nevertheless, there remain formidable obstacles to re-professionalisation. In part, these are economic, as re-equipment, retraining and payment of an adequate living wage to soldiers requires resources that are constrained under the ERP. They are partly military-political, to the extent that there remain constituencies within the Armed Forces— notably in the ranks and among more junior officers who have served the majority of their careers under the PNDC — who do not necessarily share their seniors' desire for a more neutral, 'professional' force. They are also rooted in public fear, lack of information and unwillingness to engage in debate on military and security matters. And they are partly founded in the government's own reluctance, having won the 1993 elections, to change its own procedures and practices of power, so as to breathe some life into the bodies created to supervise the military and security establishments under the Constitution, such as the National Security and Armed Forces Councils.

In theory the PNDC's shadowy parallel security apparatuses, notably the Forces Reserve Battalion (FRB), have been disbanded and their men integrated into the armed forces or elsewhere; though in reality they maintain their operational independence. State support for the CDRs and other revolutionary organs is forbidden under the Constitution; instead they are co-ordinated through a non-official 'Association of CDRs'. The BNI remains in place as the government's prime intelligence agency, but shares its responsibilities with a resurrected Department of Military Intelligence (see *Africa Confidential* 21 January 1994).

But what all this means in terms of the willingness and capacity of the government to cease spying on, and intimidating its opponents, and to rein in its security bureaucracies, is still far from certain. The opposition is not taking anything on trust, and is working through the press and the courts to prevent abuses, since it is not present in Parliament to raise defence and intelligence issues there. Parliament's Standing Committee on Defence and the Interior has been active, holding meetings in military installations up and down the country, though it is still too early to judge whether it will assure effective legislative oversight.

Though the Constitution vests responsibility for the Armed Forces in the National Security Council, Armed Forces Council and Ministry of Defence, in reality the most important decisions are taken, as before, by President Rawlings and a small circle of advisers, to a large extent bypassing the official machinery. Despite the existence in the military establishment itself of two main bodies of opinion, those who regard the return to constitutional rule as an opportunity to re-professionalise, and those who believe the military should remain a major power bloc, politically committed to the Rawlings government, the differences between them should not be exaggerated. Indeed during the transition process and 1993 election campaign, members of both camps greatly resented opposition criticism and abuse of the Armed Forces. To be sure, the military establishment is by no means as powerful and cohesive a corporate bloc, nor as resistant to efforts to bring it under greater control, as it might appear from the outside. But neither can one ignore its interests, and its potential role in the consolidation (or frustration) of democracy. For the latter is still a long way from being consolidated.

Notes

1. Sierra Leone was the sole exception, where an army revolt from the ranks in 1968 paved the way for an elected government (that of President Siaka Stevens), which then turned itself into a civilian autocracy, only for the country to come under military rule again in 1992.

2. However, the NLC and Busia regimes presided over a limited market-based revival, with 1.0 per cent real growth in GDP per head between 1966 and 1971.

3. This was the basic pattern, though it simplifies in a number of respects. For example, the core group in 1966 included more middle level than senior officers, though the latter predominated in the NLC junta. The 1978 'palace coup' by senior colleagues against Acheampong was also a deviation from the pattern, but only a temporary one.

4. Brigadiers Nunoo-Mensah and Quainoo. The latter replaced Nunoo-Mensah as Chief of Defence Staff and member of the PNDC in late 1982.

5. However, due to the large overall rise in public expenditure military spending declined as a proportion of the current budget and only slightly increased its share of the capital budget. The published estimates for military spending probably do not include much of the expenditure on Ghana's burgeoning para-military forces.

6. The study used a selected rather than a random sample. Hence its findings about the proportions of people favourable toward Rawlings and the ERP need to be interpreted with some caution.

7. At the beginning, military members included two of Rawlings' radical associates from the lower ranks as well as the GOC of the armed forces. During most of the period after the purges of late 1982, the GOC was the sole military representative, apart from Rawlings himself.

8. Only a minority of these were civil society groups that had played an active role in the previous agitation for political liberalisation.

9. During interviews with the author in August 1994, Ghanaian officials claimed there was no specific political conditionality in terms of aid being given or intended in exchange for democratic reforms. Rather, it was a case of their reading the political signals, for example in the relevant speeches by the UK Foreign Secretary, Douglas Hurd and the Minister of Overseas Development, Baroness Chalker.

10. On a visit to Accra soon after the election the British Foreign Secretary, Douglas Hurd endorsed the Commonwealth Observer Group's findings, but urged the government and opposition to find ways of working together (ARB, 39 (1) January 1993:10874).

11. Most of these are documented in Jeffries and Thomas (1993). Nevertheless, they contend the opposition had no real ground for complaint, as it had been so confident of victory that it assented to fight the election in full knowledge it would do so on an unlevelled playing field: in my view an excessively Machiavellian line of reasoning.

12. However, the NPP's presidential candidate, Adu Boahen, argues the opposition parties had little choice. Not only would they have faced more intimidation in the parliamentary elections if their leaders had decided to fight them, they would have had to contend with a mass revolt by party organisers in the constituencies: interview, June 1994.

13. Except for the Chief of Defence Staff and Service Chiefs, who were to be directly appointed by the President, in consultation with the Council of State.

14. Squadron-Leader I.S. Kadri of the Ghana Air Force.

7

The International Community and Ghana's Transition to Democracy

Kwame Boafo-Arthur

Introduction

From 31 December 1981 to 7 January 1993, Ghana was ruled by a revolutionary military regime — the Provisional National Defence Council (PNDC) under the chairmanship of Flt. Lt. Jerry John Rawlings. Until the last two years of its rule the crucial issue of when it would hand over power to a democratically elected constitutional government could not be subjected to any serious debate. This was because unlike earlier military regimes, which upon usurping political power readily announced plans for a return to civilian rule, the PNDC did not make any explicit pledge on this issue after taking power from the Limann administration on 31 December 1981. By so doing, the vexed question of returning the country to constitutional rule was left in limbo.

The PNDC's penchant for exclusiveness and secrecy in top level decision-making as well as its unabashed antipathy to multi-party democracy moved in tandem with its not too infrequent use of 'strong arm tactics' to silence political opposition. Rawlings' persistent rejection of multi-partyism, which was re-echoed *ad nauseam* by its able lieutenants, the deliberate campaign to discredit the virtues of parliamentary democracy (which was reminiscent of arguments put forward by the first generation of post independence African leaders to justify single-party rule; and the creation of political structures which were then in vogue in Libya, Ethiopia and Cuba, confirmed the regime's dislike for pluralist democratic government of the liberal hue. Accordingly, in a new year message delivered as late as 1990, Rawlings would emphatically declare that Ghana was not ready for a return to political pluralism.[1]

What then led to the PNDC's change in political course or programme? There seems to be very little doubt that the government's
decision to democratise was the outcome of a rare convergence of
domestic and external pressures, and, or influences from unanticipated
political changes in the international system.[2]

This paper examines the external factor focusing mainly on different
channels of influences, as well as specific roles played by identifiable
international governmental and non-governmental actors in the actual
transition process. We begin by briefly examining the interactive nature
of the internal and external factors leading to the transition. This is
followed by a discussion of new donor policies and its implications for
the transition process. Various roles played by international actors are
also examined in addition to post-election political developments. In the
final analysis, one cannot but agree that the role of the international
community in the transition process was unprecedented, and contributed
immensely to Ghana's transition process.

The Internal and External Interface

Military disengagement from politics, according to Claude Welch (1974),
is influenced by two main factors: a strong desire on the part of the
military to transfer power to civilians; and popular civilian agitations for a
return to democratic constitutional governance.[3] In most cases however,
military transitions are influenced by the second factor. There is no doubt
that autonomous, articulate and well organised civil associational groups
can set limits on governmental prerogatives, be it military or civilian. As
pointed out by Jean-François Bayart (1986), the political actions of civic
associations, '...invest civil society with the capacity to resist state
authoritarianism or totalitarianism'. However, the disintegration of the
eastern bloc and the general call for political changes in the Third World
in the early 1990s, seem to have given greater impetus to external donors
to support the democratic transitions. Much as one cannot so easily ignore
the role of domestic popular forces in influencing democratic transitions
through various modes, one should be candid to accept the pivotal role
played by international governmental and non-governmental actors in
various democratic transitions in Sub-Saharan Africa (SSA).

More important, any analysis of the Ghanaian transition will be
incomplete without a focus on the international community for a number

of reasons. First, the nature of the PNDC regime had greatly immobilised civic associational groups and consequently rendered them largely ineffective as pressure groups capable of compelling the military to disengage from politics. This, however, changed especially after the collapse of the Eastern bloc. One can therefore, even if obliquely, posit a correlation between general global politico-economic changes and the PNDC's acceptance of the need to democratise. Of greater significance in Ghana's transition politics was the decision by major donors to tie foreign aid to a programme of political reform towards democratic governance. This proved to be a major stumbling block to the PNDC's original goal of establishing grassroots participatory democracy.

Finally, in the light of the PNDC government's resistance to domestic pressures for democratisation, it could only be surmised that its dependence on foreign aid made it extremely vulnerable to external pressure to initiate political reforms. As Menkhaus and Kegley (1988) have observed, the behaviour of a dependent state 'manifests pronounced deference and compliance toward those powers on which it is dependent'. Therefore, the regime was bound to retreat from its opposition to multiparty democracy when further foreign aid was made conditional to the pursuit of a programme of political reforms. It is a common characteristic of economically dependent countries (as the PNDC had become) to follow certain policies in order not to lose certain economic benefits derived from ties with a dominant country. Donor dependence rendered the PNDC extremely vulnerable to mounting external pressure for change. One may thus agree with Michael Bratton and van de Walle (1992:27) that a complex array of forces which may be either structural or contingent, external or internal may create openings in authoritarian rule. In the Ghanaian situation the interactive processes between domestic and external pressures were clearly discernible especially in the latter stages of the transition process. But as Douglas Anglin (1990:6) argues, Eastern Europe 'can be credited with breathing fresh life into indigenous opposition groups which had long been struggling, with limited, if any success, to press their demands on obdurate government'. The crucial role played by external events on Africa's democratisation generally and Ghana in particular has also been emphasised by Eboe Hutchful (1992:2) who notes that:

by demonstrating that the most entrenched dictatorship can be overthrown by popular resistance and actions, the democratic movements in Eastern Europe energised civil society in Africa in ways not seen since the independence struggles.

In a nutshell, the internal environment for political protest got transformed as a result of democracy movements in countries as varied as the Soviet Union, East Germany, and South Africa (Bratton and van de Walle 1992:42).

It is arguable therefore that the liberalisation of hitherto impregnable authoritarian states in Eastern Europe served notice on the PNDC, apart from undermining its shaky legitimacy, that it could also fall. They thereby provided the hitherto disoriented internal social forces with fresh impetus to agitate for political reforms that would usher in a democratic regime and ensure respect for human rights.

Furthermore, the international changes transformed the obliging and condescending posture of western governments toward autocracy and malfeasance of so called strategic allies. Consequently, powerful international demands for 'better governance' and ultimately a 'free economy' (Decalo 1992:18) bolstered domestic political actors to struggle for change. The major issue, however, is the nature of the external factor and how it affected the transition process.

New Donor Policies

From the middle of the 1980s donors gradually realised that bad governance, broadly defined, and the repressive and intimidating political systems that generate such acts of government, constitute the most formidable obstacle to the resumption of economic growth. Consequently, political liberalisation came to be viewed as imperative for sustained economic growth (Nelson and Eglinton 1992:14). The World Bank and bilateral donors therefore became the major advocates of a new approach to external assistance that focused more on the political than it used to be. The respective positions of the major donors are briefly discussed below.

i) *The World Bank's View*

The World Bank Report of 1989 identified the 'crisis of governance' as the bane of Africa's developmental problems, and called for the promotion of pluralistic institutional structures as opposed to dictatorship or personalised rule. What is of essence, however, are the parameters of the Bank's conceptualisation of good governance. In the Bank's parlance, governance encompasses the accountability of government officials, including politicians and civil servants, openness in government transactions; transparency in government procedures; predictability in government behaviour and expectation of rational decision; and the rule of law. Thus a system of government is 'good' if it has the attributes outlined above; and the system is 'bad' if such characteristics are absent. We need to caution, however, that the World Bank's definition of 'governance' is controversial, especially among academics.[4]

The bank's major concern about governance stems from the failure of its structural adjustment programmes in many countries of Sub-saharan Africa. The most devastating index of failure is its inability to attract foreign private investments. Barber Conable, the former president of the bank, in analysing the issues involved, noted at a meeting in 1990 with African governors of the World Bank that: *..Governance is linked to economic development, and donors are showing signs that they will no longer support systems that are inefficient and unresponsive to the peoples' basic needs*[5] (my emphasis). Elaborating later on the essence of good governance especially participation in decision-making process, Barber Conable noted: 'Open political participation has been restricted and even condemned and those brave enough to speak their minds have too frequently taken grave personal risk'.[6] Without doubt, the World Bank made its position very clear and the signals could not be easily ignored by authoritarian governments that paid lip-service to democracy and popular participation in government.

ii) Bilateral Donors

Possibly taking a cue from the World Bank's position and the phenomenal global changes brought about by the demise of the communist bloc, bilateral donors also openly expressed support for the tying of aid to the initiation of political reforms by recipient countries. This shift from economic conditionalities, as espoused by the Bretton Woods institutions, to political conditionalities or the simultaneous application of both in determining who qualified for aid was prompted by the admission that good governance is essential to sustained economic growth.

From the onset of 1990, the policy of political conditionality was applied resolutely in Sub-Saharan Africa (SSA). The former colonial powers set the tone when in January and again in March, Jacques Pelletier, the French Minister for Co-operation and Development painted a gloomy picture of SSA development in the absence of democratic governance. He encouraged African countries to draw lessons from the rebirth of democracy in Eastern Europe and hinted that France was prepared to rally to the side of those 'who made and continue to make the necessary reforms' (Nelson and Eglinton 1992:16).[7] Again, a declaration at the end of the June 1990 La Baule Francophone summit meeting stressed 'the need to associate the relevant population more closely with the construction of their political, social and economic future'. He emphasised that additional aid would be granted to countries that embark on such political reforms. In informal discussions, President Mitterrand had also intimated that 'the sooner you organise free elections, the better it will be for the youth of your countries who need to express themselves' (Decalo 1992:20).

The British position on the new conditionality was articulated by its Foreign Secretary, Douglas Hurd, in June 1990 when he noted that satisfactory economic and social progress in Africa was contingent on improved political freedom and better governance. He called on major aid donors to 'look out for opportunities to support countervailing sources of power where it makes sense to do so...[8] A year later, a speech by Mrs Lynda Chalker, Minister of State for Foreign and Commonwealth Affairs, expatiated on Britain's position on political conditionality by stressing that the macro-economic policy reforms purveyed by the Bretton Woods institutions, though necessary are insufficient. The thrust of British policy would henceforth aim at promoting pluralistic systems which would, 'ensure financial accountability and freedom from political interference so that corruption and nepotism can be avoided'. In short, among others, current British bilateral aid programmes was to support 'democratic and other structural reforms'.[9]

Similarly, the US Agency for International Development (USAID) reflected the US policy-position by noting that allocation of funds to individual countries would take into consideration progress toward democratisation; that it was the US' view that:

open societies that value individual rights, respect the rule of law, and have open and accountable governments provide better opportunities for sustained economic development than do closed systems which stifle individual initiative.[10]

The US would therefore insist on democracy being placed on an equal footing with progress towards economic reforms and the establishment of a market-oriented economy. Given the history of the US government, at least until the late 1980s, as one which was noted for its unflinching support of authoritarian anti-Communist regimes, it is arguable that the changed global political situation enabled the US also to give unflinching support to the social forces agitating for democratisation in other parts of the world.

German concerns, which took shape in 1991, emphasized democratisation side by side with reduced expenditure on arms. In the same year, the Netherlands stressed on improved observation of fundamental human rights as the basis for its aid support. Along with the promotion of democracy and respect for human rights, Japanese officials stressed that the reduction of arms production as well as the pursuit of market oriented policies will be taken into account in granting aid.[11] Clearly, therefore, the major donors had shifted emphasis onto the need for recipient countries to change their mode of governance. Naturally, since most of the developing countries had become dependent on foreign assistance, few could resist the donor insistence for democratic changes. It must be stressed, however, that some of these new policy commitments by the World Bank and bilateral donors were not easily translated into action. Therefore, the idea of good governance remained mainly in theory. The French, for example, (especially after Baule) were quite flexible on the question of democratic transition. Furthermore, they were prepared to tolerate the emergence of regimes whose claims to democracy were extremely doubtful.

Implications for Policy Debate in Ghana

What then were the implications of donors' position as highlighted above on policy debate in Ghana with regard to the transition? Some problems encountered in the course of dealing with this question must first be pointed out. First, the PNDC's lack of public acknowledgement of any form of external pressure with regard to the decision to democratise makes it difficult to assess the degree of external influence on the transition process, especially when almost every policy was presented as 'home grown'. In the circumstances, one can merely speculate on the extent of external influence on the transition process. Second, much of the external pressure was exerted through 'quiet' diplomacy. This prevented public scrutiny of issues discussed and arguments raised. As a result, explicit documentary evidence of external pressure(s) could not be easily found. Third, for political reasons, the government did not want to portray itself as complying with donor pressures. The objective was to make it appear as if the transition process was wholly out of the PNDC's volition. Finally, several attempts to get information on this sensitive issue of external pressure from official sources failed basically because of the unwillingness of government officials and representatives of donor countries to open up.

Between 1990 and 1993, it was clear that the insistence by donors on good governance influenced the democratisation process in Ghana for a number of reasons. Ghana, as an aid dependent country, could not insulate itself from pressures emanating from the donor community. Due to the adoption of SAP, the PNDC's dependence on external assistance was almost total. For example, assistance to Ghana under the PNDC which was channelled through the Paris Club averaged US$420 million a year in 1984-1986 and US$740 million a year between 1987-1989. The PNDC's drawings on loans increased from approximately US$272.6 million in 1983 to US$426.8 million in 1988. Heavy dependence on external aid had also increased the nation's external debt burden. In 1980, the total external debt stock stood at US$1.4 billion which was approximately 32 per cent of GNP. This increased to US$2.7 billion in 1986 to US$4.3 billion in 1992. According to the World Bank, the ratio of external debt to GNP rose to 49 per cent in 1986 and 63.1 per cent in 1992.[12] This level of dependence obviously made the PNDC vulnerable to external pressure.

It is equally true that the World Bank/IMF as well as other donors urgently needed an African success story with regard to the implementation of adjustment policies. Ghana provided this and therefore had some amount of bargaining power *vis-à-vis* the donors. For instance, in 1986 the board of the Fund had to soften its programmes for Ghana because the PNDC was having major political problems.[13] But this was before the collapse of communism, and the 'infectious' democratisation process which was directly or indirectly accelerated by the imposition of conditionalities by the international donor community. Though one cannot underestimate the bargaining advantage of the PNDC (on account of its successful implementation of adjustment policies), this advantage was not substantial. It was, for example, clear that sanctions could have been applied as in the case of Kenya, Malawi, Benin and recently Nigeria, had the PNDC acted contrary to the expectations of the donors.

The political debate prior to, and after the elections of November-December 1992 also revealed the extent of the influence of the donors on the democratisation process. Hence, it was not by accident that the nature of the economy did not feature significantly in the campaign debates of the various parties. For instance, the New Patriotic Party (NPP) in its manifesto skirted the market-oriented policies of the PNDC with the only major bone of contention being the role of private enterprises in national development, and not the implementation of adjustment policies *per se* A leading member of the NPP affirmed this when he noted in a post-election interview noted that '...we just want to prove to the western nations who have put so much money into (P)NDC ERP-SAP that when we are given the chance we will do better than Rawlings and his people. We want them to have confidence in us'.[14] Clearly, the contestants for political power were conscious about the urgent need to appease the western donor community. This gave the PNDC further advantage in the transition politics, especially with regard to the assurance that it would vigorously pursue the economic adjustment programme. Its campaign slogan of 'continuity' (though nebulous), was intended to emphasise this and to bait the donor community to its side. Clearly, the PNDC was adept at reading the signals for change. It had a very good idea about what would please the donors. In this connection its decision to democratise could only be described as a shrewd pre-emptive strategy. In so doing it could soften the various pressures, both external and internal, for political change.

One area which the PNDC exploited fully was foreign aid for the conduct of democratic elections. As noted earlier, the World Bank in particular and the donor community in general, needed a success story to demonstrate the potency, efficiency, relevance, and the need for pursuing adjustment policies in a democratic setting. We now turn to a discussion of this form of assistance.

Direct External Assistance

In March 1991, the National Commission for Democracy (NCD) (established since 1982) which had been commissioned by the PNDC to organise regional fora on the political future of the nation submitted its report titled *Evolving a True Democracy* to the PNDC government. Based on the NCD report, a committee of Constitutional Experts was set up to work out proposals for a draft constitution. In July 1991 the committee of constitutional experts submitted its draft constitutional proposal to the government. Following this a Consultative Assembly, which was to draft a new constitution based on the work of the committee of constitutional experts, was also constituted.

The NCD report had, among others, recommended that there should be a new body to handle elections because serious concern had been expressed about the NCD's impartiality as well as its ability to conduct free and fair elections. Consequently, PNDC Law 271 dated 11 November 1991 established the Interim National Electoral Commission (INEC) to conduct the referendum on a draft constitution, as well as the presidential and parliamentary elections which followed in November-December of the same year. In the meantime, funds to implement the projected programme of democratisation had become a serious problem. The PNDC seems to have created the impression that without enough international donor support it would be difficult to proceed with the democratisation project. This was unusual because the availability of finance did not become much of a problem in the earlier transitions of 1969 and 1979. At any rate, the manner in which the PNDC portrayed the need for international support was instrumental in garnering sufficient donor commitment towards the transition.

The international community started helping the process from its embryonic stages. In April 1991, Dr. Kwesi Botchwey, the Secretary for Finance and Economic Planning and Lynn Wallis, the resident Director of the UNDP, signed a project sponsorship agreement to support the committee of constitutional experts in their work of drafting Ghana's new constitution. This was in the form of direct financial support involving an amount of $225,000. The purpose was to strengthen the capabilities of Ghana in its attempt to evolve a new constitutional order as part of its democratisation process.[15] This initial financial support from the UNDP enabled the government to push through the transition programme following the approval of the 1992 Constitution in the referendum of 28 April 1992. This success seems to have set the tone for further appeals to' the international donor community for support of various kind.

The newly established INEC took it as part of its responsibility to complement governmental appeals by approaching potential donors to obtain various forms of assistance in order to carry out the presidential and parliamentary elections. The assumption, in our opinion, appears to be that since the international community favoured democracy, it was its responsibility to help in its realisation. However, as noted above, it is likely that the quick response by the donor community was motivated by the desire to ensure that the Ghanaian model of successful economic adjustment would be translated into a peaceful transition to democracy. Therefore Rawlings' open antipathy towards multi-party democracy would not deter the donor community from providing the necessary financial support for the transition programme.

It may be argued that the same justification encouraged the Friedreich Ebert Stiftung (FES), a Germany NGO, to sponsor two studies under the auspices of the research department of the NCD to ascertain the political attitude of Ghanaians. This was done before the NCD instituted the regional fora on the same issue. The result of the studies formed an important part of the NCD report to the PNDC to the effect that many Ghanaians were in favour of multi-party democracy. FES followed up after the establishment of the Consultative Assembly with the organisation of weekend seminars on the modalities for making a democratic constitution.

Another kind of international support was in the form of sponsored studies of the Ghanaian electoral system. In response to requests by INEC, the International Foundation for Electoral Systems (IFES) came to Ghana to conduct a study of the electoral system. Its report titled, *Ghana: A Pre-Election Assessment*, submitted on 1 June 1992, was made possible by a grant from the United States Agency for International Development (USAID). From 22 April through 8 May 1992, the IFES team carried out its survey and in its recommendation drew attention, among others, to the need for an international observer team to oversee Ghana's elections. The IFES team also recommended a complete re-registration of voters.[16] In response to this, INEC submitted a budget of $2,849,908 for the re-registration exercise. IFES made a further recommendation for US assistance of $680,000 towards the re-registration exercise. Unfortunately, these requests were not granted by the US government.[17]

The Danish International Development Agency (DANIDA) also carried out another pre-election study between 1-16 September 1992. The Danish Embassy in Ghana felt that in addition to the assistance already given towards the democratisation process (see below) there was the need to assess the preparation towards the election and identify additional needs. Its final report covered all the preparations made for the presidential and parliamentary elections. The team recommended an urgent Identity Card Feasibility study. The purpose of this study was to have a thorough in-depth analysis of the various aspects and problems connected with the introduction of a national Identification Card system. This was in order to avoid various problems posed by the existing register of voters.

Other forms of assistance for the democratisation process from the international community were worked out between the representatives of the donor community in Ghana and INEC. Under the new package, the major part of donor support came in the form of financial assistance. This covered areas such as the training of election personnel for all levels of the electoral process, the provision of necessary hardware, and the publication of educational materials. A summary of various forms of assistance provided by the donor community is provided in Appendix IV.

Without doubt, the international donor community went to a great extent to help in establishing democratic governance in Ghana through direct financial support. Surprisingly, the United States, apart from the earlier support channelled through USAID for the IFES study and the provision of an amount of $25,000, did not commit additional funds to support the transition programme. The US's withdrawal of additional support may be due to the fact that in contrast to the European Community, its relations with the Rawlings regime were not very good for most of the 1980s.[18]

At best, the role of the US in the process was controversial. Most probably, the US was peeved by its inability to get the government of Ghana to embark on a new re-registration exercise in accordance with the suggestions contained in the final report of IFES. The aspects of the IFES report on what should be done to the voters register ran counter to the original US position reached after a donor's conference held at the US embassy. At the conference, the US seemed initially to have supported the view that due to financial and time constraints, the controversial voters register should be exhibited and purged of 'ghost' names. However, the IFES recommendation for a complete re-registration on the grounds that it 'is the single most important task to be completed prior to the administration of truly competitive elections'[19] seemed to have persuaded the US government later on. According to IFES, donor assistance to finalise the re-registration process would have served several important purposes such as:

a) remove a potentially contentious issue from the area of conflict;

b) make a substantial contribution to ensuring the freedom and fairness of the impending elections;

c) strengthen the independence of INEC;

d) demonstrate the US interest in the Ghanaian election process, thereby countering the impression given the IFES team in several interviews that the US government was reluctant to support a process that could unseat a 'stable' military regime.[20]

Perhaps the US was much concerned with the last two recommendations, and especially the last one. It would appear, therefore, that when it became evident that the PNDC was not prepared to embark on a new registration exercise it had no option but to refuse to give additional financial support.

International Election Observers

Another significant input made by the international donor community in support of Ghana's democratisation process was the provision of election observers. It must be stated that even though traditionally international monitoring of election has been associated with 'conflict resolution process at the conclusion of a liberation struggle or a civil war' (Anglin 1990:12), the services of observer teams have in recent times become more and more utilised by countries undergoing democratic transitions.

In the Ghanaian case, several opposition groups, members of the Consultative Assembly, the PNDC and INEC were all in favour of international observer teams.[21] The reason seems to be the prevailing air of mistrust in countries undergoing transition to democracy. In such circumstances endorsement by the international community has the value of conferring legitimacy and integrity on the electoral process. Larry Garber points out that an international election observer team may be sent for a number of reasons. These include:

a) ensuring that an independent, impartial and objective report evaluating the electoral process in a particular country is prepared;

b) to encourage participation in the electoral process by undertaking to report any significant manipulation of the electoral process; and,

c) to assist in ensuring the integrity of the electoral process (Garber 1984:13).

For these reasons (and more especially because of the apprehension expressed by Ghana's opposition groups that the elections could be rigged by the government, two main international observer teams— The Commonwealth Observer Group (COG) and the Carter Center — officially monitored the elections. Even though other nations such as Canada and organisations such as the Dakar based CODESRIA sent observer teams, non could officially report on the conduct of the election because their monitoring was not official.

Developments After the Presidential Election

The presidential election results of 3 November 1993 was the subject of dispute between the opposition parties, especially the NPP, on the one hand and the government and the INEC, on the other. Their main contention was that the election was rigged and the results officially manipulated. Consequently, complaints were lodged with the INEC. The opposition groups expected the electoral commission to resolve the issues before declaring the results. When this was not done, the opposition groups, led by the NPP, refused to participate in the parliamentary election which was then scheduled for 8 December 1993.

The claims of the opposition group ran counter in many respects to the reports of the international observer teams which sanctioned the conduct of the election as being 'free and fair'. Though the 73 page COG election report referred to the presidential election as 'a model of its kind' and noted further that none of them 'has ever witnessed a poll of such manifest transparency'[22] the report of the Carter Center was more cautious and made references to observed anomalies in the conduct of the election.

The decision of the opposition parties to boycott the parliamentary elections prompted the donor community to intervene in an attempt to persuade the parties to back out of the boycott threat. For instance, the EC ambassadors met the leaders of the opposition parties with a view to persuading them to participate in the parliamentary elections. Almost all of them were not in favour of the decision to boycott the elections. Consequently, on 18 November 1992, the British High Commission, in the UK's capacity as the president of the EC issued the following press release.

> The European Community, and its member states welcome the declaration of the international electoral observer teams that the presidential elections were broadly free and fair. The election represents a major step towards the restoration of democratic government in Ghana. They also welcome the fact that election campaigning and the elections themselves were generally free from political violence. They urge all parties to work together to ensure completion of a peaceful transition to constitutional democratic government.[23]

These interventions, including a similar appeal by the United States, fell on deaf ears.

After the parliamentary elections the donor community concentrated on ensuring that both the government and opposition parties co-operated to ensure the success of the country's fledgling democracy. For instance, Douglas Hurd, the British Foreign Secretary appealed to the opposition parties to play a meaningful role in the new constitutional era. At a meeting with the Chairman of the PNDC and other top government officials held on 4 January 1993, he identified three institutional frameworks where the opposition could fruitfully co-operate to ensure the success of democracy in Ghana. These, he said, were the courts, the press and parliament. Since the boycott effectively denied the opposition a voice in parliament, Hurd was of the view that the opposition could still participate in the affairs of the nation through the other avenues. He further called for 'genuine dialogue' between the government and the opposition on the political situation in the country.[24] It is not accidental that the opposition parties, especially the NPP, have successfully kept the government on its toes through the press and the courts.

Finally, it is probable that as a result of another threat by the opposition to boycott the 1996 elections if voter identification cards were not provided some donor countries, notably, the US and Denmark, initiated a series of meetings in the last week of March 1994 with the government, the National Electoral Commission (NEC) and the main opposition parties, on the issue of voter identification cards and related matters. Even though the stage reached in the negotiations between the government, representatives of political parties, and some donors on the vexed question of voter identification cards is yet to be officially communicated to Ghanaians, Mr. Kwame Afreh, (then Deputy Chairman of the National Electoral Commission) could announce that the US had agreed to provide $6.6 million towards the provision of voter identification cards in preparation for the elections of 1996. Mr. Afreh further announced that the European Union was prepared to provide transparent ballot boxes.[25] The expectations were that other donors might pick up part of the bill to ensure the provision of identification cards for voters.

Conclusion

Ghana's transition has been marked by very unique features. In the first place, unlike earlier military regimes, the PNDC was a reluctant convert to multi-party democracy. The most distinct feature, however, was the concerted efforts made by the government through INEC to obtain external funding in support of the process. Compared to previous transitions, the current one has received unprecedented financial assistance from the international community. This raises doubts about whether or not the PNDC would have proceeded with the transition programme without such massive external assistance. Opinion on this naturally differ. For sure, there was a domestic component to the pressure to democratise. However, there are those who, on the basis of the immediate history of the PNDC, are quick to note that but for the external financial support the transition process would have been still-born. Those who argue along these lines contend that the PNDC would have used the 'no money ploy' to either unduly delay the process or abort it altogether. After all, Rawlings is on record to have openly expressed his antipathy to multi-party democracy. Accordingly the decision to initiate political reforms towards multiparty democracy and conduct democratic elections was surely due to the external pressure which mounted rapidly in the late 1980s: the imposition of political conditionality finally overcame Rawlings' intransigence on the need for political reforms. Significantly, the PNDC's own democratic reforms which hinged on the creation of district level political authorities were not intended to establish a liberal democratic regime but a populist one. Therefore, it was the growing external pressure that forced it to concede to the demands for democratic reforms.

On the other hand, there are others who strongly believe that the government would have democratised all the same. They point to the fact that the PNDC organised the regional fora, which paved the way for the transition process, out of its volition. The various structures and measures necessary to effect the transition process, including the district assemblies, were voluntarily put in place by the PNDC. And so the establishment of democratic institutions and a democratic atmosphere was just a question of time. What is not recognised by the proponents of this view, however, is that the PNDC went through years of feet-dragging even to the last minute, and did so in spite of sporadic agitations for democracy. One major determining factor in the PNDC's political calculation, however, was its growing concern about the legitimacy of its continued rule. Having convinced itself of the inevitability of democratisation, the PNDC was quick to accede to the demands for political reforms as a means of securing its rule through democratic means and thereby, solve once and for all the vexed question of legitimacy.[26]

The next major question is related to the rapid response by the donor community. Was it borne out of genuine concern for the political transformation of Ghana? Were donors motivated by a hidden agenda? From any angle one looks at this, the inescapable fact remains that the donor community had a big stake in Ghana's transition. As noted earlier, Ghana under Rawlings was touted as a success story with regard to the implementation of hydra-headed WB-IMF SAP policies. Essentially, the donor community was interested in ensuring that this success story would not be jeopardised by a failed political transition. Surely, the implications of failure were dreaded. Thus, Jaycox, the World Bank official in charge of Africa, could not mince words when commenting on the subject:

> If they (World Bank) fail in a series of countries...then it is a failure of our approach to the economy, a failure of an institution, a failure of our political will, and there is no way that we'll be able to say that it is just a failure of Africa! So we have a very big stake in this.[27]

No wonder that few months after the transition to democracy, Ghana received a commitment of $2.1 billion in assistance for 1993-1994 at a donor's conference in Paris chaired by the World Bank. This commitment, in our view, was an absolute vote of confidence in the adjustment programme and an endorsement of the democratic transition irrespective of the queries raised by the opposition on the integrity of the process.

But there was another equally relevant consideration. In view of current global political and economic changes, the donor community must have been motivated by the imperative for global political stability which is necessary for the health of the global economy. As explained by John Holmes of the Canadian High Commission, 'donors value the political stability of the nation because it is through this that any fruitful and mutually rewarding relationship that could lead to development could be forged'.[28]

This position rhymes with Barber Conable's assertion in 1990 that:

> ...the political uncertainty and arbitrariness evident in so many parts of Sub-Saharan Africa are a major constraint on the region's development. Investors will not take risks, entrepreneurs will not be creative, people will not participate — if they feel they are facing capricious, unjust or hostile political environment.[29]

Apparently, all this meant the need to support friendly, howbeit, autocratic governments provided such governments were willing to undergo some kind of political reform. In the Ghanaian case, this produced the miracle of self-succession by the PNDC which logically raises questions about the nature of the country's transition to democracy.

Notes

1. See *Africa Confidential*, Vol. 31, No. 2, 1990, p.2.

2. See for example Samuel Decalo, 'The Process, Prospects and Constraints of Democratisation in Africa', in *African Affairs*, Vol. 91, No.362, January 1992, pp.7-35; Eboe Hutchful, 'The International Dimensions of the Democratisation Process in Africa', Paper presented at CODESRIA 7th General Assembly, 10-14 February, 1992; Michael Bratton and Nicholas van de Walle, 'Towards Governance in Africa: Popular Demands and State Responses', in Goran Hyden and Michael Bratton (ed.), *Governance and Politics in Africa*, Lynne Rienner Publishers, Boulder and London, 1992, pp. 27-55.

3. For further details on this point, see Claude E. Welch, 'The Dilemma of Military Withdrawal from Politics: Some Considerations from Tropical Africa', *African Studies Review*, xvii (April 1974).

4. For aspects of this controversy, see *Good Government?* IDS Bulletin, Vol.24, No.1, Jan. 1993.

5. Cited in Carol Lancaster, ' Governance and Development: The Views from Washington', in *Good Government? IDS Bulletin*, Vol. 24, No.1, January, 1993.

6. Ibid.

7. Nelson, J. M. and Eglinton, S. J., 1992, 'Encouraging Democracy: What Role for Conditioned Aid?' Policy Essay No. 4, Overseas Development Council, Washington, DC.

8. Nelson and Eglinton (1992:20).

9. See Lynda Chalker, 'Good Governance and the Aid Programme', ODI Chatham House, London, June 25, 1991, reproduced in *Ashanti Pioneer*, August 22, 23 and 29 editions, 1991.

10. Nelson and Eglinton (1992:16-17).

11. Ibid.

12. For details on Ghana's current external debt situation and related issues see Charles Jebuni and Abena Oduro in this volume.

13. Matthew Martin, 'Negotiating Adjustment and External Finance: Ghana and the International Community, 1982-89', in Donald Rothchild (ed.)*Ghana: The Political Economy of Recovery*, Lynne Rienner Publishers, Boulder and London, 1991, pp.249 and 256.

14. See *The Ghanaian Voice*, 25/27 October, 1993.

15. UNDP Project Doc. GHA/91/004/A/01/99.

16. See International Foundation for Electoral Systems (IFES) Report- *Ghana: A Pre-election Assessment*, 1st June 1992, p.45.

17. Several visits to the US Embassy and the offices of USAID to ascertain why the US government declined the IFES request proved futile.

18. For detailed information on Ghana-US relations in the 1980s, see Kwame Boafo-Arthur, ' Ghana's External relations Since 31st December, 1981', in E. Gyimah-Boadi (ed.) *Ghana Under PNDC Rule*, CODESRIA Books, 1993.

19. IFES report, *op.cit.*, p.45.

20. Ibid., p.19.

21. IFES report, *op.cit.*, p. 40.

22. Commonwealth Secretariat, *Report on the Presidential Election in Ghana*, 3rd Nov. 1992, pp.63 and 72.

23. EC Press Release, No. 2, 18th November, 1992.

24. Record of Meeting between the Chairman of the PNDC and the British Foreign Secretary on Jan. 4th, 1993. See also *Daily Graphic*, Jan. 5th 1993.

25. See *Daily Graphic*, 4th May, 1994, p.3.

26. For a perceptive discussion on the question of PNDC's legitimacy crisis, see Kwame A. Ninsin, 'The PNDC and the Problem of Legitimacy', in Rothchild (ed.) *op.cit.*, pp.49-67.

27. Cited in Thomas M. Callaghy, 'Towards State Capability and Embedded Liberalism in the Third World: Lessons for Adjustment', in Joan Nelson (ed.) *Fragile Coalition: The Politics of Economic Adjustment*, Transaction Books, Oxford, 1989, p.135.

28. Interview with John Holmes (on March 2, 1993) who was the First Secretary of the Canadian High Commission before his re-posting.

29. Barber Conable, quoted in Adebayo Olukoshi, 'The World Bank, Structural Adjustment and Governance in Africa: Some Reflections', mimeo, Dakar, CODESRIA, 1992, p.5.

8

The Press and the Transition to Multi-Party Democracy in Ghana

Kwame Karikari

Introduction

Just as the press was central to the anti-colonial movement, so has it always played a critical role in the struggles for a pluralist political order based on a multi-party parliamentary democracy in Ghana. It has always been an indispensable ideological and mobilising factor in the struggles against authoritarian political rule. However, its efforts have been as short-lived as the pluralist political regime it has espoused; because prior to the 1992 multi-party elections, Ghana's 35 years post-colonial history had altogether only about 10 years in which the independent press could operate freely. The rest were characterised by one party 'socialist' rule and military regimes under which, by legislation and or extra-legal means, the state monopolised the media and restricted press freedom and pluralism. The quarter-century of authoritarian rule and corresponding authoritarian control of the press included eleven years under the Provisional National Defence Council (PNDC) of Flt. Lt. J.J. Rawlings, (1981-1992) the longest reign by any post-colonial regime.

This paper discusses the resurgence, character, and problems of the press; its contribution to the restoration of multi-party constitutional politics in Ghana, and to the advancement of democratic ideas from 1990 to 1992, a period that saw the revival of a vigorous independent press activity. The paper focuses on the print media, though where necessary some reference is made to the broadcasting media.

Background — Press and Constitutional Development

Ghana's independence (Order in Council, 1957) and first republican (1960) constitutions made no explicit provision for press freedom beyond general references to 'freedom of conscience'. The only constitutional provision that comes closer to our concern could be found in Article 13(1) of the 1960 Constitution which stated:

> Subject to such restrictions as may be necessary for preserving public order, morality or health, no person should be deprived of freedom of religion or speech, of the right to move and assembly without hindrance or the right to courts of law.

Bennion's (1962) interpretation is that this provision included freedom of 'speech' through the media of mass communication. The 1969 Constitution introduced explicit provisions guaranteeing press freedom and press pluralism (Article 22). The 1979 Constitution went beyond these guarantees in Article 28, explicitly prohibited the enactment of any laws requiring licensing for publishing newspapers (Article 93), and introduced the Press Commission (Articles 192-195) which was empowered to take measures to preserve press freedom, protect journalists from external interference and also protect citizens from abuses by the press.

As far as the independent, privately-owned press is concerned, the two intervening multi-party regimes, the 1969-72 regime under Busia's Progressive Party, and the 1979-81 regime under Limann's People's National Party generally adhered to the liberal constitutional provisions on press freedom. Nonetheless, they also showed varying degrees of intolerance of independent judgement by editorial managements of the state-owned press, especially when the latter expressed positions which went contrary to the regimes' perspectives on issues of politics and economic policy. They also showed the tendency to place in editorial chairs of the state-owned press journalists who were politically sympathetic.

But by far the most pernicious legal instrument against press pluralism and freedom has been the various newspaper licensing laws and decrees enacted over the past several years. The first one, the 1963[1] newspaper licensing law legalising state monopoly under the Nkrumah government was repealed by the multi-party parliament in 1970. It was resurrected in

1973,[2] repealed again in 1979, and was restored again by the PNDC in 1985 (PNDC Law 211). The re-enactment of the newspaper licensing law in the latter periods, both by military regimes, revived the discretionary powers of the Minister (Commissioner or Secretary) for Information to interfere with the establishment and operation of the press when the latter expressed views contrary to the regimes' own views regarding matters of politics and economic policy.

Throughout its history, however, the Ghanaian press has been marked by a short life span explained by low readership (due mainly to widespread illiteracy and low incomes), poor advertising climate, and very limited investment capital. Before independence, colonial laws and economic factors significantly retarded the development of the independent press;[3] after independence the 'interventionist' politics of the post-colonial state account primarily for the fact that only four papers founded before independence have survived — and precariously so — up to now. Of these, three are church-owned: *The Standard* which is owned by the Catholic Church, *The Christian Messenger*, which is owned by the Presbyterian Church of Ghana and is over 100 years old, and *The Methodist Times*. The fourth is the Kumasi-based *Pioneer* whose 57 years of existence have been scarred by banning orders, censorship, libel suits, and the detention and exile of editors.

The *Pioneer* was the first casualty of the first post-colonial regime's propensity to curtail press pluralism and editorial independence. The paper was banned in 1962,[4] five years after independence, in favour of party and state monopoly of the press. It was a logical development in that regime's one-party socialist scheme. For President Kwame Nkrumah, the justification for finally limiting press freedom after 1961, was that:

> This was not freedom of expression. This was irresponsible license, and if allowed to continue unbridled, it would have undermined our state, our independence and the people's faith in themselves and their capacities (Nkrumah 1963:76).

The Political Background

Ghana has had most of the regime types that have characterised the post-colonial state in Africa: one-party 'socialist'; (advocacy for) 'no-party' system of government; conservative/right-wing military junta; variations of radical populist military juntas; and a 'liberal' multi-party constitutional regime. The tendency of all these types has been to maintain, at varying degrees, a docile state-owned press and, to varying degrees, muzzle the independent press even as they have all or mostly ridden to power largely or partially by exploiting the militancy of the independent press. The two liberal multi-party regimes (Busia 1969-72; Limann 1979-81) that have shown relative tolerance for a pluralist press were short-lived. But they too showed evidence of the 'interventionist' tendency of the state in post-colonial Africa which manifests itself in 'attempts to curtail and restrict the social life of citizens, often employing the most draconian and sometimes petty means available' in order to effect an overwhelming presence in social, economic and political life of the people (Goulbourne 1987:26-47).

It is however, the country's military regimes which have shown the most blatant disposition towards press control and repression. The military's propensity to suppress press pluralism and monopolise media practice is due, among others, to the greater need they have for the media as instrument for building public support, mobilising legitimacy, and securing acceptance for their policies. This dependency syndrome is itself the result of their political weakness — the lack of a tangible political base in the form of mass civil organisations such as political parties which might articulate them to civil society. It is also due partly to the prevailing military culture which thrives on a top-down communication system. This authoritarian culture is compatible with the mass media's essentially or top-down method of operation. Hence, the government-controlled, state-owned media became an easy and natural target of control by military regimes (Karikari 1990). Once the public sector media are controlled those elements of the private-sector press which insist on expressing independent — especially critical and opposing views — automatically court repression. Therefore, under the military regimes, the potential for conflict with the press, especially those in the private sector, is extremely high.

It seems, though, that the overall objective of authoritarian control of the state-owned press, that is, as an instrument for perpetuating the political and other interests of significant sections of the privileged social groups, does not diminish much with a change in regime from military to civilian. For, despite the wide differences of forms and in the levels of intervention which the state-owned press experience between military and multi-party regimes, the social class orientation of these press has tended to remain the same under both types of political regime. The state-owned press under both regime-types marginalises the rural (peasant) populations and urban working classes in overall news coverage and editorial perspectives. The implication here for popular democratic involvement is obvious. According to Twumasi,

> It is becoming increasingly clear that our newspapers are being used by the well-connected in underwriting the privileged status of urban social classes — politicians, and administrative, military and professional elites ... But the elitist orientation of the press possibly hinders the use of our newspapers for development (Twumasi 1985).

Thus, on one hand, state media under military authoritarian rule inhibit and disrupt expressions of pluralist ideas; and on the other, the same media under multi-party government tend, or appear to provide the means for expressing pluralistic views. However, under both political conditions the working classes and the rural poor are not adequately represented. The reason is that journalists and editors represent and/or are oriented to the class viewpoint of the ruling groups in the country; and the 'pluralism' of the media under liberal constitutional conditions tend to be the expression of varying and contrasting viewpoints of members of these ruling groups. This shows that the press, even under constitutional political regimes, would hardly articulate or make room in their columns for articulating the political perspectives of the marginalised social classes in the discourses on 'democracy' both during the transitions from authoritarianism to liberal constitutionalism; and after.

The PNDC and the Press

State repression attained its apogee under the PNDC government. It was so far, the only government that used systematically the death penalty (and secret executions) as a weapon against political opponents of all types. Its initial populist rhetoric notwithstanding, that government established the most authoritarian regime compared with the record of earlier military governments. This government pursued the most right-wing economic policy in which the role of the state in the economy was rejected on ideological and political grounds. It pursued the same dependency economic development policy with greater zeal and courage than its predecessors ever did. In a manner that is consistent with current policy practice in Africa, the government pursued a conservative economic policy — structural adjustment programme — under close supervision of the IMF and the World Bank.

The principal premise of its economic policy was the expansion of primary and extractive commodity production for export, dependence on foreign consumer imports, destruction of local manufacture— in sum the rehabilitation and strengthening of the colonial economic structure and production relations. The social crisis which this policy produced and its political ramifications led to greater political control and repression. The result was the narrowing of the boundaries of political freedom.

The government's dogged pursuit of the IMF/World Bank-led structural adjustment programme nonetheless earned it the adulation of Western donors, which repeatedly cited Ghana as a model of economic progress (Anyang' Nyong'o 1987). Under such conditions, it was not possible to expect a democratic attitude towards the press.

In social terms, the PNDC regime, represented or facilitated the rise to ascendancy of what Mafeje (1995) has described as 'a new class of compradors', who 'try their best to ingratiate themselves with the World Bank and to give its Structural Adjustment Programme in Africa a larger lease of life'. Though 'less nationalistic, more pro-West,' the important characteristic of this new comprador class in Ghana is that its members showed neither inclination nor pretension to 'espouse some naive and anachronistic ideas about liberal democracy'. Rawlings himself not infrequently pronounced his aversion to constitutional democracy.

The operation of the press under the PNDC government was conditioned by three broad factors:

i. the authoritarian political environment;

ii. the wide discretionary or interventionist powers of the office of the Secretary (Minister) for Information, and

iii. The *Newspaper Licensing Law 1985* (PNDC Law 211), which gave legal backing to and systematised the arbitrariness inherent in the PNDC regime.

In times of authoritarian rule, the media are first in the line of attack: journalists are intimidated, repressed, or co-opted. However, the press does not become submissive as a result of legal restrictions and political repression alone. Just as the whole of society relapses into a 'culture of silence' in reaction to widespread state repression, so does the press often recoil into a shell of caution, self-censorship and, in several cases, sycophancy and acquiescence in an atmosphere of generalised persecution. Hence, on the PNDC's seizure of power, some independent newspapers voluntarily ceased publication in anticipation of the new regime's hostility towards the press. Some of such newspapers like *The Palaver*, were confiscated while others were forced to close down (e.g. *The Echo*) by organised groups of militant PNDC supporters who found the critical and uncompromising stance of those papers intolerable. The government undertook other high-handed measures against the press: the arrest and detention without trial of the publisher and editors of the *Free Press*; the arrest and imprisonment of reporters, and forced exile of a number of editors of both state-owned and the independent press; the unexplained and unprovoked dismissal of others in the state media, and the dismissal of others for their views. All of these were threatening enough to deter the press from taking inquiring and daring positions on public policy issues.

The PNDC's method of controlling the media involved strengthening the hands of the Secretary (Minister) for Information, as well as setting up, almost parallel to the Minister's office, a semi-official body which combined oversight as well as elements of censorship and policing of the press — the Castle Information Bureau (CIB). For example:

> Much of the use of the editorial page (of the state-owned media) to curb expression of critical and contrary opinion under the PNDC has been laid at the doors of the Castle Information Bureau, a body whose existence has objectively paralleled (and perhaps contested) the supervisory authority of the office of the Ministry of Information, and has been used to prod editors into line without the administrative encumbrances of a ministry (Karikari 1990).

The CIB was set up in the office of the PNDC Chairman without any enabling law. It acted as both a quasi-censorship board and propaganda unit, and a watchdog to ensure press subservience to the regime. It seems also to have been set up as a counter to the control of the management of major state-owned media which was then under 'leftist' elements in the regime. The CIB's role became increasingly insidious after Rawlings' public denunciation of the leftist editorial heads of the media in March

1983.[5] For instance, it manufactured a number of readers' letters and editorials in the state-owned press; these were then used to intimidate critics in and outside the press, and generally curtail freedom of the press and expression.[6]

This arrangement guaranteed for the government loyalty and complete subservience from the press. The Secretary for Information, aware of the countervailing power of the CIB, could ill-afford to encourage the development of independent attitudes, and/or harbour any tendency to cultivate independent thought and viewpoint among the media practitioners and editorial leaders. Editors, who were aware of the various centres of power, and that several policing agencies existed to enforce unquestionable submission, could only remain loyal to the head of the PNDC government — J. J. Rawlings, who came to be referred to as the 'leader of the revolution'. Though press managers were aware of the Secretary's established authority, knowledge that the CIB was Rawlings' personal creation worked to discourage any tendency toward defiance of Rawlings' authority or dissent. This undermined the authority of the Secretary for Information; but it did not necessarily translate into an increase in the authority of the CIB. The latter existed at the caprice of Rawlings. It nonetheless created among the media both fear and scorn normally reserved for all censoring institutions.

One significant method of ensuring the Information Secretary's absolute loyalty was to keep the tenure of the office holder in a state of permanent insecurity. This made the Ministry of Information one place in the state bureaucracy with the highest turnover of appointees under the PNDC. During the first four years of the PNDC there were as many as five Secretaries.[7] The high turnover of managers of the state-owned Ghana Broadcasting Corporation (GBC) — whose radio broadcast reaches all corners of the country and is thus the most important mass medium — can also be explained as the PNDC government's insistence on absolute control of the media. In the decade of its rule up to the 1992 elections for constitutional pluralism, the PNDC chairman appointed six different chief executives of the GBC. For the state-owned *Daily Graphic*, it once appointed a member of the CIB as supervising editor.

The *Newspaper Licensing Law 1985* (PNDCL 211), was decreed at a time of widespread arbitrary detention of people expressing critical views, and wanton execution of others for allegedly plotting against the regime. The law demanded that anyone wishing to publish a newspaper or magazine should obtain a licence from the Secretary for Information. It also empowered the Secretary to revoke the licence of a newspaper publisher and/or suspend the publication of a newspaper for an indefinite period. The result of this draconian law was the growth of a private press which was dominated by tabloids that specialised in reporting quasi-pornographic stories, mysticism, superstition, sports, and lottery as the only publishable issues. It is remarkable that the Secretary for Information justified this decree on grounds of safeguarding 'journalistic standards'.

Generally, the authorities used this law to abort attempts to start new papers.[8] *The Revolutionary Banner*, a weekly newspaper of the Ghanaian left, ceased publication soon after its publisher — the June Four Movement, a former ally of the military government, came into conflict with the regime and its members were either sent into prison or forced into exile. Between 1987 and 1989, the nascent independent press employed methods of coping with such hostile conditions, including an ingenious and cunning method of journalism: sports commentaries acquired serious political undertones, sometimes couched in aesopean/satirical terms, and aimed at sending a protest message to the government. Because of the prevailing oppressive environment, for the most part of the 10 years that the PNDC government was in power there were only three private secular newspapers of any significance — *The Pioneer*, published in Kumasi and *The Echo* and *Ghanaian Voice* which were published in Accra.

Admittedly, there was also a number of mimeographed periodical publications which, though short-lived, were put out by several community and workplace mass organisations largely spawned by and supportive of the PNDC. One of such mimeographed publications was by the Bank of Ghana Workers Defence Committee. But these were either sycophantic, insignificant, or both.

By 1990, however, this authoritarian regime was wearing thin, and several private newspapers were appearing on the scene even though they exercised a great deal of caution in their editorial positions and news reporting; but they gradually came out to pose questions which were very critical to the regime. This spirit of re- awakening among the press was a direct outcome and an intrinsic part of the movement for political liberalisation and pluralism which had been growing over the years and, which in August 1990, was galvanised by the formation of the Movement for Freedom and Justice (MFJ).

The Reform Movement

All political systems, irrespective of the subjective desire of their architects, are quite often shaped by the character of the processes that gave birth to them. According to Nsouankeu (1991) the outcome of the struggle for pluralist democratic reform in Africa between the late 1980s and early 1990s has so far followed one of the following broad patterns.

(a) negotiated between the incumbent regime and the organised opposition

(b) imposed by the struggles of popular forces, or

(c) imposed by the regime in power.

Ghana under Rawlings seems to have followed the third path. The Rawlings government could sense mounting dissension and imminent trial of strength between it and its opponents; it tactically seized the initiative and carried through political reforms without consulting the leadership of the reform movement. Furthermore, the activities of the reform movement were obstructed, and often suppressed.

As a result of such repressive environment the reform movement could not attain sufficient political strength and momentum. For example, it could only marginally attract to its fold the most politically organised and conscious political forces in society — the working classes of both urban and rural sectors. The MFJ which led the organised opposition and demanded political reforms, was an alliance of forces from radically different political orientations. It brought together representatives of all the political parties that had been suppressed by the Rawlings government, and of leftist groups, some of whom had earlier collaborated with the regime but had later been violently suppressed by it.

This alliance of existing political elites represented the broad spectrum of political ideas in the Ghanaian society. But it could not mobilise the social forces whose political weight could have enabled it to impose its programme on the transition process. Accordingly, apart from the organisation of students, the mass organisations of teachers, civil servants and of the working classes which had waged months of strikes and struggles for economic objectives in 1991-92, stayed outside the political alliance as well as from organised political struggles. Its political demands were couched in the traditional liberal democratic language; because, as indicated earlier, the alliance was dominated by representatives of the ruling groups whose political organisations had been suppressed by the regime immediately it seized power. Among their demands were the restoration of multi-party parliamentary government and constitutionalism with emphasis on the rule of law, freedom of association and of the press, religion and other traditional liberal political freedoms. As elsewhere in Africa, the movement hardly raised the need for locating the democratic state they envisaged in an equitable socio-economic framework. Clearly therefore, the crux of the demands of the reform movement was simply a return to the status quo ante with new players in the saddle of the state.

Given its programme of merely replacing the existing dictatorship with a multi-party parliamentary democracy, the dominant forces in the alliance were more anxious for a change of regime than for a protracted programme of reform. Having had little time to organise; limited by resources; and unable to ensure an independent institutional arrangement to expedite a programme it had no control over, the alliance quickly fragmented, and the opposition lost out in the struggle. The military government retained the political initiative throughout the length of the process which culminated in the general elections of November-December 1992. It was not surprising therefore that when the regime lifted the ban on political parties, the alliance easily broke up into its original squabbling and competing interest groups of the old power-seeking political parties for whom the struggle for 'democratisation' translated merely as the struggle for the control of state power.

The Press and the Transition Process

Nineteen ninety-two was Constitution-making and election year. When *The Newspaper Licensing Law 1985* was repealed in May, 1992, it was obvious that the regime could no longer contain the pressure for the expression of dissent. The *Daily Graphic*, the more widely read state-owned daily for example, without any change in editorial leadership, had begun covering opposition groups and the activities of previously blacklisted persons and groups. It became popular enough for readers to rally to the staff's support, when the latter protested the transfer of certain journalists by management, on the ground that it was an attempt to victimise independent-minded editorial staff. Instantly, the *Daily Graphic* became a source of credible news on the political process leading to presidential and parliamentary elections. Despite an increase in cover price of 100 per cent, the paper's circulation quickly recovered from less than 70,000 to about 120,000 in three months.[9]

Similar changes in orientation occurred on the editorial staff of the *Weekly Spectator* leading to management-editorial staff conflicts over editorial independence. These tensions not only signalled the changing times; they represented efforts against state interference in media reporting, and an attempt to insulate the media from governmental control.

The effect of the movement for political liberalisation on the position of the press was considerable. It opened up the political space well enough for the press to function in support of the overall movement for change. The media industry responded to this democratic opening by starting a large number of new independent newspapers during the 1990-93 period. No comprehensive and reliable record is available of newspapers and magazines licensed before the repeal of the law, or of those that have registered since then. From a grossly incomplete and obviously dated list obtained from the Ministry of Information, and from unwritten accounts of officials of the Private Newspaper Publishers Association of Ghana, about 34 independent weekly socio-political newspapers and a dozen magazines appeared on new stands between 1991 and early 1993. Altogether about 40 such papers were published between 1991 and the general elections in November-December 1992. Also, between 15-20 newspapers were started from mid-1991; but later ceased operation.

In general, the ownership pattern and structure of the newspaper industry in Ghana has remained virtually the same throughout most of the twentieth century: 'a trinity' of private entrepreneurship, church sponsorship, nationalist movement (political party) venture and, from the

1930s the significant addition of government participation (Ekwelieh 1985). The emergent press of the late 80s and early 90s showed two noteworthy exceptions.

First, during this round of the transition to multi-party constitutional rule, no political party invested in a newspaper as an instrument of mass mobilisation. There were papers started by individual leaders of parties but they were not party organs financed, staffed and provided with editorial direction by the parties, though the papers were more than sympathetic to the opposition parties. For the government-sponsored party, the NDC, this was not necessary since the incumbent regime still controlled the state-owned media. The leading opposition party, the NPP, may also have considered that since most of the private papers supported change and opposed the PNDC, investing in a newspaper should not be a priority. In the circumstances the opposition parties paid dearly for neglecting this important area. They deprived themselves of the medium for consistently propagating or articulating their programme, or reporting for the electorate their campaign activities, and providing consistent direction for their supporters and general mobilisation for electoral activity.

Second, the new press was owned by entrepreneurs of the small-scale business stratum. This translated into several factors which limited their effectiveness. Unable to recruit adequate staff to provide nation-wide coverage of events, coverage of the regions was obviously thin and patchy. The quality of journalism was equally suspect. Also, for a long time, only one or two of the independent newspapers had their own, albeit dilapidated, printing press. This also affected their operations as established and well-equipped printing houses refused to handle the printing of the more vociferous newspapers for fear of losing lucrative government contracts or political reprisal.

These and other economic factors contributed to low circulation figures. Average individual weekly circulation ranged between 5,000 and 8,000, though a few, such as the *Ghanaian Chronicle*, *The Statesman*, *The Independent*, *Ghanaian Voice* and *Free Press* circulated on average 25,000-45,000 copies.[10] These papers printed 12 pages, but the majority ran eight pages, usually with banner front-page headlines in 96 points or more. Advertising in the three leading 12-page independent weekly newspapers scarcely covered four pages; usually three. The eight-pagers run from no-advertisements to two pages of advertisements on the average. Advertisers generally shunned the independent press for political as well as strictly business reasons. Some feared government reprisal; and others did not find the low professional quality and poor circulation record attractive enough for their business operations.

These constraints notwithstanding, the new independent newspapers defied the traditional notion that newspapers could only thrive on advertising revenue: indeed, they survived in the face of poor advertising revenues. Some even prospered principally on the basis of circulation sales. The remarkable thing about this emerging press culture is that even those which were timid before 1990 all of a sudden picked up courage. Overnight, the content of such newspapers was quite different: critical, polemical, and combative. Particularly in 1992, and increasingly so during the months leading to the elections, the independent press raised such issues with the PNDC that were hitherto unheard of. Indeed, what sold these papers were the mutual competition for muckraking regarding issues of morality and accountability in public life, especially issues which involved members of the PNDC government and its functionaries.

A prominent feature of the revived independent press was the opinion column. Usually, there were more pages for opinion than news. There was more advocacy than detailed information and factual analysis. The line between news and editorial comment was often hard to discern. *The Pioneer*, for instance, would often use reader's letters or private contributions which were critical of the regime as front page lead items, especially if the author was a known critic of the regime. In so doing, the private press became an integral part of the movement to dethrone authoritarian rule and restore liberal, democratic political institutions; and they made no apologies about it. In pursuit of the democratic order the press gave ample space to human rights abuses by the regime. The security agencies came up for some scrutiny and monitoring. Everything that exposed the regime's undemocratic practices was newsworthy and made bold headlines. Anything that raised doubts on PNDC officials' moral and political integrity was sought after, particularly as the presidential elections drew closer. Nothing was now 'sacred', and the PNDC had its back to the wall. Never in the history of Ghana, since the twilight of colonial rule, was a ruling regime so pilloried by the press.

Their tone and style were so polemical, aggressive and controversial that sometimes they raised professional and ethical questions. The fact, however, is that the sluice gates of freedom had finally been forced open by the reform movement, and what came out could not be controlled.

But the excitement to print which often threw professionalism to the wind, ought to be seen in context. First, officials of the regime resorted to the use of violent language and every means to libel opponents through the state-owned media. Second, a few of the journalists had been victims of the regime's policy of detention without trial; and so the new press was naturally eager to fight an authoritarian regime which was historically unequalled in the use of violence against its opponents. It must be emphasised that the regime itself could not expect a friendly press after suppressing them for so many years. The situation therefore seemed ripe for the press to fight back, at least, for its own survival.

The Press and the Elections

As was to be expected, the private press assumed a watchdog role in the country's progress to the elections of November-December 1992. They raised doubts about the regime's commitment to ensuring free and fair elections, and were full of reports about alleged moves to rig them. The private press backed the opposition firmly, and openly campaigned for votes against the regime. Some of them even made excursions into public opinion polling, albeit of dubious scientific value, to test the popularity of presidential candidates.[11]

The state-owned press, on the other, showed mixed attitudes towards the elections and the entire reform process. The tensions between journalists' desire for editorial independence and the government's determination to control it came to the fore on the management of the *Daily Graphic*. In early October, about a month to the presidential and parliamentary elections, the rumpus between management and editorial staff compelled the editorial section and the board of directors to produce differing versions of guidelines for coverage of the elections.[12]

The coverage of party campaigns in the state-owned press is indicative generally of their respective positions on the political reform process. The following data show the amount of square centimetres of space which the two state-owned dailies, the *Daily Graphic* and *Ghanaian Times*, devoted to coverage of the political campaigns of the parties. The data covers the period from May, when the ban on party activities was lifted, to December 1992 when the parliamentary elections were held. The study examined news coverage, news assumed to be non-subjective presentation of events and occurrences, and finally news on the NDC and NPP as they appeared on the front page, page 3 and the centre pages, where news on political affairs is regularly and strategically reported in the two papers.

Table 1: Space Allocation and Number of Articles on the NDC in the *Daily Graphic*, May-December 1992 Election Campaign

	Space Allocation in Square cm	Number of News Stories
Front Page	1803.00	8
Page 3	6825.61	75
Centre Page	19678.18	23
Total	28306.79	106

Table 2: Space Allocation and Number of Articles on the NPP in the *Daily Graphic*, May-December 1992 Election Campaign

	Space Allocation in Square cm	Number of News Stories
Front Page	1185.20	5
Page 3	8352.57	84
Centre Page	4481.80	6
Total	14019.57	95

Table 3: Space Allocation and Number of Articles on the NPP in the *Ghanaian Times*, May-December 1992 Election Campaign

	Space Allocation in Square cm	Number of News Stories
Front Page	102.50	1
Page 3	5942.87	64
Centre Page	-	-
Total	6045.37	65

Table 4: Space Allocation and Number of Articles on the NDC in the *Ghanaian Times*, May-December 1992 Election Campaign

	Space Allocation in Square cm	Number of News Stories
Front Page	834.25	6
Page 3	8105.52	77
Centre Page	12623.40	10
Total	21563.17	93

The figures show that the two state-owned papers gave more space to the incumbent government's party than to the principal opposition party, the NPP. In the *Daily Graphic* the NDC took twice as much space as the NPP, and published NDC-related reports on the front page more often than it did for its main contender. The NDC also took more space than the NPP in the centre spread — space which has usually scored the highest in readership preference. The difference in the total number of articles on the two major parties in the *Graphic* does not appear significant: in percentage terms it is about 10 per cent, and assumes greater significance when the total space taken is considered together.

The *Ghanaian Times* showed greater discrimination in its coverage of the two principal contending parties. It gave only one front-page reporting of news on the NPP, gave no space for it in the centre-pages, and altogether gave more than three times as much space to the NDC as to the NPP. Similarly, the total number of articles about the two major parties varied quite significantly. Throughout the period, the *Ghanaian Times* showed no evidence that it had been affected by the movement for editorial independence as evidenced on the editorial board of the *Daily Graphic*, or its own sister paper, the *Weekly Spectator*. On the whole, both the *Daily Graphic* and the *Ghanaian Times* showed considerable bias in favour of the NDC and its allies of the Progressive Alliance in their coverage of the election campaigns.

Contribution to Political Discourse

The state-owned press hardly opened their pages to debates and discussions on questions pertaining to democracy. The few contributions which were published concerned the formal processes of constitution-making. On the other hand the private press was implacably opposed to the military government of the PNDC. But its input into the debate and process of political reform, with particular reference to the type of democratic system of government for the country, was indeed negligible. The poverty of the discourse carried out in the columns of the independent press was significant. The debates were more or less a chorus on a return to either the British or American model of constitutionalism. At any rate the justifiable fury of the private press against the PNDC's violent and arbitrary rule helped mobilise some amount of popular support against the PNDC government and its authoritarian economic and political regime.

Despite its relentless stand against this military government, the private press remained a protest press; it was not an 'alternative press', if by the latter is meant a press that articulates a 'countervailing discourse (alternative interpretation of political events) to that preferred by politicians'; engages 'in permanent dialogue with the oppressed in a language that is part of the 'social practice of the people'; 'articulates a "return to sources" or "cultural renaissance" among the culturally alienated', or encourages the 'exploration of utopia' (Masilela 1994). While the state-owned press by-and-large worked to maintain the old regime, the private press advocated mainly the conventional ideas and institutions of liberal democracy. They posed no fundamental and critical questions about the regime's economic and political policies and programmes. Invariably they implied by their silence a tacit acceptance of the underlying philosophy of the government's economic policies since 1983.

On the whole, the Ghanaian press showed two main tendencies. First, all the newspapers were biased in their reporting. A recent study by Gadzekpo and Denkabe (1995) makes conclusions which are applicable to the press during the period covered by this paper. They observe in this study that journalism in Ghana is

> aimed at persuading readers towards a particular political interpretation of the news. Even in the case of straight news reports traditionally devoid of opinion, there is a good amount of opinionating that creeps in ... The situation is further exacerbated when language becomes emotive and inflammatory.

Second, they were polarised along the prevailing political divide. The full impact of the press' message on their readers seems therefore to have been undermined by the particular language and style employed by either of the factions. As Gadzekpo and Denkabe rightly argue:

> ... newspapers in Ghana are challenged in their use of language and this may have negative implications for the manner in which their message is conveyed to the general public. The manner in which language is sometimes misused, misapplied and abused by the press in Ghana can distort the socio-political reality newspapers reflect, especially in the coverage of issues that are highly important and controversial.

In addition to this disadvantage, the use of the English language, instead of the vernaculars, by the Ghanaian press has also become a fundamental limitation of the press as instrument for political mobilisation and ideological orientation, whether it is democratisation or something else. The limited or non-use of indigenous languages in the mass media generally, not only renders the press an elite cultural institution but it also raises disturbing implications for the masses' participation in the democratic process itself (Karikari 1993). It above all raises questions about the prospect for what Masilela has called 'cultural renaissance' as an essential and central condition for a successful and authentic democratisation process.

Regime Response

The almost sudden avalanche of press exposures of allegations of corruption and human rights abuse against a regime previously basking in self-constructed and highly publicised claims of 'honesty' and 'accountability' excited public interest and sympathy. For the regime, it was obviously destabilising. The regime's response, in a situation in which it could not as easily as before resort to illegal and arbitrary methods, was to invoke repressive laws that had remained unused for some time. In the short period of May-December 1992, as many as 42 libel cases were brought to court against a number of private newspaper publishers and editors.[13] The significant ones were suits filed by persons closely associated with Rawlings against the regime's critics among the private press. The most celebrated case was a criminal libel case brought against the editor of the *Christian Chronicle*, George Naykene, who was later convicted and sentenced to 18 months imprisonment. The case involved the *Christian Chronicle's* report that some people associated with Rawlings during his short reign as head of the Armed Forces Revolutionary Council, June-September 1979, had been party to money deals from questionable sources. Another was a suit brought against the *Ghanaian Chronicle* by Rawlings' closest adviser and friend, Tsatsu Tsikata, concerning a series of articles which alleged impropriety and lack of accountability in the public-owned Ghana National Petroleum Company which Mr. Tsikata headed. Given the political circumstances of the moment it could be argued that:

> ... libel suits [were] frequently brought for reasons that [were], at best, tangential to the protection of someone's reputation. Some plaintiffs [had] political aims or [were] interested in discouraging or punishing unfavourable coverage; others may simply be fishing for damage awards (Demac 1988:24).

Outside the courtroom some newspapers came under the brute and clandestine force of the state. *The New Republic*, a weekly publication which attempted to be a spycatcher, folded after thirteen issues. The publisher/editor went into 'voluntary' exile in November, 1992, following orchestrated harassment by the Bureau of National Investigation as well as pressures from family members who had been intimidated by this agency.[14] This was not an isolated case. Reports of harassment or surveillance of editors of the private press by agents of state security were not uncommon. But in the face of such threats and harassment by the state, most editors of the new crop of private press and their publishers proved indomitable.

The regime, having 'won' the presidential elections and gained control over parliament, believed that it could amend the constitution and institute legal ways of curbing the private press. In his inaugural speech as the first elected president of the Fourth Republic, Rawlings proposed the amendment of the section of the constitution which deals with the composition of the National Media Commission (NMC) to 'expand' its membership. The National Media Commission seemed a strategic instrument to attempt a constitutional control of the press, contrary to the 1992 Constitution's unambiguous provisions baring governmental control and censorship of, as well as interference in media independence generally. The new Rawlings government sought to accomplish this constitutional control in various ways. The Constitution empowers the new Parliament to establish the NMC within six months of the Constitution coming into force. First, parliament did not enact this law until 7 months later (on 6 July 1993); and then 10 months after this date the NMC was inaugurated. Second, the PNDC had, before the November-December elections, passed a decree (PNDC Law 299, 1992) empowering itself to appoint the executive secretary of the NMC, which it did on 6 January,[15] a day before it dissolved itself to pave the way for the inauguration of the Fourth Republic. Even though the plan to control the NMC failed, the Rawlings constitutional government had, by this ingenious use of the law, virtually established the legal basis for controlling the NMC.

Furthermore, some weeks before the Constitution came into force, and presumably acting under PNDC Law 299, the board of directors of the Graphic Corporation, publishers of the *Daily Graphic*, appointed Rawlings's personal press secretary as the paper's new editor. Though he had been the deputy editor of the paper, the appointment seemed to conflict with the provisions of the Constitution of the Fourth Republic, and sparked off virulent criticism against the government. Despite these insidious actions, the political environment has remained relatively open and free for the press to open the frontiers of political freedom much wider.

Conclusion

The Fourth Republic started with uncertainties about the prospect for political democracy. For the press it was compounded by the false start of the Media Commission, and the existence on the statute books of several laws criminalising freedom of speech and the press, acts which were still defined broadly as 'sedition' or 'libellous'. Most of these laws, originally introduced in 1934 (*Criminal Code Amendment Ordinance No. 21*), were reproduced in the *Criminal Code 1960* (as amended) making the exercise of certain freedoms an offence against the state. If there is one law that has been invoked to suppress the press, it is the *Criminal Code* (Ekwelieh 1978).

The movement for restoration of multi-party parliamentary democracy in Ghana has produced a complex political situation. The PNDC was returned to power as the dominant party in Parliament, supervising a liberal, democratic constitution. The utterances of the new Rawlings government soon after assuming office raised questions about its commitment to constitutional rule. On the one hand, the state-owned press, after its initial signs of self-assertion against state control, immediately relapsed into its old culture of singing the tune of the government due largely to the reimposition of controls from the president's office. On the other hand, the private press, which played a decisive role in the movement for reform, appeared extremely vulnerable; open to numerous forms of pressure, intimidation and brazen use of state coercion. In spite of such pressures, and the negative attitudes and actions of the new Rawlings government the private press has remained the single most important force in the enormous task of keeping open and wider the frontiers of political freedom.

Notes

1. This was the *Newspaper Licensing Act 1963*, (Act 189) and the accompanying *Newspaper Licensing Regulations*, 1963 (L.I. 296).

2. The National Redemption Council passed *The Newspaper Licensing Decree*, 1973 (NRCD 161) and the *Newspaper Licensing Regulations* 1973, (L.I. 810).

3. This author has argued elsewhere that the introduction of the *Daily Graphic* in 1950 by the London Mirror Company contributed to creating conditions favourable for the first post-colonial regime's dismantling of press pluralism in Ghana. See, Kwame Karikari. The 'Anti-White press' campaign: the opposition of the African press to the establishment of the *Daily Graphic* by the British Mirror Newspaper Company in Ghana, 1950. *Gazette* 49:215-232,1992.

4. The *Ashanti Pioneer* (as it was then known) had become an organ of opposition to the Nkrumah government. Under the *Emergency Powers Act, 1961 (Act 56)*, the Nkrumah government imposed censorship on the paper. The Act itself was passed by the CPP-dominated Parliament after a major railway and port workers' strike in Sekondi-Takoradi in reaction to the austerity budget of September of that year.

5. Radio and TV broadcast by the Chairman of the PNDC, Independence Day, 6 March 1983.

6. This was the case especially with the *Ghanaian Voice*. In May, 1987, it published 'news' planted by state security personnel falsely accusing individuals, who were critical of the regime, of engineering acts of arson committed on the premises of the state-owned New Times Corporation, publishers of the *Ghanaian Times*.

7. The instability of that office would seem to emphasise the strategic importance of that position for authoritarian state control of the media. In fact, the high turnover of the office was not peculiar to the PNDC. In the first 30 years of independence there were 28 Ministers of Information. Two of them, one each under the military government of the National Liberation Council and the PNDC, spent exactly 20 days each in office.

8. A prominent example is Kabral Blay Amihere's *Independent* which was not allowed to publish beyond three editions.

9. Interview with Mr. Asani, Managing Director of Graphic Corporation, Accra, 13 August 1992.

10. This is based on conversations with editors and publishers in 1993, and may be overestimated. No independent record exists for circulation, and the proprietors are generally averse to giving out circulation figures.

11. The professional merit of these exercises elicited the following sarcastic comment from the popular columnist of the *Mirror*, Kwatriot: 'God has given him (the journalist) the talent of opinion polling, such that he can decide to opinion-pull you down today, and opinion-pull you up the next day'. In,

Kwesi Yankah (1996) *Woes of a Kwatriot: Beloved Let Us Laugh*. Anansesem Publications, Accra, 1996, p.74.

12. See the *Daily Graphic*, 8 October 1992.

13. According to Mr. G.B.K. Owusu, Editor, *Christian Messenger*, and General Secretary of the Private Newspaper Publishers Association of Ghana, at a seminar on 'Reporting the Fourth Republic', Golden Tulip Hotel, Accra, 23 December 1992.

14. Interview with George Anamolga, an assistant to Kofi Bawiah, Editor-in-Chief/Publisher of the *New Republic*, Accra, 21 November 1992.

15. See this author's letter to the *Daily Graphic* 27 January 1993, questioning the constitutional basis of the appointment.

9

Postscript: Elections, Democracy and Elite Consensus

Kwame A. Ninsin

On 7 January 1997, Ghanaians made history. Jerry John Rawlings was sworn-in for a second term of office as president of the country and leader of his political party, the National Democratic Congress (NDC). He and the NDC had won the December 1996 presidential and parliamentary elections with the largest majority. It was the first time in the history of the country that a civilian government had run its full term in office and sought the mandate of the people through the ballot box. In other words, for the first time, leadership or political succession was decided by constitutional means. The presidential and parliamentary elections which returned Rawlings and his party to power for another term of office had come off smoothly; it was also free from most of the acrimonious exchanges which had bedevilled the 1992 elections.

In the presidential elections, Rawlings had won in all the regions, except Ashanti, with 56.8 per cent of total votes cast, and had obtained majority votes in 142 constituencies. Rawlings' closest rival, J. A. Kufour of the New Patriotic Party (NPP) had won only in Ashanti; he had received 40.3 per cent of total votes. In the parliamentary election the National Democratic Congress led by Rawlings had also swept the polls with 135 of constituency seats against 64 for the opposition. The voter turnout in the presidential election was an astounding 73.5 per cent compared to just 48.3 per cent in 1992. The beginning of the life of the Rawlings government and new parliament had been marked by tense moments as government and opposition members quickly disagreed on whether or not the new parliament should approve cabinet ministers of the previous Rawlings government who had been re-appointed by Rawlings to serve on his new cabinet. At one point, the opposition members of parliament had felt compelled by their conviction to boycott parliamentary proceedings. Notwithstanding those developments, the life of the new parliament has proceeded uninterrupted; and from all indication, it is going to continue smoothly. What do such impressive electoral and parliamentary performance mean in the context of Ghana's fourth attempt to institutionalise democracy in their country?

In the preceding chapters of this book a number of issues were raised which counselled caution against any unbridled optimism about the country's successful transition to democracy. Among them are the fragility and instability of pro-democracy civil society; the strong authoritarian current which underpins the country's politics especially as was expressed in the PNDC's calculated attempt to monopolise political power and tightly control the political space, as well as use state and quasi-state organs to benefit it and ensure its retention of power through the 1992 elections; the fragile consensus among the political elites, and in particular, the failure of those contending for political power to agree on bargaining, negotiation and compromise as the means to resolve differences in their struggle for power, and to agree on the rules of mutual trust and fair play in the political sphere. The almost ubiquitous threat of the military was also raised.

Positive factors which undergird multi-party democracy were also identified. These include party political traditions which have endured and seem to have established the normative framework for a multi-party political system; the press which has also developed a tradition of pluralism, independence and freedom of expression; the vigour of a small group of civil society actors and the resilience of pro-democracy civil society generally in spite of its fragility and instability. Of equal importance is the role of foreign governments in creating the enabling environment for the growth of democratic institutions. Clearly absent from the chapter is any discussion and analysis of the role of elections and electoral politics generally in nurturing democratic norms, attitudes and practice. In this postscript, I focus on the recent presidential and parliamentary elections and how a number of issues in those elections bear on the country's transition to democratic politics. I will examine the environment in which multi-party electoral politics occurred, and assess the elections as an exercise in democratic choice by citizens of the country. I will also examine the role of relevant institutions and bodies in facilitating the process to the point it has now reached. I approach the subject from two related angles: (i) the elections as an exercise in consensus building and political legitimation by the political elites; and (ii) the election as an exercise in sovereign decision-making by ordinary citizens. I argue that, as an exercise in democratic choice by the sovereign people of Ghana concerning who should govern them — whether they were guided by a latent or explicit ideology or not — the elections were of much less value to the advancement of the transition process. For, Ghanaians are wont to vote for reasons which are largely instrumental and totally unrelated to democratic precepts provided the political elites created the enabling environment. But as an exercise in consensus building and power legitimation, Ghana's political elites used the moment of the 1996 electoral politics to forge the institutional bases for a stable and orderly democratic politics.

Legitimation of Power and Consensus-Building

The controversy and crisis surrounding the 1992 elections were potentially disruptive of the fledgling democratic political order that had been established under the 1992 constitution. If this young political order based on multi-party democracy was not secured on the basis of consensus among the political elites, the exercise of power by any fraction of the Ghanaian elites might not be considered legitimate both internally and internationally. The normative vacuum arising from the lack of consensus was most likely to encourage any group of political adventurers to arrogate to itself the sovereign right of the people, seize power and pretend to exercise it according to the will of the people; as for example, the action by military cliques.

Especially for the leaders of the opposition political parties the pressure to achieve some consensus with Rawlings and the leaders of his party was much stronger. Consensus was needed on the rules of the electoral contest to ensure that the country would have a smooth transfer of power from one leadership group to another whenever necessary. There was also the need to inspire confidence in the multi-party democratic system as one that provides a better method for changing leaders as well as a better system of government compared to military coups and military regimes. Furthermore, there was the probability that prolonged disagreement over the rules of electoral politics and elite succession to power could encourage the organised sections of the lower classes to embark on militant and radical political agitation which might jeopardise the new constitutional order as was the case just before the fall of the 1979 constitutional order.[2] Already, the level of mass political mobilisation was substantially high both as a result of the dire socio-economic circumstances of ordinary Ghanaians, and as a result of multi-party politics. Above all, there was the stark possibility that if the stand-off with the Rawlings government on the conduct of the 1992 elections remained unresolved, that government might seize the opportunity to perpetuate itself in power. The declaration of the New Patriotic Party, the leading opposition party, barely a year after the 1992 elections that it was prepared to do business with the Rawlings government was the strongest signal of the determination of the leaders of the opposition parties as a whole to agree with their counterparts of the National Democratic Congress on how to settle their differences through negotiation rather than confrontation and non-co-operation, and in so doing build the necessary consensus over the rules of political competition and elite succession.

The 1992 elections had exposed how some of the leading democracy commissions like the electoral commission lacked the moral bases to command compliance with rules of fairness, equity and transparency in spite of the constitutional provisions which guaranteed their independence. It was clear that as a result of that situation the entire process of rebuilding a democratic order had taken off on mistrust, intolerance, fear and intimidation. Clearly, the appropriate norms of fairness, transparency, mutual respect and trust as well as voluntary compliance had not been clearly defined and agreed to. This had to be rectified. The rules of electoral politics had to be defined and agreed to, and the necessary commitment to compliance with, as well as confidence in their impartiality, firmly secured. It meant that a fresh start had to be made to build trust in the impartiality of key political institutions which regulate electoral contest, like the National Electoral Commission (NEC), and secure general respect for their conduct. The legitimacy of the electoral commission was bound to strengthen the role of elections and the multi-party system as institutions for choosing and changing government. The process of legitimation and consensus building therefore took the form of institution creation.

Margaret Levi (1990:409) has argued that:

...the most effective institutional arrangements incorporate a normative system of informal and internalised rules.

(However) the norm of fairness regulates behaviour by offering a rule for when one should comply. It generates a kind of compliance that possesses both normative and utilitarian element: (what he calls 'contingent consent'). If current arrangements represent an acceptable bargain and if others are doing what they can reasonably be expected to do to uphold the bargain, the institutional arrangements can be considered 'fair'. If individuals are convinced that the norm of fairness is operating, they are more likely to act in accordance with rules of conduct, the norm of fairness implies.

The 'norm of fairness develops through a social process and in a social context; it is relational and contextual' (Levi 1990). The National Electoral Commission provided leadership in creating the social context in which dialogue among the feuding political party elites would take place. The major political parties came together to form the Inter Party Advisory Committee (IPAC) in March 1994. Under chairmanship of a representative of the NEC, this body became an important mechanism for dialogue, consultation, and consensus- building. During the following two years the IPAC became the forum where disagreements, suspicions, and fears were addressed at regular monthly meetings. The goal of making the conduct of future elections conform to the highest canons of democratic elections — to be free and fair — guided deliberations. A major outcome of the deliberations was the agreement to design an electoral system that would be acceptable to all and sundry, and administer that system to ensure fairness, equity, and transparency in elections. In the end the political elites became not just consumers of policies prepared cut and dry for them by a remote and suspicious body; they became part of the decision-making body and 'made decisions' that would ensure the success of the elections. Ultimately the deliberations of the IPAC became a major exercise in confidence-building among the country's political elites.

The idea that elections in a democracy should be free and fair requires that all contenders for power should be free to organise and engage in lawful activities pursuant to the objective of wining political power; and that they should all be accorded equal rights by the state and quasi-state institutions whose conduct affect the outcome of elections either directly or indirectly. Among the rights that political actors have claimed are equal access to the state-owned media and other state controlled resources that are crucial to success in an election. These principles of freedom and equality are clearly spelt out in the country's 1992 Constitution. In Article 55(1) the Constitution provides: 'The right to form political parties is hereby guaranteed'. While it states in Article 55(11) 'The State shall provide fair opportunity to all political parties to present their pro-grammes to the public by ensuring equal access to the state-owned media'. Such constitutional provisions formed the ideological basis within which especially the opposition party leaders pressed their demands for a satisfactory electoral arrangement for the 1996 elections. Their experience of the 1992 electoral politics gave ample impetus for insisting on the need for an even playing field for all contenders for political power.

In 1992, a major complaint against the electoral process was that the voters register had been inflated allegedly to favour the outgoing military government. To give all contestants an equal chance of wining the 1996 elections, it was agreed that a new voters register would be compiled with the active participation of all the registered political parties. The participation of the parties involved the training of about 80,000 party agents — two each from the alliance of government and opposition political parties. Four trained party agents, representing the two party alignments, were assigned to each registration centre to monitor the registration exercise. The party agents kept a daily record of the number of persons registered per day to ensure that the register would not be tampered with.

The importance which the political elites attached to the voters register as a means to ensure equality of opportunity at the polls was evident in the interest showed in the authentication of names on the register when it was opened to the public from 28 April to 7 May 1996, at all the 20,000 registration centres. Out of the 9,185,660 names on the voters roll, 6,709,989 (or 73.0 per cent) were verified; 361,180 (3.9 per cent) corrections were made; 6,157 (0.06 per cent) objections were registered; and 22,849 (0.24 per cent) missing names were restored.[3] Second, the party leaders agreed that voter identification cards would be issued to every voter with voters in the ten regional capitals and ten rural constituencies, selected nationwide being issued with photo identification cards. Third, the use of transparent ballot boxes was finally accepted as a means to allay fears of possible vote rigging on polling day. These and other measures agreed upon at the IPAC enhanced the confidence of all the key actors in the electoral politics and ensured the conduct of elections that would be accepted by the contending parties as free and fair. Surely, there were several problems and incidents which might have raised doubts especially among leaders of the opposition parties. But the spirit of trust in the fledgling electoral institutions had become sufficiently grounded to guarantee the integrity of the process. Rawlings' acceptance speech reflected the seed of the democratic ethic of mutual trust and fair play, a most remarkable transformation in norms and attitudes of Ghana's political elites:

> I wish to thank each and everyone of you for making the election peaceful, fair and transparent. Together we have established the tradition of orderly democratic procedure and every Ghanaian should take satisfaction in its accomplishment.

> To our brothers and sisters in the opposition, let us believe that the majority of you entered the electoral contest with the interests of our nation as your primary consideration. In this respect, I congratulate Dr. Edward Mahama of the People's National Convention and Mr. John Agyekum Kuffuor of the New Patriotic Party and the other parties for their competitive spirit. For me, all the political rivalry came to an end when Ghanaians cast their vote on the 7th December.

> ... We must all make an effort to put the past behind us. It is my hope therefore that in all that we say or publish, we will stress more on the things that unite us as a people rather than those which tend to divide us.

> In the true spirit of reconciliation, I wish to assure the nation that we bear no grudges... I pledge the government's commitment to draw upon the experience and expertise of all men and women of integrity, no matter their political leanings, in our common effort to improve upon our national performance (Rawlings 1996).

The donor community was actively involved in the inter-party negotiations. Their aim was to ensure that the bargaining between the alliance of government and opposition parties would succeed in facilitating an enabling environment. Representatives of the principal donors either participated in the meetings of the IPAC, or gave technical assistance, or did both; or they influenced proceedings from behind the scenes. The range of material aid given by the donor community is significant. Together, the donor community gave 12.03 million cedis to the NEC to facilitate the conduct of free and fair elections. The USA contributed $6.5 million; Denmark — $3.0 million; UK — $0.8 million; Canada — $0.745 million; European Union — $0.5 million; Germany — $0.185 million; The Netherlands — $0.164 million; Friedrich Ebert Foundation — $0.079 million; and China — $0.057 million (Afriyie Badu and Larvie 1996:75-76). Such forms of direct material assistance went into the procurement of a variety of election materials which contributed directly to the confidence building processes. It, above all, enhanced the technical capacity of the NEC to manage the elections admirably (Ayee 1997:6-14).

Apart from the donor community there were several international and local election monitoring and observer teams whose intervention in the electoral politics also enhanced the legitimacy and overall success of the process. Among them were the Commonwealth Observer Group, National Democratic Institute, and the Ghanaian election monitoring body — the Network of Domestic Election Observers (NEDEO), an umbrella organisation of civic groups, religious and professional bodies. Its members included the Ghana Journalists Association, Ghana National Association of Teachers, Civil Servants Association, Federation of Moslem Councils, the Christian Council of Ghana, National Catholic Secretariat, Ghana Trades Union Congress, and National Union of Ghana Students. Other indigenous groups and organisations which monitored and/or observed the elections are the Institute for Economic Affairs, Ghana Legal Literacy and Resource Foundation (established by the Ghana Bar Association), Ghana Alert, and the Ghana Committee on Human and People's Rights. All of them contributed immensely to the success of the elections.

The activities of these domestic bodies and the international election monitoring and observer groups complemented one another to inspire extra confidence in the electoral process, and ensured a peaceful and orderly exercise in the long run. The NEDECO, for example, was able to train and deploy about 2,331 election observers to all the 10 regions of the country on election day; while the National Democratic Institute observed the elections in about 300 polling stations, both rural and urban, throughout the country. When these developments are compared to what prevailed in the 1992 elections, it becomes quite significant that by the 1996 elections domestic election monitoring and observer groups had been formed. It shows growing consciousness among Ghanaian interest groups (pro-democracy civil society) that free, fair, transparent and reliable elections are important for the success of pluralist democracy.

Two other equally important features of the 1996 elections were the formation of a plurality of political organisations and a vigilant pro-democracy civil society. Jonah (in this book) emphasised the importance of political party tradition in reviving and sustaining the multi-party political system in the country. But in fact, it is clear from both 1992 and 1996 electoral politics that it normally requires more than *the political party as tradition* to re-invent the multi-party system in the country. During the immediate post-election period when the political situation was tense the leading pro-democracy civic associations like the Christian Council of Ghana, Catholic Bishops Conference and the Muslim Representative Council played a major role in reconciling the leaders of the government and the opposition political parties: they made several attempts to bring the leaders to the negotiating table to dialogue over a number of contentious issues. It is however significant that several political parties, despite the prevailing two principal political party traditions, were formed and most of them registered for both the 1992 and 1996 elections. In 1992, not less than 13 political parties were formed immediately after the ban on party political activities was lifted; 9 political parties were registered to contest the 1996 parliamentary elections. The following table shows a breakdown of registered political parties and party nominations per region.

It is true that a large number of these registered political parties did not command enough resources to function autonomously in the very competitive political arena which prevailed. That is why only 2 of the registered political parties could mobilise the manpower as well as material resources to contest seats in more than 150 out of the 200 constituencies. But the fact that this good number of political parties could be formed at all is indicative of a strong commitment to pluralist and competitive political life. As Appendix I shows, the formation of a broadly based multi-party system in the 1992 and 1996 elections was not the first in Ghana's political history. Since the 1950s the country's political elites have always seized the opportunity to form political parties as the primary instrument for the pursuit of political power.

Party Nominations by Region for the 1996
Parliamentary Election*

Party	W	C	GA	V	E	A	BA	N	UE	UW	Total
NPP	16	16	21	15	25	32	20	18	8	8	179
NDC	19	17	22	19	26	32	21	23	12	8	199
PNC	9	6	16	12	21	19	14	11	11	8	127
NCP	10	7	7	3	14	6	7	10	4	3	71
DPP	0	1	3	4	6	4	2	2	0	0	22
EGLE	2	0	0	0	4	0	2	0	0	0	6
GCPP	0	0	1	0	0	0	0	0	0	0	1
PCP	12	16	18	13	17	12	7	15	6	0	115
I/C**	2	1	16	12	6	5	7	5	2	1	57
Total	70	64	104	78	119	110	80	84	43	28	780

Source: Afriyie Badu and Larvie (1996:39).

* There was no election in the Afigya Sekyere East Constituency due to a court order secured by some citizens of the area.

** Independent Candidates who constituted 7.3 per cent of the nomination.

The success of the tedious and protracted negotiations at the IPAC produced consensus in several key areas of electoral politics. The most important outcome of it was that the elections would be free and fair and that all the parties would enjoy an equal chance of wining political power.

Consensus building like this is fundamental to institution creation which is essential to the stability of the democratic process. Once the leading politicians agreed on the fairness, transparency and reliability of the basic rules and procedure governing the conduct of public affairs, a good foundation was laid for the sustainability and stability of the institutions of multi-party politics. Hence the lapses, conflicts and uncertainties of the transition process notwithstanding, all the major actors accepted the outcome of the elections as a valid, and true expression of the sovereign will of the people of Ghana.

The success in consensus building notwithstanding, there were enough adverse developments to emphasise the fragility of the normative foundation of the new democratic order. It was clear that the norm of fairness would not always be reciprocated by the major players. Nor did certain key state and quasi-state institutions whose conduct affect the electoral process believe entirely in the value of fair and impartial conduct. The belief that politics is a game of the strongest, and should be played to the disadvantage of the weaker actors persisted, and was manifested in the conduct of, for example, the state-owned media. Despite the fact that the National Media Commission had issued guidelines on impartial political reporting to all the media houses, those guidelines were flouted with impunity: 'the state-owned print and broadcast media favoured the incumbent president. Allegations of the incumbent party having greater access to public resources were consistently made by the opposition parties' (NDI 1996). Furthermore, political indiscipline and a variety of political violence characterised electioneering campaigns of all the leading parties. It was these coupled with the uncertainty about the intentions of certain leading actors in the electoral process which resulted in mass hysteria on the eve of voting. According to one shrewd political observer,

> The whole country had been sitting on tender-hooks. There had been real fear (mostly unexpressed) as what would happen if Rawlings and his henchmen were to lose the election. This, of course, was no idle fear, knowing the kind of people they are. As matters turned out he won an election that, in the narrow Western sense, was free but which, in my books, were certainly not fair. ... The rigging of the elections have been ongoing since about 1990. The level of the use of patronage and state resources for glorification of a few is scandalous. ... It is really a new form of mass corruption or myopia. In some ways the country breathed a sigh of relief when it became clear that Rawlings had won and they would be spared any disruption of their already stressed lives. In fact, a number of people ... had been so scared they had hoarded food against possible shortages brought on by feared post-election disturbances. So in a certain perverse sense we should be grateful to little mercies.[4]

The elections of 7 December 1996 were held in this mixed atmosphere of elite consensus and a current of mass hysteria. But the knowledge that the contending political leaders had agreed on the basic rules of electoral politics and that the elections would proceed, encouraged Ghanaians to troop to the polls. Elite consensus was enough guarantee for the democratic game to be consummated in the casting of votes to elect representatives and a government. This accounts for the impressive voter turnout of 73.5 per cent.

Elections and Democratic Consolidation

Elections do not necessarily make a political system democratic. Hence, under Africa's one-party regimes of the 1960-1980 period, elections were denounced as undemocratic because they did not avail the electorate the necessary freedom of choice. Recent multi-party elections, especially those held in the wake of the scramble by military and single party regimes to become democratic, have also raised several questions. For example, military regimes which were determined to transform themselves into elected civilian governments have manipulated the electoral process to perpetuate themselves in power. Even civilian regimes have provoked a storm of protest from their political opponents about their handling of multi-party elections. It has been alleged that elections were rigged even before they were held. As the controversy surrounding Ghana's 1992 elections results shows, the results of most of Africa's recent elections have either been disputed, repudiated or denounced outright in spite of a certificate of 'free and fair' conduct usually issued by foreign election observers and monitors. That most of the recent multi-party elections have simply reproduced the old power configurations and legitimised old oligarchies as well as their styles of government, is due to this crucial fact of generally flawed elections. Indeed the old Leviathan has, in most of such cases, been reborn with the connivance of foreign election observers, foreign experts and foreign money. This is why the recent wave of so-called democratic elections notwithstanding, the dream of politically empowering citizens of nation-states through liberal democratic politics has not been realised, and the elections have merely succeeded in reviving the old and maligned patron-client relationships.

Whatever the magnitude of the lapses in recent elections may be, it is true that multi-party elections promise to promote a democratic culture in the long run — especially the freedoms of choice, association, speech, etc. Having said this, I must immediately caution that the average Ghanaian sees the meaning and function of elections differently from his or her US counterpart. In Ghana, where the vast majority of voters are peasants, illiterate, and live in closely knit communities, the *vote* is not the embodiment of the sovereign equality of the individual. Instead it represents the collective power and interests of the community of which the individual is part.[5] Accordingly, the majority of Ghanaians have usually voted neither to express individual political preferences, nor as autonomous citizens of the state acting in association with other autonomous citizens to choose a government and thereby influence, howbeit indirectly, the direction of future policies of the country. People have voted as part of a political collective — the community — to register either their collective appreciation for material benefits like development projects (a road, clinic, electric power, piped water, a school bloc, etc.) received in the past. The vote either expresses confidence in the ruling political class; or it forges a new social contract with incoming political leaders. In the event of the latter, the vote is intended to ensure that the community would also benefit from the distribution of development projects in the future. The vote may therefore be described as the medium by which communities reaffirm or affirm the *social contract*[6] with the political leadership.

The use of the *vote* to express the collective interest of the community is a perfectly rational electoral behaviour even though fundamentalists of liberal democracy may disagree. The fact, however, is that if democratic elections provide a mechanism for regulating elite behaviour, then Ghanaian voters make a democratic point when they employ their collective voting power to compel their political leaders to be sensitive to their community needs and aspirations.

This electoral behaviour emphasises a peculiar elite-mass nexus prevailing in Ghanaian politics that is mediated by material expectations, the expectation that the leaders would share the national wealth equitably with citizens according to their local community identities. This instrumentalist voting behaviour synchronises with elite political norms and behaviour. Ghanaian politicians are notorious for employing state power to cultivate political loyalties on the basis of largely communal solidarity much less on the basis of either tribe (ethnicity) or religion, and definitely not on the basis of class solidarity. This peculiar nature of the elite-mass nexus is not restricted to electoral politics; it pervades the entire Ghanaian political behaviour under both elected and non-elected governments. It may even be argued that the Ghanaian elite — whether in public or private service, appointive or elective position — are regarded and used by their communities as vital rods in the political bridge linking them into the elite dominated world of material or developmental resources (Chazan 1987).

The government of the National Democratic Congress led by J. J. Rawlings had by the 1996 election year established a reputation for a populist type of redistributive politics. From 1982 when it ruled the country as the Provisional National Defence Council through to 1992-96, the Rawlings government excelled in employing the limited resources of the state to provide development projects, especially, in rural communities, which could be described as historically disadvantaged or deprived. It has been estimated that 'Community and Social Services' accounted for the highest percentage of government expenditure under the previous Rawlings regime. 'Prior to 1991 expenditure on ... community and social services averaged 45 per cent' (ISSER 1995:22). From 1988 to 1993 its share in total government expenditure per annum was 44.7 per cent, 45.5 per cent, 46.4 per cent, 41.7 per cent, 41.5 per cent and 40.1 per cent respectively. Education, health, and social and welfare services consumed the bulk of such expenditures. Works and roads and waterways constituted another major set of items of expenditure among economic services (ISSER 1994: 24-28).

This policy has generally been regarded as a product of Rawlings' populism. But it is also true that the Rawlings government is adept at legitimating itself by co-opting economic discontent and exploiting it as political discontent: it finds political scapegoats for such discontent projecting itself as the one that cares and is able to mitigate or correct past injustices. In the name of redistributive justice, the Rawlings government has allocated development projects to neglected, deprived, or poor rural communities. The reward has been a resounding popularity among the beneficiary communities: the government has won solid loyalty and support among them. In the event of any challenge from the political opposition, it is able to mobilise the support of such communities. The prospect of multi-party electoral politics raised the political value of this strategy affording the government a perfect justification for expanding public expenditure for purposes of legitimising itself.

Wright (1978:157) has argued that the strategy of legitimating a government or regime through massive expenditures could be counter-productive:

> There is a certain logic to legitimation which means that the political apparatus gets progressively diminishing returns in added legitimation for a given programme over time. *Once a programme becomes seen as a right, the continuation of the programme adds little to the legitimacy of the state where as a cutback in the programme would constitute a source of delegitimation* (Emphasis is mine).

On the eve of competitive electoral politics in 1992, the logic of political survival and self-succession heightened the value of regime legitimacy for the Rawlings government and drove it to embark on more public spending on rural and community development projects regardless of the negative effect of uncontrolled public spending on the public budget. The increased legitimacy accruing from this politics of redistribution was translated into victory at the 1996 elections.

This particular nature of the elite-mass nexus forms the key to the understanding of why Ghanaians turned out in large numbers to vote in the elections of 7 December 1996 in spite of the mass hysteria which had gripped the nation and why, above all, they voted for Rawlings. Regarding the latter the logic was simple: every community was aware of the strategic development resources which are controlled by the national political leadership who have held political power since January 1982. They were conscious of the fact that any community that desired access to those limited national resources for its development should not be seen in opposition to the ruling party. All such communities should rather become part of a reconstituted social contract with the Rawlings government.

It must be emphasised that the logic of legitimation operates both ways: it is a duality. That the electorate should respond enthusiastically to the politics of patronage which merely serves the legitimation project of the ruling political elite has become more than compelling; it is an iron law of Ghanaian politics. Part of the reason for this pattern of behaviour is the poverty of most Ghanaian communities. A recent *Ghana Living Standards Surveys*[7] have revealed that the level of poverty among both urban and rural communities has been growing at an alarming rate in spite of the alleged success of the government's structural adjustment programmes. The new local government units which were established under the *Local Government Law 1988 PNDC Law 208* are also largely poor, and lack the economic base necessary to generate adequate revenue. This situation has not been mitigated by the 1992 Constitution's provision (Article 252) for a mandatory transfer of not less than 5 per cent of the state's annual budgeted revenue into a local government fund — the District Assembly Common Fund — for development purposes. The bulk of the local government units are still poor financially. As Ayee (1995:292-306) has argued, the local government units are so weak that they are unable to respond to the needs of their communities and so their legitimacy as units for local self-government still remains shaky.

Consequently, the burden of rural and community development generally still rests with the central government. This is why in 1994, for example, the government paid a hefty C38.3 billion into the District Assembly Common Fund. This huge payment was one of two expenditure items which amounted to '54.0 per cent more than the budgeted C55.7b' (IEA 1995:30). Because of this pivotal role played by central government in rural and community development, local communities are obliged to strive hard to win the central government's attention and sympathy in the distribution of development projects. National elections provide a singular opportunity for them to do so.

In so far as Ghanaian elections are linked to access to development projects and other material benefits for communities, they may be regarded as instrumental, not in the narrow sense of personal gain. People vote for the greatest good of the community: they do not vote for the abstract individual freedoms of liberal democracy. It is this instrumentalist-utilitarian role of Ghanaian elections which distinguishes Ghanaian elections from elections in developed societies. But it is also arguable that this distinctive function of elections may provide fertile grounds for the rise of a one-party dominant multiparty system in Ghana.

In so far as elections are perceived as the ultimate means for ensuring access to the limited national resources which a group of national political elite control for strategic distribution, it is those who control access to such limited national resources who have the greatest possibility of winning votes at an election. Rawlings and his party men won the 1996 elections because the electorate perceived them as the ones who control the scarce resources needed for the development of their communities. They were also the ones with demonstrable capacity and commitment to either deliver or punish communities that do not show sufficient support at the polls.

The problem arising from this kind of electoral behaviour is that the stability of the political order then hangs precariously on the capacity of the political elite to distribute patronage, or fulfil the terms of the social contract. The implications of this linkage are grave. Where the elite's patronage capacity is high, their legitimacy and that of key state institutions are high. But where they are unable to fulfil public expectations under the social contract their own legitimacy and that of state institutions is jeopardised.

In the past, this *economic rationality of Ghanaian elections* has acted as a predictable barometer of regime legitimacy as well as political stability. The level of voter turn-out had correlated to the level of economic well-being of the nation-state: voter turn-out was low when the economy was in crisis and high when there was relative well-being (Ninsin 1993:184-185). In this age of economic austerity, this correlation could spell crisis for the fledgling liberal democratic order, especially where the ideology of liberal democracy has not been sufficiently instilled in the consciousness of the larger society. To avert this potential danger, liberal economic policy has to be designed in such a way that society could produce adequate wealth for the good of the greatest majority. This will go a long way to weaken the link between regime legitimacy and distribution.

Conclusion

In so far as the election of 7 December 1996 had any meaning for liberal democratic practice in Ghana, implying the consolidation of freedom of political association, organisation and action; freedom of speech, information, and choice; freedom to periodically choose one's government, and so on, two developments occurred to make the elections successful. The Ghanaian political elite demonstrated considerable determination and commitment to institutionalising appropriate norms and procedure which will ultimately stabilise a liberal democratic regime. Between the 1992 and 1996 elections, they succeeded in laying the foundations of liberal democracy as a normative system and a political method. The character of the institutions which provided the framework for the election and the overall political environment showed a marked improvement from what prevailed during the 1992 electoral politics. This qualitative change was amply reflected in the attitude of the leading political actors in the elections, especially, the presidential candidates— Rawlings, Kuffour, and Mahama. In contrast with the negative perceptions, attitudes and utterances of the leading actors in the 1992 elections, these three presidential candidates showed enough respect for the rules of the game and, most especially, for the sovereign will of the people as expressed through the ballot box. Rawling's acceptance speech, part of which has been quoted above, is a good example of the remarkable change which has occurred since the 1992 elections.

What has changed? From the evidence adduced above, it is clear that there has been significant normative shift in the beliefs of the political elite — a shift towards politics of reconciliation, bargaining, and, above all, consensus. The tough inter-elite bargaining which followed the post-1992 election crisis afforded a fresh opportunity to strengthen the institutional bases of liberal democracy. Institution-building immediately brings to the fore consensus building; and consensus building occurs around critical norms like *fairness*.

The process also underscored the ultimate responsibility of Ghana's political leadership to either consolidate liberal democracy as a normative system and method; or undermine it. Between March 1994 and the elections of 7 December 1996, they demonstrated positive leadership by strengthening the institutional bases of the fledgling democratic order. In this process pro-democracy civil society actors could only play either a facilitating role or the role of a watchdog. The actual job of institution-creation was undertaken by the political elite; because clearly the success of legitimising the liberal democratic order served their own aspirations for power. Once the institutional framework for liberal democracy had been agreed upon, the electorate could be expected to faithfully act as referee in deciding which of the contending groups of elite should become party to a reconstructed social contract. The success of the latter also depended on the success with which the political elite provided structured alternative leaderships through their respective political organisations to facilitate the choice between alternative leaderships by an electorate whose primary concern is with securing access to the limited state-controlled resources for the development of their respective communities. Or, in liberal democratic jargon, the emergence of a reasonably well organised multi-party system afforded the electorate a simplified framework for *periodically influencing* leaders in the redistribution of development projects.

Notes

1. See Beetham (1991:3-41) where it is argued that the primary ground for the legitimation of power is that it is secured and exercised in accordance with established rules and procedure.

2. A foreboding development during the 1979-1980 period when Ghana's political elites squabbled and disagreed endlessly over basic rules of consensual government was creeping political disorder and the emergence of radical political groups whose activities were aimed at discrediting and delegitimising the new democratic political order. Refer to Ninsin (1985:89-110) for a discussion of these developments which were a precursor to the fall of the Third Republic.

3. The data used in this paragraph were taken from Afriyie Badue and Larvie (1996:29-30).

4. Private communication from a very intelligent observer of Ghanaian politics.

5. Austin (1975:10) explains this as the result of tradition, and the closely knit communal bonds that unite members of Ghana's traditional communities.

6. Nugent (1996) has described the elite-mass nexus in Ghanaian politics as based on a social contract by which the political elites are bound to ensure distributive justice in public affairs. Nugent seems to view the social contract as a relationship between the citizens and ruler *à la* Locke. I would argue that the *social contract* is indeed an unwritten political agreement between community and the ruler concluded mainly through elections; because for Ghanaians liberal democracy could be attained primarily 'through the representation of various communities (in parliament) and through equitable access to the nation's resources. Ghana's parliaments may therefore be described as coalitions of little community interests which are subsumed under electoral constituencies' (Ninsin 1993:186). This instrumentality is not individualistic contrary to Maxwell Owusu's view. See Owusu (1970). It is driven by utilitarianism.

7. See Ghana Statistical Service, *Ghana Living Standards Survey, 1995.*

Appendix I

Profile of Political Parties, 1946-1994

1945-66	Convention People's Party (CPP)
1954-57	Anlo Youth Organisation (AYO)
	Ghana Action Party (GAP)
	Ghana Congress Party (GCP)
	Ghana Nationalist Party (GNP)
	Moslem Association Party (MAP)
	Northern People's Party (NPP)
	Oman Party (OP)
	Togoland Congress (TC)
1957	Ga Shifimo Kpee (GSK)
1957-64	United Party (UP)
1969	All People's Party (APP)
	Black Power Party (BPP)
	Labour Party (LP)
	Progress Youth Party (PYP)
	Republican Party (RP)
	Saviour's Party (SP)
	United Jehovah Party (UJP)
1969-72	All People's Republican Party (APPRP)
	National Alliance of Liberal (NAL)
	People's Action Party (PAP)
	Progress Party (PP)
	United Nationalist Party (UNP)
1979	Combined Politicians Party (CPP)
	Development Filosofa Kongress (DFK)
	Ghana United Movement (GUM)
	Mother Ghana Solidarity Party (MGSP)
	Patriotic Alliance (PA)
	People's Democratic Party of Ghana (PDPG)

                    People's Revolutionary Party (PRP)
                    People's Vanguard (PV)
                    Theocratic Restoration Party (TRP)
                    United Liberal Party (ULP)
                    Welfare Party (WP)

1979-81	Action Congress party (ACP)
	People's National Party (PNP)
	Popular Front Party (PFP)
	Social Democratic Front (SDF)
	Third Force Party (TCP)
	United National Convention (UNC)
1992	Democratic People's Party (DPP)
	New Generation Party (NGP)
1992-93	Ghana Democratic Republican Party (GDRP)
	National Independence Party (NIP)
	People's Heritage Party (PHP)
1992-94	Eagle Party (EP)
	National Convention Party (NCP)
	National Democratic Congress (NDC)
	New Patriotic Party (NPP)
	People's National Convention (PNC)
	People's Party for Democracy and Development (PPDD)
1994	People's Convention Party (PCP)

Appendix II

Government Ghana 1957-1994

Date	Government	Head of Government	Type
1957-66	CPP	K. Nkrumah	Civilian; Multiparty One-Party
1966-69	NLC	E. Kotoka/ A. A. Afrifa	Military
1969-72	PP	K. A. Busia	Civilian; Multiparty
1972-89	NRC/SMC	I. K. Acheampong/ F.W.K.Akuffo	Military
1979 (June-Sept.)	AFRC	J.J. Rawlings	Military
1979-81	PNP	Hilla Limann	Civilian; Multiparty
1982-93	PNDC	J.J. Rawlings	Military
1993-present	NDC	J.J. Rawlings	Civilian; Multiparty

Appendix III

A Chronology of Major Political Events Since 31 December 1981

DATE	EVENT
1981	
31 December 1981	31 December coup d'état which overthrows the PNP Government.
1982	
11 January 1982	PNDC Establishment Proclamation Decree (Law). Promulgation of PNDC Law 4: Preventive Custody Law.
1984	
4 November 1984	Inauguration of National Commission for Democracy (NCD).
30 November 1984	People's Defence Committees (PDCs) and Worker's Defence Committee's (WDCs) renamed Committees for the Defence of the Revolution (CDRs)
1985	
February, 1985	Formation of Public Education Committees on the Democratic Process.
1987	
February-May, 1987	NCD Demarcates country into 110 Districts including 45 new ones carved out of the existing 65 Districts.
1 July 1987	Launching of Blue Book and Modalities for the District Level Elections.
4-8 August 1987	National seminar on public education to prepare Regional and District Public Education Committee members for their work.

1987
1 September-November   Intensive nationwide publicity
                        1987 campaign on the voters registration
                        exercise.

1987
1-30 October   Registration of voters 11th November,
                        NCD hold press conference and invites
                        the public to submit views on the future
                        system of government. Responses included:
                        TUC, GNAT, NUGS, etc.

1988
February, 1988   Culture of silence smashed by Professor
                        A. Adu Boahen at the J.B. Danquah Memorial
                        Lectures.

16-18 March 1988   3rd Quadrennial Delegates Congress of TUC,
                        calls on the government to respect the
                        fundamental human rights of Ghanaians and
                        to convene a constitutional conference to
                        write a new constitution for Ghana.

3-7 May 1988   The Annual Congress of NUGS calls on the
                        government to respect basic human rights,
                        repeal all draconian laws and to restore
                        the country to constitutional rule.

18-31 July 1988   Exhibition of voters register for impending
                        First District level elections.

1988-1989
6 December 1988   First District level elections 28 February
                        1989 held by the NCD.

13 January-17 March   Inauguration of First District
                        1989 Assemblies.

1990
March-April 1990   Outreach Program to find out the type
                        of government to be superimposed on
                        the District Assemblies (DA's).

5 July-19 November	Regional fora on the theme: 'The District Assemblies and the evolving Democratic Process'.
1 August 1990	Formation on Movement for Freedom and Justice (MFJ).

1990
October-December 1990	The Christian Council of Ghana (CCG) issued a document titled: 'Ghana's Search for a New Democratic System'.

1991
February, 1991	The Catholic Bishops Conference issued a document titled: 'The Catholic Church and Ghana's Search for a new Democratic System'.
25 March 1991	NCD presents its report on the regional fora on the theme: 'The District Assemblies and the Evolving Democratic Process'.
13 May 1991	Government issues its statement on the NCD report. Consultative Assembly Law signed. Constitutional Committee of Experts appointed.
6 August 1991	Formation of Coordinating Committee of Democratic Forces (CCDF).
26 August 1991	Inauguration of Consultative Assembly to consider Constitutional Draft Proposals by the Committee of Experts.
27 September 1991	Non-Aligned Movement Conference held in Accra.
8 November 1991	Promulgation of Interim National Electoral Commission (INEC) Law.

1992
February, 1992	Inauguration of INEC.
March, 1992	Consultative Assembly finishes its work.

28 April 1992	Referendum on the Draft Constitution.
18 May 1992	Lifting of ban on political party activities.
1 July, 1992	Inauguration of Kwame Nkrumah Mausoleum in Accra.
14-30 July September, 1992	Registration of Political Parties by INEC.
13-30 August	Political Parties hold Congresses.
3 November 1992	Presidential Election.
29 December 1992	Parliamentary Election.
1993 7 January 1993	Inauguration of the 4th Republic.
7 August 1993	Inauguration of National Electoral Commission (NEC).
1994 22 March 1994	2nd District Level Elections Conducted by NEC.
28 April 1994	The Ghana Bar Association (GBA) inaugurates Legal Literacy Resource Foundation to educate Ghanaians on the law and the constitution.

Appendix IV

Other Forms of Direct Foreign Assistance

BRITAIN: Provided items and services valued at one million pounds sterling. The items included; 20 photocopiers, 20 air conditioners, 120 manual typewriters, 20 electronic typewriters, 20 personal computers, 40 computer work stations, spareparts for typewriters and photocopiers, 3,500 collapsible booths etc.

CANADA: Items worth one million Canadian dollars provided included reams of special paper for printing, ink pads, endorsing ink, indelible ink, twine balls, ruler and glue paste.

FRANCE: Computer mainframe and 23 work stations. Training personnel for the computers.

SWEDEN: Standby electric generator with KVA capacity, 15 fax machines, PABX telephone set with 140 extensions, 1 electric and 1 thermal binding machines, 3 shredding machines, 2 computer decollators.

ITALY: Nine vehicles worth $350,000 in addition to a sum of $66,000.

GERMANY: Training of registration and polling assistants, printing of 200,000 copies of 'A Guide to the Voter' and 60,000 copies of 'A Guide to the Candidate'.

EU: Training of trainers of polling assistants, holding of national seminars, printing of 120,000 of manual for election staff and polling agents.

SWITZERLAND: Provided 15.6 million cedis through its Consul General which was used to print additional copies of Manual for election staff.

NEW ZEALAND: 120,000,000 cedis which was used for the printing of 800,000 copies of 'A Guide to the voter'.

DENMARK: $100,000 for the procurement of security pulltight seals and other materials. A further 65 million cedis was provided for voter awareness educational programme.

CHINA: 200 bicycles.

References

Abdulai, N. (ed.), 1995, *Ghana: The Kumepreko Demonstrations*, London, Africa Research and Information Bureau.

Afriye Badu, K. and Larvie, J., 1996, *Elections 96 in Ghana*, Part 1, Accra, Friedrich Ebert Foundation.

Ahiakpor, J. C., 1991, 'Rawlings, Economic Policy Reform and the Poor: Consistency or Betrayal?', *Journal of Modern African Studies* 29(4), 583-600.2

Ake, C., 'Rethinking African Democracy', *Journal of Democracy* 2, 1, 32-44.

Anglin, Douglas, G., 1990, *Southern African Responses to Eastern European Developments*, mimeo., June, p.6.

Anglin, Douglas, 1990, *International Monitoring as a Mechanism for Conflict Resolution in Southern Africa*, mimeo., July, p.12.

Anyang' Nyong'o, Peter, 1987, 'Introduction', in Anyang' Nyong'o, ed., *Popular Struggles for Democracy in Africa*, The UN University/Zed Books Ltd., London and New Jersey.

Anyang' Nyong'o, Peter, 1991, 'Democratisation Process in Africa', Dakar, CODESRIA Bulletin 2, 2-4.

Apter, D., 1963, *Ghana in Transition*, Atheneum Press, New York.

Asante, Y., 1994, *Determinants of Private Investment Behaviour in Ghana* Interim Report presented at the African Economic Research Consortium Workshop, Nairobi.

Austin, D., 1964, *Politics in Ghana*, London, Oxford University Press.

Austin, D. and Luckham, R., (eds.) 1975, *Politicians and Soldiers in Ghana, 1969-1972*, London, Frank Cass.

Austin, D., 1976, *Ghana Observed*, Manchester, Manchester University Press.

Ayee, J. R. A., 1995, 'Financing Sub-National Governments in Ghana: The District Assemblies Common Fund', *Regional and Federal Studies* 5 (5).

Ayee, J. R. A., 1997, *Ghana's 1996 General Elections: A Post-mortem*, AAPS Occasional Paper Series, Volume 1, Number 1.

Bangura, Y. and Gibbon, P., 1992, 'Adjustment, Authoritarianism and Democracy: An Introduction to Some Conceptual and Empirical Issues' in Gibbon, P. *et al.*, (eds.), *Authoritarianism, Democracy and Adjustment: The Politics of Economic Reform in Africa*, Uppsala, Scandinavian Institute of African Studies.

Bates, R. H., 1983, 'Governments and Agricultural Market in Africa' in D. Gale Johnson (ed.), *The Role of Markets in the World Food Economy* Part 4, Westview Press, Boulder, Colorado.

Bayart, Jean-François, 1986, 'Civil Society in Africa', in Patrick Chabal, *Political Domination in Africa*, Cambridge, Cambridge University Press.

Bayart, Jean-François, 1993, *The State in Africa: The Politics of the Belly*, Essex, Longman.

Baynham, S., 1984-1985, 'Civil-Military Relations in Ghana's Second Republic', *Journal of Contemporary African Studies* 4(1-2): 71-88.

Baynham, S., 1985, 'Quis Custodiet Ipsos Custodies?: The Case of Nkrumah's National Security Service', *Journal of Modern African Studies* 23(1), 87-103.

Baynham, S., 1988, *The Military and Politics in Nkrumah's Ghana*, Boulder, CO and London, Westview Press.

Beetham, D., 1991, *The Legitimation of Power*, London, Macmillan.

Bennion, F. A. R., 1962, *The Constitutional Law of Ghana*, London, Butterworths.

Bluwey, G. K., 1991, 'Obstacles to an Orderly Transition to Constitutional Rule Under the PNDC' in K. A. Ninsin and F. K. Drah, (eds.), *Ghana's Transition to Constitutional Rule*, Accra, Ghana University Press.

Bluwey, G. K., 1992, 'Democracy at Bay: The Frustrations of African Liberals' in B. Caron, A. Gboyega and E. Osaghae (eds.), *Democratic Transitions in Africa*, Ibadan, CREDU.

Bluwey, G. K., 1993, 'The Opposition in Democratic Government: Reflections on the Ghanaian Experience' in K. A. Ninsin and F. K. Drah (eds.), *Political Parties and Democracy in Ghana's Fourth Republic*, Accra, Woeli Press.

Boafo-Arthur, K., 1992, 'Prelude to Constitutional Rule: An Assessment of the Process' in F. K. Drah and K. A. Ninsin (eds.), *Ghana's Transition to Constitutional Rule*, Accra, Ghana Universities Press.

Boafo-Arthur, K., 1993, 'Ghana's External Relations Since 31 December 1991', in E. Gyimah-Boadi (ed.), *Ghana Under PNDC Rule*, Dakar, CODESRIA.

Boahen, A. A., 1989, *The Ghanaian Sphinx: Reflections on the Contemporary History of Ghana, 1972-1987*, Accra, Ghana Academy of Arts and Science.

Bozeman, A.B., 1976, *Conflict in Africa: Concepts and Realities*, Princeton, Princeton University Press.

Bratton, M. and van de Walle, 1992, 'Toward Governance in Africa: Popular Demands and State Responses' in Goran Hyden and Michael Bratton (ed.), *Governance and Politics in Africa,* Lynne Reinner Publishers, Boulder and London.

Callaghy, T. M., 1989, 'Towards State Capability and Embedded Liberalism in The Third World: Lessons for Adjustment', in Joan Nelson (ed.), *Fragile Coalition: The Politics of Economic Adjustment*, New Brunswick, NJ, Transaction Books.

Callaghy, T. M., 1990, 'Lost Between State and Market: The Politics of Economic Adjustment in Ghana, Zambia and Nigeria', in Joan Nelson (ed.), *Fragile Coalition: The Politics of Economic Adjustment,* New Brunswick, NJ, Transaction Books.

Catholic Bishops Conference (CBC), 'The Catholic Church and Ghana's Search for a New Democratic System' in K. A. Ninsin, 1996, *Ghana's Political Transition* 1990-1993 (Selected Documents), Accra, Freedom Publications.

Central Bureau of Statistic, 1980, *Economic Survey of Ghana 1977-1980,* Accra.

Chazan, N., 1983, *An Anatomy of Ghanaian Politics: Managing Political Recession 1969-1982,* Boulder, CO, Westview Press.

Chazan, N., 1989, 'Planning Democracy in Africa: A Comparative Perspective on Nigeria and Ghana', *Policy Sciences* 22:325-57.

Chazan, N., 1987, 'Anomalies of Continuity: Perspectives on Ghanaian Elections Since Independence' in Fred Hayward (ed.), *Elections in Independent Africa,* Boulder, Westview Press.

Chole, E. and Ibrahim, J., eds., 1995, *Democratisation Processes in Africa: Problems and Prospects,* Dakar, CODESRIA Book Series.

Christian Council of Ghana (CCG), 'A Memorandum to the Government of the Provisional National Defence Council from the Christian Council of Ghana on 'Ghana's Search for New Democratic System of Government', in Ninsin, *Ghana's Political Transition.*

Christian Council of Ghana and Catholic Bishops Conference (CCG/CBC) 'Memorandum from the Heads of the Member Churches of the Christian Council of Ghana and the Catholic Bishops Conference on the Release of the Report on the Evolving Democratic Process' in Ninsin, *Ghana's Political Transition.*

Coleman, J. and Carl, R., (eds.) 1964, *Political Parties and National Integration in Tropical Africa,* Berkeley and Los Angeles, University of California.

Commission on Security and Economic Assistance, 1983, *A Report to the Secretary of State.* Washington, DC.

Committee of Experts, 1991, *Report of the Committee of Experts on Constitution Proposals for a Draft Constitution of Ghana,* Accra, Government Printer.

Decalo, S., 1989, 'Modalities of Civilian-Military Stability in Africa', *Journal of Modern African Studies* 27(4):547-78.

Decalo, S., 1991, 'Towards Understanding the Sources of Stable Civilian Rule in Black Africa: 1960-1990', *Journal of Contemporary African Studies* 10(1), 66-83.

Decalo, S., 1992, 'The Process, Prospects and Constraints of Democratisation in Africa', *African Affairs,* Vol. 91, No. 362, pp. 7-35.

Demac, Donna, A., 1988, *Liberty Denied. The Current Rise of Censorship in America*, Pan American Centre, New York, p.24.

Diamond, L., 1994. 'Toward Democratic Consolidation', *Journal of Democracy*, Vol. 5, No. 3, July.

Dotse, M., 1992, 'Recruitment Policy Administration in the Ghana Civil Service', *Greenhill J. of Public Administration*, Vol., No. 2, July.

Ekwelieh, S. and Dympna, E. U., 1978, 'The Genesis of press control in Ghana', *Gazette*, 24:196-206.

Ekwelieh, S. and Dympna E.U., 1985, 'Ownership patterns of Ghana Newspapers. An Historical Perspective', *Gazette*, 35:49-59.

Fitch, B., and Oppenheimer, M., 1966, *Ghana: End of an Illusion*, Monthly Review, New York.

Folson, K. G., 1993, 'Ideology, Revolution and Development-The Years of J. J. Rawlings' in E. Gyimah-Boadi, (ed.), *Ghana Under PNDC Rule*, Dakar, CODESRIA Book Series.

Fosu, K. Y., 1993, 'Domestic Public Policy and Ghana's Agriculture, 1982-89', in Gyimah-Boadi (ed.), *Ghana Under PNDC Rule.*

Frimpong-Ansah, J., 1991, *The Vampire State in Africa: The Political Economy of Economic Decline in Ghana* James Currey, London.

Gadzekpo, A. and Denkabe A., 1995, *What's fit to print? The Language of the Press in Ghana*, (Forthcoming), School of Communication Studies and Friedrich Ebert Stiftung, Ghana.

Garber, Larry, 1984, *Guidelines for International Election Observation*, Washington DC, p.13.

Ghana Bar Association (GBA), 'Statement of the Ghana Bar Association Made at an Emergency General Meeting of the Bar on 23 February 1991, on the Programme for a Return to Constitutional Rule' in Ninsin, *Ghana's Political Transition.*

Ghana Bar Association (GBA), 'Statement of the Ghana Bar Association Made at an Emergency General Meeting of the Bar on Saturday 11 May 1991 on the NCD Report and the PNDC's Statement on the Said Report' in Ninsin, *Ghana's Political Transition.*

Ghana Trades Union Congress (GTUC), 'The Trade Unions and Democracy in Ghana', Paper presented to the National Commission on (sic) Democracy by the Trades Union Congress, in Ninsin, (op cit.).

Gills, B. Rocamora, J. and Wilson R. (eds.), 1993, *Low Intensity Democracy: Political Power in the New World Order*, London, Pluto.

Goldsworthy, D., 1981, 'Civilian Control of the Military in Black Africa', *African Affairs* 80 (8), 49-74.

Goldsworthy, D., 1986, 'Armies and Politics in Civilian Regimes', in S. Baynham (ed.), *Military Power and Politics in Black Africa*, London, Croom Helm.

Goulbourne, H., 1987, 'The State, Development and the Need for Participatory Democracy.' in Peter Anyang' Nyong'o (ed.), *Popular Struggles for Democracy in Africa*, The UN University/Zed Books Ltd., London and New Jersey, pp.26-47.

Government of Ghana (GG), 'Government's Statement on the NCD Report on Evolving True Democracy' in Ninsin, *Ghana's Political Transition*.

Government of Ghana, *Constitution of the Republic of Ghana 1992*, Accra, Government Printer.

Graham, Y., 1989, 'From GTP to Asene: Aspects of Industrial Working Class Struggles in Ghana, 1982-1986', in Hansen E., and Ninsin, K. A., (eds.),*The State, Development and Politics in Ghana*, Dakar, CODESRIA Book Series.

Green, D. M., 1991, 'Structural Adjustment and Politics in Ghana', *TransAfrica Forum* 8 (2), 67-89.

Green, R. H., 1988, 'Ghana: Progress, Problematics and Limitations of the Success Story', *IDS Bulletin* 19(1), 7-15.

Gregor, A. J., 1979, *Italian Fascism and Developmental Dictatorship*, Princeton, NJ, Princeton University Press.

Gyimah-Boadi, E. and Essuman-Johnson, A., 1993, 'The PNDC and Organised Labour: The Anatomy of Political Control', in Gyimah-Boadi (ed.), *Ghana Under PNDC Rule*, Dakar, CODESRIA Book Series.

Gyimah-Boadi, E. and Rothchild, D., 1982, 'Rawlings, Populism, and the Civil Liberties Tradition in Ghana', *Issue: A Journal of Africanist Opinion* XII(3-4): 64-69.

Gyimah-Boadi, E., (ed.), 1993, *Ghana Under PNDC Rule*, CODESRIA Book Series, Dakar, CODESRIA.

Haggard, S. and Kaufman, R.R., 1989, 'Economic Adjustment in New Democracies' in J.M. Nelson (eds.) *Fragile Coalitions: The Politics of Economic Adjustment*, New Brunswick, NJ, Transaction Books.

Hansard, *Proceedings of the Consultative Assembly of Ghana 1991-92*, Accra, Government Printer.

Hansen, E., 1987, 'The State and Popular Struggles in Ghana, 1982-1986', in *Popular Struggles for Democracy in Africa* (ed.), Anyang' Nyong'o, London, ZED/UNU.

Hansen, E? and Ninsin, K. A. (eds.) 1989, *The State, Development and Policies in Ghana*, Dakar, CODESRIA Book Series.

Hansen, E., 1991, *Ghana Under Rawlings, Early Years*, Oxford, Malthouse Press for African Association of Political Science.

Haynes, J., 1991a, 'Inching Towards Democracy: The Ghanaian 'Revolution', the International Monetary Fund and the Politics of the Possible', in R. Cohen and H. Goulbourne (eds.), *Democracy and Socialism in Africa*. Boulder, CO, Westview Press.

Haynes, J., 1991b, 'Human-Rights and Democracy in Ghana - The Record of the Rawlings Regime', *African Affairs* 90 (36): 407-425.

Hofmeier, R., 1991, 'Political Conditionalities on Development Aid in Africa: A New Form of Intervention or Legitimate Support for Democratic Efforts?' *Economics* Vol. 44, pp. 100-111.

Holmquist, F., 1989, 'Why Democratic Forms of Rule in Africa are Necessary and Possible', in *Beyond Autocracy in Africa* (The Inaugural Seminar of the Cater Centre Governance Program, 17-18 February 1989).

Huntington, S.P., 1957, *The Soldier and the State: The Theory and Politics of Civil-Military Relations*. New York: Vintage Books.

Huntington, S. P., 1968, *Political Order in Changing Societies*. New Haven, CT, Yale University Press.

Huntington, S. P., 1984, 'Will More Countries Become Democratic?' *Political Science Quarterly*, 99, No.2.

Huntington, S. P., 1992, 'How Countries Democratise', *Political Science Quarterly*, 106, 4.

Hutchful, E., 1979, 'Organisational Instability in African Military Forces: The Case of the Ghanaian Army', *International Social Science Journal* 31(4): 606-18.

Hutchful, E., 1987, 'New Elements in Militarism: Ethiopia, Ghana and Burkina Faso', *International Journal* 41(4): 802-30.

Hutchful, E., 1991, 'Reconstructing Political System: Militarism and Constitutionalism' in Issa G. Shivji (ed.), *State and Constitutionalism - An African Debate on Democracy*, Harare, SAPES Trust.

Hutchful, E., 1992, *The International Dimensions of the Democratisation Process in Africa*, Dakar, CODESRIA.

Hutchful, E., 1993, 'Institutional Collapse and the Rise of the Military Mass Movement in Ghana', Unpublished paper. Detroit, IL: Department of Africana Studies, Wayne State University.

Ibrahim, J., 1992, 'The State, Accumulation, and Democratic Forces in Nigeria' in Lars R., (ed.), *When Democracy Makes Sense*, Uppsala, AKUT.

Imam, A., 1991, 'Democratisation Processes in Africa: Problems and Prospects', *CODESRIA Bulletin*, No.2.

Institute of Economic Affairs, 1995, *1994 Economic Review and Outlook*, Accra, IEA.

Institute of Statistical Social and Economic Research, 1994, *The State of the Ghanaian Economy in 1993*, Legon, Accra, ISSER.

Institute of Statistical Social and Economic Research, 1995, *The State of the Ghanaian Economy in 1993*, Legon, Accra, ISSER.

Jebuni, C. D., Oduro, A. D. and Tutu, K. A., 'Trade and Payments Regimes and the Balance of Payments in Ghana' World Development (forthcoming).

Jeffries, R., 1991, 'Leadership Commitment and Political Opposition to Structural Adjustment in Ghana' in D. Rothchild (ed.) *Ghana: Political Economy of Recovery* SAIS, African Studies, London.

Jeffries, R. and Thomas, C., 1993, 'The Ghanaian Elections of 1992', *African Affairs* 92 (368): 331-366.

Jeffries, R., 1992, 'Urban Popular Attitudes Towards the Economic Recovery Programme and the PNDC Government in Ghana', *African Affairs* 91 (363): 207-226.

Jeffries, R., 1993, 'The State, Structural Adjustment and Good Government in Africa', *Journal of Commonwealth and Comparative Politics* 31(1): 20-35.

Jonah, K., 1992, 'The Monopolisation and Manipulation of the Constitution-Making Process in Ghana' in K. A. Ninsin & F.K Drah (eds.), *Ghana's Transition to Constitutional Rule*, Accra, GUP.

Jonah, K., 1994, 'Ghana's Industrial Towns and the Election of President Rawlings in 1992', Accra: Seminar Paper, Department of Political Science, January.

Karikari, K., 1990, 'Media Policy: A Factor in the Search for Democracy', *Africa Media Review.* Vol.4, No.1, pp.27-41.

Karikari, K., 1993, 'Africa: The Press and Democracy', *Race and Class*, Vol.34, No.3, January-Arch. pp.55-66.

Kimble, D., 1963, *A Political History of Ghana*, Clarendon, Oxford University Press.

Kumado, Kofi, 'Legislation on Political Parties', *Political Parties and Democracy in Ghana's Fourth Republic* , Ninsin and Drah, *Political Parties and Democracy in Ghana's Fourth Republic.*

Lal, D., 1987, 'The Political Economy of Economic Liberalisation', World Development Vol. 1, No. 2, pp. 273-300.

Lancaster, C., 1993, 'Governance and Development: The Views from Washington', *IDS Bulletin*, Vol. 24, No. 1.

Leith, J. Clark and Lofchie, M. F., 1993, 'The Political Economy of Structural Adjustment in Ghana', in R.H. Bates and A. O. Krueger (eds.) *Political and Economic Interactions in Economic Policy Reform*, Blackwell, Oxford.

Lemarchand, R., 1992, 'Africa's Troubled Transitions', *Journal of Democracy*, 3, 4.

Lindblom, C. E., 1977, *Politics and Markets*, New York, Basic Books.

Luckham, R., 1971, *The Nigerian Military - A Sociological Analysis of Authority and Revolt 1960-67.* Cambridge, Cambridge University Press.

Luckham, R., 1978, 'Imperialism, Law and Structural Dependence: The Ghana Legal Profession', *Development and Change* 9(2): 201-244, April.

Luckham, R., 1982, 'French Militarism in Africa', *Review of African Political Economy* 24, 55-84.

Luckham, R., 1985, 'Militarization in Africa', *SIPRI Yearbook 1985*, Chap. 9. Stockholm, Stockholm International Peace Research Institute.

Luckham, R., 1990, *American Militarisation and the Third World: The End of the Cold War?* Working Paper No.94, Canberra, Peace Research Centre, Australian National University.

Luckham, R., 1994, 'The Military, Militarization and Democratisation in Africa: A Survey of the Literature and Issues', *African Studies Review* 37 (2).

Mafeje, A., 1995, 'Theory of Democracy and the African Discourse: Breaking Bread with my Fellow-travellers', in Eshetu Chole and Jibrin Ibrahim, (eds.), *Democratisation Process in Africa, Problems and Prospects*, CODESRIA, Dakar, pp. 5-28.

Mamdani, M., 1995, 'A Critique of the State and Civil Society Paradigm in Africanist Studies' in Mamdani, M. and Wamba-dia-Wamba, E., (eds.), *African Studies in Social Movements and Democracy*, Dakar, CODESRIA Book Series.

Manu, T., 1993, 'Women, The State and Society Under the PNDC' in Gyimah-Boadi, *Ghana Under PNDC Rule*.

Martin, M., 1991, 'Negotiating Adjustment and External Finance: Ghana and the International Community, 1982-1989', in Don Rothchild (Ed.),*Ghana: The Political Economy of Recovery*, Boulder, Lynne Reinner.

Martin, G., 1993, 'Democratic Transitions in Africa', *ISSUE*, Vol. XXXI, No. 1-2.

Masilela, T. S. B., 1994, 'Alternative Media and Political Change in Africa.' A paper prepared for the ACCE Pre-biennial Conference on 'Rethinking Development: The Legacy of Paulo Freire', Accra, 16-17 October.

Meier, G., 1991, 'The Political Economy of Policy Reform', in G.M. Meier *Politics and Policy Making in Developing Countries. Perspectives on the New Political Economy*, International Centre for Economic Growth, USA.

Menkhaus, Kenneth J. and Charles W. Kegley Jr., 1988, 'The Compliant Foreign Policy of the Dependent State Revisited', *Comparative Political Studies*, Vol.21, No. 3, Oct., p.316.

Ministry of Trade *Annual Report*, various issues, Accra.

Mkandawire, T., 1988, 'Comments On Democracy' *Africa Development* 12, 3.

Movement for Freedom and Justice (MFJ), 'Announcement of the Formation of a Broad Based National Movement The Movement For Freedom and Justice (MFJ) at a Press Conference on Wednesday 1 August 1990. Embargoed for Automatic Release on 1 August 1990 - 11 a. m.' in Ninsin,*Ghana's Political Transition*.

Movement for Freedom and Justice (MFJ), 'Statement by the Movement for Freedom and Justice (MFJ) on the New Year Broadcast of the PNDC Chairman and Other Related Matters at a Press Conference in Accra, 11 January 1991', in Ninsin,*Ghana's Political Transition*.

Movement for Freedom and Justice (MFJ), 'Statement by the Movement for Freedom and Justice (MFJ) on the PNDC's Statement on the 'NCD Report and the Constitutional Proposals', Accra, 17 May 1991', in Ninsin, Ghana's Political Transition, National Commission for Democracy (NCD), 'Evolving A True Democracy: Summary of Memoranda Submitted to the NCD', in Ninsin, *Ghana's Political Transition.*

Movement for Freedom and Justice (MFJ), 'Executive Summary. Regional Seminar on 'District Assemblies and the Evolving Democratic Process' in Ninsin, *Ghana's Political Transition.*

National Commission of Democracy, 1987, *District Political Authority and Modalities for District Level Elections* Accra: Government Printer.

National Commission of Democracy, 1991, *Evolving A True Democracy: A Summary of NCD's Work Towards the Establishment of a New Democratic Order*, Accra, Government Printer.

National Democratic Institute, 1996, *Preliminary Statement by the NDI International Observer Delegation to the December 7 Elections in Ghana* (Press Release), Accra, December.

New Patriotic Party, 1993, *The Stolen Verdict.* Accra, New Patriotic Party.

Ninsin, K. A., 'State, Capital and Labour Relations, 1961-1987' in Hansen E., and Ninsin, K. A., *Op.cit.*

Ninsin, K. A., 1989, 'The Impact of the PNDC's Economic Reform Policies on Ghanaian Politics and Society', *Legon Journal of The Humanities.* Vol. 5 1991.

Ninsin, K. A., 1991, 'The PNDC and the Problem of Legitimacy', in Rothchild, ed., *Ghana: The Political Economy of Recovery.*

Ninsin, K. A., 1991, *The Informal Sector in Ghana's Political Economy,* Accra, Freedom Publications.

Ninsin, K. A., 1992, 'NGOs and Democracy in Ghana', Paper prepared for the International Conference on Democracy in Africa, organised by the Friedrich Ebert Foundation, Bonn, 1-3 June.

Ninsin, K. A., 1993, 'The Electoral System, Elections and Democracy in Ghana' in K. A. Ninsin and F. K. Drah, *Political Parties and Democracy in Ghana's Fourth Republic.* Accra, Woeli Publishing Services.

Ninsin, K. A., 1996, *Ghana's Political Transition 1990-1993* (Selected Documents), Accra, Freedom Publications.

Nkrumah, Kwame, 1963, *Africa Must Unite,* Panaf Books, London, p.76.

Nugent, P., 1996, *Big Men, Small Boys and Politics in Ghana: Power, Ideology and the Burden of History, 1982-1994*, London/New York, Printer.

Nyerere, K., 1963, *Democracy and the Party System,* Dar-es-Salaam, Government Printer.

Nzimande, B. and Sikhosana, M., 1995, 'Civil Society: A Theoretical Survey and Critique of Some South African Conceptions', in Lloyd Sachikonye, (ed.), *Democracy, Civil Society and the State - Social Movements in Southern Africa.* Harare, SAPES Trust.

Nzouankeu, J. M., 1991, 'The African Attitude to Democracy', *International Social Science Journal,* No. 128, May, pp. 373-385.

O'Donnell, G., 1978, 'Reflections on Patterns of Change in the Bureaucratic-Authoritarian State', *Latin American Research Review* 13 (1), 3-38.

O'Donnell, G. and Schmitter, G., 1986, *Transitions from Authoritarian Rule: Tentative Conclusions About Uncertain Democracies.* Baltimore, MD., Johns Hopkins University Press.

O'Donnell, G. A., Schmitter, P. C. and Whitehead, L., (eds.), 1986, *Transitions from Authoritarian Rule: Latin America. Baltimore,* MD., Johns Hopkins University Press.

O'Donnell, G., 1994, 'Delegative Democracy', *Journal of Democracy* 5 (1): 55-69.

ODI, 1994, 'Political liberalisation and Economic Reform in Developing Countries' Briefing Paper, No. 1, London.

Olukoshi, A., 1992, *The World Bank, Structural Adjustment and Governance in Africa.* Mimeo.

Onimode, B., 1992, *The Democratisation Process and the Economy,* CODESRIA Working Paper No. 23.

Oquaye, M., 1993, 'Law, Justice and The Revolution' in Gyimah-Boadi E., *Ghana Under PNDC Rule.*

Osaghae, E., (ed.), 1994, *Between State and Civil Society in Africa,* Dakar, CODESRIA Book Series.

Oyugi, W. O., *et al.,* 1988, *Democratic Theory and Practice in Africa,* London, Heinemann.

Peil, M., 1972, *The Ghanaian Factory Worker,* Cambridge, Cambridge University Press.

Pion-Berlin, D., 1992, 'Military Autonomy and Emerging Democracies in South America', *Comparative Politics* 25 (1): 83-102.

Przeworski, A. and F. Limongi (1993) 'Political Regimes and Economic Growth', *Journal of Economic Perspectives,* Vol. 7, No. 3, pp. 51-69.

Przeworski, A., 1991, *Democracy and the Market: Political and Economic Reforms in Eastern Europe and Latin America.* Cambridge: Cambridge University Press.

Ravenhill, J., 1980, 'Comparing Regime Performance in Africa: Limitations of Cross National Aggregate Analysis', *Journal of Modern African Studies* 18(1), 99-126.

Rawlings, J. J., 1986, *The New Direction, Selected Speeches of Flight Lieutenant Jerry John Rawlings*, 1 January - 31 December 1986, Accra, Ghana Publishing Corporation.

Rawlings, J. J., 1996, *Address by H. E. President Jerry John Rawlings on the Occasion of His Re-election*, Thursday, December 12.

Remmer, K. L., 1985-6, 'Exclusionary Democracy', *Studies in Comparative International Development* 20 (4).

Riddel, R. C., 1987, *Foreign Aid Reconsidered* James Currey in association with ODI, London.

Rimmer, D., 1991, *Staying Poor. Ghana's Political Economy, 1950-1990* Pergamon Press, Oxford.

Rodrik, D., 1990, *Trade Policies and Development: Some New Issues* CEPR Discussion Paper Series, No. 447, London.

Ronen, D., 1990, *Democracy and Pluralism in Africa*, Boulder, Lynne Reinner.

Rouveroy van Nieuwaal, n.d., 'The Togolese Chief: Caught Between Scylla and Charibdis' in *Journal of Pluralism and Unofficial Law*.

Rueschemeyer, D. and Stephens, E., and J., 1992, *Capitalist Development and Democracy*. Cambridge, Polity Press.

Sangmpam, S. N., 1993, 'Neither Soft Nor Dead: The African State is Alive and Well', *African Studies Review* 36(2).

Seligman, A. B., 1992, *The Idea of Civil Society*, New York, Free Press.

Shearman, P., 1987, 'Gorbachev and the Third World', *Third World Quarterly*, Vol. 9, No. 4.

Shillington, K., 1992, *Ghana and The Rawlings Factor*, London, Macmillan.

SIPRI, 1992, *SIPRI Yearbook 1992: World Armaments and Disarmament*, Stockholm, Stockholm International Peace Research Institute.

Sklar, R., 1987, 'Developmental Democracy', *Comparative Studies in Society and History* 20 (4).

Stepan, A., 1988, *Rethinking Military Politics, Brazil and the Southern Cone*, Princeton, NJ, Princeton University Press.

Tanzi, V., ed., *Transition to Market Studies in Fiscal Reform*. Washington, DC, IMF.

Tilly, C., 1985, 'War and the Power of Warmakers in Western Europe and Elsewhere 1600-1980', in P. Wallenstein (ed.), *Global Militarisation*. Boulder, CO., Westview Press.

Twumasi, Yaw, 1985, 'Social class and newspaper coverage in Ghana', in Frank Okwu Ugboajah, ed., *Mass Communication, Culture and Society in West Africa*, Hans Zell Publishers, New York, London, Paris, pp.211-220.

Weffort, F. C., 1993, 'What is a New Democracy?', *International Social Science Journal* 136, May.

Welch, C. E., 1974, 'The Dilemma of Military Withdrawal from Politics: Some Considerations from Tropical Africa', *African Studies Review,* XVII.

West Africa, various issues, London.

White, G., 1994, 'Civil Society, Democratisation and Development', Mimeo IDS, University of Sussex, Brighton.

World Bank, 1989, *Sub-Saharan Africa: From Crisis to Sustainable Growth. A Long-Term Perspective Study,* Washington DC, pp. 60-61.

World Bank, 1992, *Governance and Development,* Washington DC.

Yankah, K., 1986, *The Trial of J. J. Rawlings* Tema, Ghana Publishing Corporation.

Yeebo, Z., 1991, *Ghana: The Struggle for Popular Power*, London, New Beacon Books.

Zaverucha, Z., 1993, 'The Degree of Military Autonomy During the Spanish, Argentinean and Brazilian Transitions', *Journal of Latin American Studies* 25 (2).

Ghanaian Newspapers: *The Ghanaian Times - The Peoples Daily Graphic - The Ghanaian Chronicle - The Statesman - The Independent,* etc.

Lightning Source UK Ltd.
Milton Keynes UK
UKOW01f0625201017

311327UK00009B/223/P

9 782869 780910